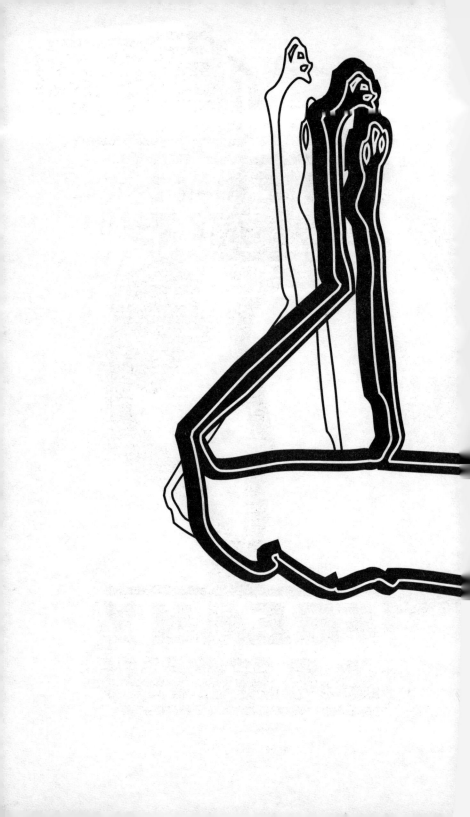

PAN BOOKS

First published 1998 by Pan Books

an imprint of Macmillan Publishers Ltd
25 Eccleston Place, London SW1W 9NF
and Basingstoke

Associated companies throughout the world

ISBN 0 330 37054 5

Copyright © Mark Berry and Deborah Faulkner 1998

The right of Mark Berry and Deborah Faulkner to be identified as the
authors of this work has been asserted by them in accordance
with the Copyright, Designs and Patents Act 1988.

5 7 9 8 6 4

A CIP catalogue record for this book is available from
the British Library.

Typeset by SX Composing DTP, Rayleigh, Essex
Printed and bound in Great Britain by
Mackays of Chatham plc, Chatham, Kent

THANKS TO EVERYONE

CONTENTS

PROLOGUE

I'm makin no apologies, let's get that straight right now, not even to myself. The past is irrevocable an there's no point in even tryin to make amends now for somethin that happened over a decade ago. I'm simply tellin it like it was an thankin God that I emerged from it all relatively unscathed with my sanity an my family intact. I'm not condemnin an I'm not condonin either, I'm simply relatin an era in which I was blissfully unaware of my catalystic qualities as a full-on hedonist: pleasure for pleasure's sake was my only maxim. I never asked no one to adhere to my lifestyle: I was simply takin to the rostrum an shakin my stuff 'cos it felt so fuckin good. So I stand accused of bein BEZ – what can I say – alright, it's me, I admit it, but who else *could* I be, tell me that.

We were the dissident youths that sprang forth from the bowels of Salford durin the late 70s an early 80s, growin up at a time when there were no prospects of havin a job at the end of our turbulent school years. An overall atmosphere of despondency ran right the way through school, not made any more palatable by a team of teachers that could barely conceal their despair at the futile task of tryin to get us through the system an steer us towards an attainable goal. Not much different from today, except that our generation were the first to encounter this fast track to poverty en masse an we found ourselves reviled by a society that had not previously had to deal with the unemployment of its young school leavers on such a large scale.

The struggle to provide ourselves with the means to survive led whole armies of young lads like myself to take to the streets in search of the missin ingredient, an we found it in a happy marriage of music an drugs. Then the drug culture, like the unrepentin demoniac mechanism that it is, took away other life options as it enveloped us in endless rounds of parties an raves, claimin more an more for its disciples as time for the ordinary things in life, like jobs an families, got squeezed out: the country was failin its young big style an so they turned to partyin to relieve the boredom of the listlessly long an empty days. Everyone knows that if you party all night, the days take care of themselves: the readjusted body clock no longer incorporates the daylight hours. You sleep to avoid the day an all its depressing reminders that you don't even belong in the category of workin class: you are actually wallowin at the very bottom of the pile in some sub class that doesn't even have a label.

There are flaws in this scheme though. Most notably, the small matter of gettin to the dole office to sign on becomes a major concern when you're strugglin with yet another amphetamine come down an can't make it out of your pit. An if you do make it to the counter, the effort to communicate, to fill in the endless forms, to spell out your inadequacies in BIG FUCKIN CAPITAL LETTERS for all to see, is a fuckin soul-destroyin nightmare. Also, you never get a suntan, a meal is somethin that lives in a tin an has the words VALUE *before* the food description, an as we are what we eat, you always look like shit – a crap situation to be in then.

An then the E scene came along.

The party explosion was, ironically, one of the biggest outcries from the young in recent times that they were not happy with their lot, even though, strangely enough, everyone appeared to be ecstatic at the time.

As well as the scene takin over the clubs, massive open-air parties were organized that littered the countryside with young adults completely off their rockers on E. The Government, seein an underlyin subversive force on a scale never encountered before, panicked at the uprisin of their future electorate an banned partyin with the speedy introduction of the Criminal Justice Act.

Why did thousands of people take to poppin a pill an ravin the weekend away in a field? Because they had no serious expectations of gettin anythin better out of life: it took the monotony out of bein on the dole or sinkin under the pressure of tryin to cope on criminally low wages in a desperate bid to maintain dignity.

The results of various experiments into the long-term effects of takin ecstacy suggest that there is a real danger of the user depletin their stores of the brain juice known as seratonin. In layman's terms, this substance is akin to the lubricants needed to keep engines runnin smoothly – the oil runs out, the engine seizes. Likewise with the human brain. Runnin out of seratonin early, they say, can lead to memory loss, depression, anxiety, panic attacks, insomnia, violent outbursts an many other symptoms associated with bein emotionally unbalanced.

So what are the long-term effects of bein out of a job, or of having a job an still bein so poor that you can't afford to pay the bills or eat properly an going out with your mates requires big sacrifices all the way down the line. Well, I'd say the long-term effects are likely to be: depression, anxiety, anger an violence within the home, lack of proper nutrition an insomnia, along with other symptoms of bein emotionally unbalanced. An you can only wish that you could blot out the memory of all the crap in the past.

Not much of a risk then, considerin the outcome can be pretty similar, whether it is the result of the external effects of livin in a run-down community or the internal effects of takin drugs within that same community. Of course, there is always a real chance that you can literally drop down dead from consumin drugs, but what of the slow agonizin death of sufferin poverty day in, day out, an the increased risk of developin fatal illnesses in such an atmosphere?

The sad fuckin truth is that there is widespread POVERTY an people are starvin in Britain, but it's not just food they are hungry for, but a chance to see what life could really be like.

But enough of my layman's politics an soap-box orations.

I don't pretend to know what the answer is myself an it's obvious that, me bein me, I can't possibly take the moral high ground on such matters, but I do know that the key to it all is understandin an educatin, not ignorance an condemnation. There aren't many lives that aren't tainted with the problem in one way or another an that can't be ignored.

I concede I was an amazingly lucky bastard in that I found myself on a stage an I could view the growin tide of supporters of the party-on vibe from that platform. It's a scary thought that an arena full of educated an talented kids are all lookin up to the biggest bunch of fuckin villainous low-life Beelzebubs with the most ridiculously twisted an knorled historics an, ironically, they are really gettin off on our performance of life on the dark side, soakin it all in as an antidote to their learned objectivity – a momentary escape from the safety of their carefully structured lives. We were comin at it from completely the opposite direction: an antidote to the poverty an deprivation we'd seen; an escape from the hand-to-mouth existence we feared an loathed that threatened to suck us in an swallow us whole.

This is the life I was tryin to escape from by takin the paths that I did. Some of them were dead ends with damp sheds at the bottom an some of them were fuckin great big tree-lined avenues flanked with mansions.

This is the story of my misspent youth, an early adult life, a pendulous life of extremes, but none the less, one that travels a steady if meanderin incline from poverty an despair to hope an salvation via the unlikely vehicle of a ramshackle band known as the Happy Mondays.

There is hope.

DRUGS = life
DRUGS = stimulated life
DRUGS = simulated life
DRUGS = escapism
DRUGS = captivity
DRUGS = money
DRUGS = no money
DRUGS = sex
DRUGS = broken families
DRUGS = confidence
DRUGS = paranoia
DRUGS = energy
DRUGS = inertia
DRUGS = glamour
DRUGS = deprivation
DRUGS = generosity
DRUGS = deceit
DRUGS = social circles
DRUGS = antisocial circles
DRUGS = love
DRUGS = violence
DRUGS = wicked nights
DRUGS = wasted days
DRUGS = enlightened thoughts
DRUGS = banal conversations
DRUGS = somethin other than this life
           – death maybe?

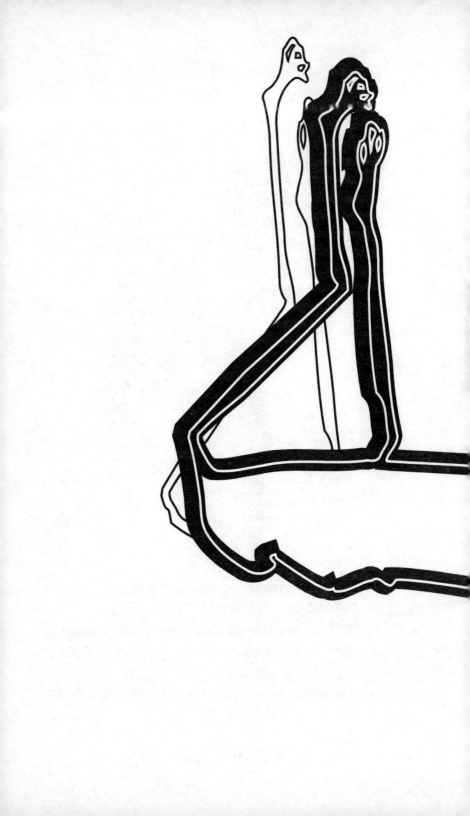

AND GOD
CREATED BEZ

There has got to be some mistake, though. I wanted to be a footballer. 'Pop celebrity', it sounds so fuckin puffy, but life's a twisted conundrum for all of us an who am I to cast the first stone?

No, there has definitely got to be some genuine mistake! An what was all that baggy bollocks about? Surely it was borne only from a need to look fatter than the skinny bastards we were. The lifestyle we led didn't account for the need for food; my much publicized ribs an concave stomach were testament to the fact, an anyway, it's bloody cold an pissin it down most of the time in Manchester; a second layer of clothing never goes amiss.

Okay, let's take a Freudian sidestep an look for some clues in my childhood.

A pretty normal set-up in my view, all the usual ingredients were there like a mam, a dad, a sister, a nice three-bedroomed detached house, plenty of food, washed an ironed clothes; in fact everything was perfect, just perfect – an therein lies the crux of the problem. I was not perfect. I spoiled the flawless little set-up that my mam an dad had perfected; my parents were the ultimate perfectionists an I was not. A perfect excuse to become the recusant little upstart from hell. Let's get this clear though, I never intended it to be that way, it just sort of happened, the way these things do.

My mam, she's great, everything co-ordinates in her little world. She won't have her picture taken at Christmas unless her clothes are co-ordinated, she won't serve a meal unless it all co-ordinates with the dinner service – I love her to bits, but that doesn't co-ordinate with her poise, it's a messy emotion to be showing, that love thing. Neat an tidy, clean an ironed, washed an fed – to stray from this tried an tested formula would be nothing short of a recipe for a nervous breakdown for my mam. Perhaps it's something to do with their generation, or perhaps it's just that I'm reluctant to accept that I'm a lazy bastard. My girlfriend says it's my mam's fault, she made it all too easy for me: school clothes on the radiator warming every morning, never having to think about feeding myself or pushing a Hoover round. I'm an irresponsible git, I can't deny it, but it's all a matter of instillin some trust an confidence in a kid, an I was bestowed a hefty zilch of both. Probably because I couldn't be trusted, come to think of it!

So now we're gettin somewhere, it's all beginnin to come back to me; the poor school reports: 'Mark has the ability but does not seem interested in his school work.' I fuckin hated school, all that authoritarian bullshit, it never worked for my old fella, so why in the hell should I be subjected to it at school as well. I felt an outcast from the word go, never graspin the fundamentals of the 'Me teacher, you small child who shall learn' ethics of education. I'll give you a small example. My mam gave me some money to buy my daily snack at school an instructed me to buy a packet of crisps. I was buzzin with this new found independence an duly asked for my packet of crisps when my turn came. The teacher in all her wisdom told me the price of a packet of crisps. This meant nothin to me, I could barely spell my own name at this point in time. I handed the money over in all innocence an was just about to move off when I got a pull: I didn't have enough to buy the crisps. A small error for a five-year-old I think, but she was adamant that I buy somethin else.

Now here's the rub, my mam had told me to buy crisps an crisps I was buyin, or else, by my reckonin, I was in deep shit. The teacher wasn't havin it, so I did what any self-respectin tearaway would do an bit her hand to show I meant business. In my little mind I was merely expressin the deep desire to please my mam, no matter what. The teacher didn't see it as thus an ran out of the room screamin. Fuckin hell, it couldn't have been more difficult for a kid to get his crisps. The buzz went around that I should be expectin the cane – just what was this cane? I was really shittin my pants by now an gettin more indignant by the minute. I imagined a cage made out of canes an everyone throwin rotten fruit an veg at me: I was five years old for God's sake! I can't remember the actual outcome, but a letter was drafted an sent out to my mam an dad. That was the start of a very tetchy relationship between myself an the authorities that never enjoyed a reunion.

An so the seeds were sown.

I think I'll throw in a bit of the old background nonsense here so you'll understand a little more of where I'm comin from, maybe.

I was born on the 18 April 1964 in a hospital somewhere in Bolton. That makes me an Aries; a stubborn ram runnin head-long into each new thing that comes my way – I'm sure those around me would agree.

My mam an dad are both from Liverpool; my dad from Norris Green an my mam from Fazakerly. They moved to Manchester when they got married an my dad took up the profession of policeman. When I was born, I came complete with the biggest pair of fuck-off manic, starin eyes ever seen on a babe of such a tender age; the chemical additions to my nervous system in later years were NOT the makin of my peepers! Inter-estingly, or maybe not so interesting, my dad has a very similar bone structure, with skull-enhancin, hollowed-out cheeks an piercin, steely-blue eyes set in a deep scowl, an not a single narcotic has ever passed into his bloodstream. Now, all you bandwagon reporters, just how do you account for that?

My mam, Norma Berry, is the oldest of a family of four. She's really dinky, with size three feet but, fuck me, she can give a proper clout out when she feels like it, or rather, when she was driven to the point of no return by her little devil of a son. I remember that through all of my childhood, she would effort-lessly get on with all that mundane shit like washin an ironin an makin sure the dinner was on the table at the 'proper' time an all that bollocks. I mean I am grateful for it all now but, back then I assumed it was what every good mam did for their offspring.

It is of course one way of showin love an it is bein a good mam but, now I'm older, I can see a multitude of ways to show your love to your kids. Sometimes it's okay to say fuck the routine way of doin it, we're goin to just enjoy ourselves today 'cos that's what life should be about; a little bit of supervised anarchy is good for the soul. Nothin too radical, you understand, simply allowin a bit of fun to happen once in a while to get it out of their system; a kind of a safety valve, you might say, to let the build up of craziness out in short, sharp bursts.

There was no room for this kind of behaviour in my child-hood an as a result, the craziness accumulated an bubbled below the surface until I couldn't suppress it any longer an the whole fuckin lot came floodin an frothin out of me, takin many unde-sirable forms an gettin me in some seriously stinkin, deep shit. It's all a question of findin a balance; you might think I'm a reck-less person instillin such values in my own boys, but I know how harmful it is to stifle your kids with unbendin rules an regula-tions, an they know I'll be their friend no matter what.

My old fella, Tony Berry, is a tall geezer with pretty much the same features as myself, as I've said earlier. He is the younger of two brothers an bein a member of the dibble squad, has a ten-dency to lean a little heavily on the serious an strict side of things. Because of this trait in his personality, I always found it very difficult to please him, an quickly realized it would be vir-tually impossible to do so even with a 100 per cent effort. I soon stopped tryin an resigned myself to the fact that it was better to just keep out of his way, not that I really saw that much of him as his job kept him workin all hours. I'll give him his dues though, he did try to do some of those treasured father/son things like playin football an cricket. I remember him settin me off on two wheels for the first time in the back garden in Swinton. Come to think of it, he did have a subtle streak of humanity in him when he chose to show it, the old bastard.

My sister, Michaela, I'd say she's pretty goddam ACE. She looks nothin like me, the only similar feature we used to share was a big gap in our front teeth. I foolishly lost mine at fifteen one school lunchtime when I decided it would be a top laugh to go rippin about on my mate's motorbike an – just for good measure – leave the helmet behind. How was I to know a stupid fuckin mongrel of a dog, hell bent on the same death trip as me, would make a B-line for my front wheel? Road burns hurt like fuck, especially when all that's between you an the tarmac is a flimsy but fly Harrington jacket. Both sides of the zip stuck in either shoulder, I lost my trademark gappy teeth an had angry red burns from head to foot. On arrival at hospital, I tried the old concussed an can't remember my name line. They weren't havin it, an neither were the police. I'd lost my best jacket, my teeth an my freedom – I was severely grounded for what seemed like a whole year.

So our kid still has hers an quite cute it is on her too, the gap that is. My eldest son has inherited similar teeth, so I might get to see what I would have looked like in later years if he manages to hang on to his that long.

I must have been a top thorn in our kid's side most of the time, especially as she seemed to feel obliged to stick up for me when the shit hit the fan, which was quite a regular occurrence in our house. What more could you ask for in a sister? For some strange reason though, our kid never seemed to get into trouble on the same scale as me, breezin through school with great reports an goin on to university to eventually become a lawyer. I must admit, I'm totally in awe of what she has achieved – very handy too for a rogue such as myself, not that I'd ever use her or put her on the spot, except to ask advice on legal matters, you understand.

She did actually grass me up the one time over some money that I brought home from school, a grand total of four pence that had been an overpayment of dinner money or somethin. I should have given it to my mam but, bein the rascal that I was, I took our kid an myself down the road to the sweet shop. Four pence in those days, you have to appreciate, could buy you a shitload of toffees.

Tea time found us sat round the table with my mam an dad tryin to force the food down our stuffed gullets. My dad, the ever watchful an observant dibble that he was, soon sussed the pair of us out. Next thing, I can't believe my ears as our kid proceeded to put me right on the spot, tellin them I'd bought her some sweets. The one-man crime squad got on my case immediately, an employin all of his police trainin tactics, quickly pushed through the blatant lies to get to the truth. The saddest point to this little drama is that when he did finally squeeze the truth out of his six-year-old son, he didn't believe that I'd come by the money by such innocent means. Needless to say, the punishment did not fit the crime an it was the first an last time our kid ever grassed me up. A few good lessons were learnt by all that day in our house; havin been accused, tried an punished beyond the point of acceptable, I resolved to cover up my boyhood endeavours a little better next time.

Don't get me wrong now, not all my childhood memories are of the 'I'm so hard done by' kind. In fact I would say that I had a reasonably comfortable upbringin with plenty of food to eat, holidays every year, nice sensible shoes that were fitted properly at Clarks, an all that responsible parentin kind of stuff that goes on in most average households up an down the land.

We had quite a large family if you included all my uncles an aunts, nanas an grandads an all the cousins that we used to visit on a regular basis, which I really used to look forward to as a kid. We were a close family which I suppose is somethin in these days of isolated family units. My favourites had to be my grandparents on both sides, whom I loved an still love dearly for standin by me an havin faith in me more than anythin, when every other single member of the family had me down as the proverbial bad-assed black sheep. They always gave me their support an did their best to help me through some really shitty times.

Family holidays were the best times, campin in England an Scotland, on various caravan sites, always in Britain though; holidayin abroad was purely the mark of the privileged round our way. Actually, I can honestly say that those were some of the best holidays I've ever had; hangin round on beaches in the daytime an goin to nightclubs after dark – they possibly formed the blueprint for the recurrin patterns in my life in later years! Alright, so it was the local equivalent to the Wheel Tappers an Shunters but, to a mere kid, it was disco heaven with lashins of shandy Bass an as many bags of KP nuts as possible in an attempt to uncover the scantily dressed woman on the card on which the packets were hung behind the bar. This was in the days before Britain was gripped with a prudent fear of offendin the fairer sex by admirin bodily curves in a public place. Shame. My ancestors were of French origin, possibly accountin for my hot-blooded passion for oglin just such luscious sights without remorse.

As we got older, the old fella took to hill walkin, takin me an our kid out in all sorts of weather; stormin up an down mountains was a breeze with his six-foot one-inch frame an fanatically trained an toned physique. For short-arsed fledglins such as us, it was a completely different story, our faces turnin purple an our legs burnin with the effort of keepin him in our sights. At the time it was pure torture an I hated every piece of land that had the impudence to be juttin upwards with anythin more than a 2 per cent incline, but, lookin back, it was a fuckin gem of an experience to be outdoors an worryin about nothin but pissin into the wind an gettin wet shoes.

One of the best times was up in Scotland, a whole clan of us takin over a few little cottages for a few activity-crammed weeks. My old fella took our little tribe of cousins an myself out nice an early one mornin, determined to show us the ins an outs of fishin. We were located right on a loch that led out to an estuary a quarter of a mile or so from the North Sea coast.

We hired a little rowin boat down at the loch an set off in the early mornin haze on the mission designed to make real men of us. With such complicated equipment as a handline spinner an a net, we sat in silence waitin for the first bite. The silence was killin me an I started to fidget about like bored little kids do; I was stuck out there in a forced union, with my mentor flashin unapprovin looks at my inability to control my impatience. I tried whistlin – the look said it wasn't on to whistle. I reached for the packet of crisps that my mam had lovinly slipped in my lunch box – rattlin crisps bags apparently is a mortal sin in the codes of fishin conduct.

Finally, I got a bite.

My adrenalin kicked in an before I knew it we were breathless, with involuntary 'ughs' an 'aghs' escapin our wide-open mouths as we wrestled with the big, ugly, scaly creature that was flappin furiously on the end of my line. Top fuckin buzz as it left the water an I manoeuvred it into the net. I was nervous but exhilarated by the frenzied reaction of this strange life force that I'd plucked from its natural habitat; a cod up until that point had only ever been a fillet of flaky white stuff wrapped in greasy batter, but this mother fucker had bulgin eyes an toilet-rim-white lips on a big, fat 'orrible mouth that opened an closed revealin a set of razor-sharp tiny teeth. I'd never considered the livin entity in its watery home in comparison to the supper on my plate from the chippy. So this is what he meant by makin a man out of me; showin me how to tease an torture lesser life forms before tossin them mercifully back, secure in the knowledge that we rule the Earth as men. *Fuckin ACE!* I mean let's be right, I was a big, bad twat with a sharp hook to this poor little fish an, fuck me, was I gloatin about it. Yes, I thought, I could quite get used to this sadistic sport, if you didn't have to wait so fuckin long for the rush that is. An it's never guaranteed, an that's the real bummer.

My first fish.

Chuffed from our first result, we continued to fish for some time, not knowin that the next fish we were to catch sight of would be a fuck-off baskin shark. Obviously right on the power trip we'd been complacent enough to wallow in, it decided to jump right out of the water just a hundred yards from the boat to make a point about nature always gettin the upper hand. My old fella took a split-second to grab the oars an make the Oxford/Cambridge oarsmen look like they propelled pleasure boats in the park for a livin.

Our moment of glory had passed. We had to concede, as men, we weren't so superior after all.

I was havin a particularly interestin introduction to the joys of discoverin wildlife that summer – my next victim bein a black-adder snake which I inadvertently stood on an consequently battered to death in a bout of superhuman strength caused by sheer terror. My little heart had skipped a beat as I glanced to the ground to see what the unfamiliar sensation under my trainer-clad, city feet was. What I had assumed to be a stick of some sort moved in a strange writhin motion.

FUCK ME – A SNAKE.

In my limited knowledge of the world, I assumed snakes only existed in the more exotic lands, not up here in safe old Scotland. The reaction was that of any kid in a blind panic; I lunged at it with my walkin stick, which I'd fashioned earlier from a stray branch.

WHACK WHACK WHACK WHACK WHACK WHACK WHACK WHACK WHACK WHACK WHACK.

I didn't stop till I could be sure of its certain death. The local farmer's wife shit herself when I told her the story of my triumphant battle in the wilds an I proved my glory by danglin the offendin limp corpse in front of her face. How was I to know they were poisonous? Fuckin good job I sorted it out then if you ask me. If it's goin to be me or Mr Snake, I think it's only fair to say – batter the motherfucker.

I spotted my first real submarine on that holiday, too, just off the coast of Scotland. It bobbed up from out of nowhere, a huge, bullet-shaped, grey metal vessel with all the features of, well, a submarine I suppose. It took my breath away as it rose silently an majestically from the waves, the sun bouncin late-afternoon rays off its metallic turrets givin it the appearance of a red-hot poker. It looked indescribably powerful as it glided out of sight; it was way beyond any concept I had formed of the way things are in the world an how they are kept that way. The whole scale of the meaning of havin an American war vessel in my midst was too much for my immature mind to take in. I just marvelled at the vision in front of me; it was *Stingray* for real an I was a lucky little bastard who couldn't wait to tell my mates back in Swinton.

Summer holidays were a constant battle for freedom, with the old fella layin down the rules of conduct in his little domain. Playin out for the sheer joy of it didn't come into the equation. First, it was times tables to be learnt, bein tested every day before I could go out. Then, as I got older, the tasks to be performed before leisuretime was entered into became more seriously home orientated, like cuttin the grass before joinin my mates who were all happily playin footie across the road in the local DSS grounds. All character-buildin stuff I'm sure, but when you've got a game of footie to attend with your mates it's a fuckin liberty innit, or it's a sad loss of fuckin liberty, or both. To add insult to injury, my dad, as I suppose all dads do, would embarrass me further by turfin the lads off this revered piece of enclosed grass an stoppin the game altogether. Life's a twat, even when you're a kid.

Skateboards, bikes, roller-skates – all were alien concepts to me an I wanted in badly. I did get a bike once, when I was five – a Raleigh R II, red with white wheels an stabilizers. It was ACE an I was made up to fuck. I treasured that bike an a good job too because I never got another one. Now where's the logic in that? I split a gut learnin to ride a bike an then what – nothin. I tell you, I was sorely pissed off.

In later years, I remedied the situation by stockpilin bike parts from all manner of places – the back of the bike shop, the tip, bits that my mates were discardin, anywhere. The styles were nothin if not imaginative an some of them turned out to be an acceptable mode of transport – some of them were simply death traps. Now both my boys have bikes – nice, shiny, comfortable, safe ones from a proper bike shop – which we take to the park along with their safety helmets an clip-on drinkin bottles an they ride to their hearts' content, confident as fuck an lovin every minute. It's a joy to see.

The importance of music hit me around the age of seven thanks to my uncle George, a real Beatles devotee who got himself a new stereo an kindly donated his old mono set from the 60s along with all the old mono records. Afternoons were spent listening intently to timeless classics such as 'Strawberry Fields', 'Yellow Submarine', 'Lucy In The Sky With Diamonds' an 'Norwegian Wood' – my underdeveloped knowledge of the world an its stimulants led me to believe that all these tunes were written for kids. I couldn't believe that adults could get on the fantasy vibe that screamed from the nonsense lyrics – how could they understand all that with their clean-cut rules an sundry sensible explanations for every goddamned thing that was?

All I knew was that they turned me on an lit up my little life like nothin had before. I was proper buzzin-to-fuck over my new acquisition – a real record player, wow did I think I was the coolest kid in the street – YES. The record player looked like an old wooden suitcase but it delivered me to a place more wondrous than ever before, as I locked myself in my bedroom with stars like Buddy Holly beltin out his greatest hits. The cover was purple an inside there were black an white photographs of Buddy himself – brilliant.

The Bay City Rollers – now there's a band I can't forget. I remember bein really impressed when I saw them on the television an goin into school the next day I was aware of an explosion of interest among all my friends as we compared notes about what we'd seen the night before. The lads decided to adapt one of their biggest hits – 'Bye Bye Baby' – to somethin like – 'You're the one girl in town I'd marry, big tits an a hairy fanny.' It became a bit of an anthem that lasted for many months in our little posse. Samplin an twistin the original, it's the essence of art. An why not?

Secondary school: Wardley High – a flat pack, single-storey buildin made from hardboard, holes gapin everywhere, where bored, Docker-shod feet had tested the fabric of the walls, an countless broken windows where bricks had been hurled in disgust at the ugliness of the stark, barren structure.

As I've said earlier, the relationship between school an myself was an uncomfortable forced union, with my constant efforts to leave by any means possible counteracted by the head-master's stubborn determination to keep me there till the bitter end – no matter how bad my actions became. By the time I'd entered the fifth form, I was desperate to get out into the big wide world to join my mates, all of whom had triumphed in gettin expelled before their time was officially up. I couldn't understand it, here I was bein the biggest, single most disruptive element in the gaff an, no matter what I got up to, they wouldn't succumb to defeat an accept I was an irredeemable lost cause. The headmaster called me into his office for the umpteenth time in the final term of the fifth year.

'Berry, I will not give you what you want. You want to be out there with your mates, but I'm not goin to sanction it. You might as well stop trying to get expelled because you will be stayin right here, with us, until it is the proper time for you to be leavin, an that is my final word on the matter.'

Fuckin pompous bastard.

God knows, I'd tried my damnedest, pullin tried an tested stunts like floodin the toilets. That's bound to get their goat, I reasoned, an set off the instant the thought had popped into my head to put the plan into action. I was feelin particularly disillu-sioned by the education system that day an was convinced the school an myself could benefit from my absence; at least the other kids could get on with their studies if I wasn't constantly interruptin the classes with my belligerent ways. Driven by my honourable sense of martyrdom, I proceeded to put the plug into each sink an, one by one, turn on each tap to its fullest before standin back to reflect on my handiwork. I was filled with a sense of gratification as the water began to cascade over the tops of the sinks an spill on to the pissy floor, the individual puddles soon joinin to form one giant pool, creepin slowly towards the door.

'Berry! What do you think you're doin! Turn those off an go to the caretaker to get a mop an bucket to clean up this mess.'

I'd been rumbled in my finest hour, but resolved to stand my ground. This they couldn't forgive, surely. I retorted with a suitably arrogant negative, just to ensure the punishment would be the final marchin orders I was hankerin after. 'No, fuck off. I ain't cleanin no mess up, we 'ave cleaners to do that.'

Just to emphasize my intolerable nature, I pushed past the teacher, sendin his pile of books into the sonny cesspit, which by now was coverin the whole floor. Another teacher who had been passin at the time an had heard the commotion came bawlin into the bogs an ran headlong into my scrawny frame – I was completely charged with adrenalin an again managed, in my heightened emotional state, to mow him down with one angry swipe. I made it to the door, focused on gettin the hell out of there an through the school gates, but on openin it the silhouette of the biggest, bastard games teacher stopped me dead in my tracks an he instantly lunged at me with a serious rugby tackle, bringin me down hard on the concrete steps.

Shit! This wasn't supposed to happen. The plan had backfired badly. I was escorted to get the mop an bucket an watched over as I sullenly cleaned up the water, mumblin obscenities with each wring of the mop. My humiliatin task completed, I was frog-marched to the head's office to receive my retribution. The 'whack' was administered with a hefty dollop of righteous indignation at my subordinate behaviour.

An still they would not expel me. Bastards. What does a kid have to do to get right under their skin an make them scratch me off the list for good?

The corporal punishment only served to strengthen my resolve. The impact of havin to clean the toilets had, to be honest, been a far bigger pain. Chastisin me with corporal punishment, however, only confused the issue, creatin a relentless cat an mouse scenario of: I tease the teachers, they catch me an give me a good hidin an then I go on my way, smartin slightly but still smilin, back into the system. We used to laugh at the futility of the routine, sometimes makin a competition out of who could get the most whacks in one day. I ask you, fancy treatin juveniles like juveniles an expectin a reformation of character to ensue. Ridiculous.

My behaviour after school hours wasn't gettin any better either as I became more an more embroiled with the criminal-minded youth in our district. I was, I confess, gettin right out of hand, hell bent on causin as much disruption an chaos in every area of my life. Teenage angst wasn't even in it. I was careerin down the slippery slope at full throttle into a life of petty crime when most kids my age were safely contemplatin which career path they were goin to take in the respectable world of employment.

Blinkered to the harm I was about to inflict upon my future, I found myself one typically mischievous evenin 'borrowing' a bike along with a friend. A particularly amiable passer-by, well known round our way for his dexterity in mechanical matters of this kind, stopped to enlighten us with a few handy tips, havin witnessed our pathetic struggle to get the fuckin thing in motion. Cheers mate!

We'd got a taste for ridin bikes in the summer, when we'd borrowed one, legit, from this other mate of ours but then he'd gone away, takin his bike with him, leavin us high an dry. We needed that fix that the bikin around had given us an hit upon the idea of findin another bike to get our kicks on. Don't ask me why, it was just written into the scheme of things in those days. I knew I was doin wrong but the momentum of the moment carried us along an before you could say, 'don't forget your helmet', we were off, buzzin into the night, minus the required headgear, of course. My parka billowin like the Michelin man an the wind rushin in my face, I sped through the night feelin invincible, or was that invisible; I can't believe we didn't get pulled by the old bill. A few hours of mayhem passed in this manner before we realized we were pushin our luck a little too far, an put the bike to rest in a carefully concealed spot, hopin to return for more of the same the next day.

I ran the short distance back home an paused at the top of the drive to compose myself. The adrenalin rush was still full on, coursin through my veins, makin my heart jump wildly about in my chest. I bent over, takin deep breaths so that I could enter the house in a relaxed an innocent manner. Fuck me if the old man didn't pull into the drive, shinin his headlamps full on my gaspin, crumpled figure, catchin my eyes in the beam as they spun in wild delirium, transfixed with terror like a rabbit in the road. He was just back from work an was still in detective mode, smellin a guilty rat from ten paces.

'What you doin son?'

He knew by instinct that whatever I'd been up to, it was seriously wrong an before I could answer, I was in the confines of the kitchen bein accused of takin all manner of drugs. Now I can forgive him for comin to such a logical conclusion, considerin the state I was in at the time; eyes rollin an frothin at the mouth, but I look like that whenever I get seriously out of breath an I vehemently protested my innocence on the drugs allegation. My sleeves were rolled back for evidence, but obviously I came up clean on the inspection. Top one; this gave me bonus time to get it together an I once more proclaimed my innocence, with slightly more confidence this time. For once, he'd been barkin up the wrong tree. True I'd taken a couple of tokes on a spliff, but nothin more. To be honest, I never even used to smoke that much, maybe just the odd few drags of someone else's bifter in the Smokers' Corner at school an gettin stoned to a few tunes with my mates now an then. I was still right into playin footie an stayin healthy so that I could play for St Paul's, the local youth club team.

After much eyeballin durin the interrogation I realize he believes I'm tellin the truth, an good job as, on this particular score, I was. I quickly regain my confidence, makin up a rapid blag about havin to put a sprint on it home as I'd been chased by a gang of other kids.

This wasn't too far from bein unfeasible, rememberin the

incident a few weeks previously when I'd been jumped by a gang from Cheetham Hill. It was an unresolved territory feud between the Salford an Cheetham kids. We were obviously viewed as the new, younger blood that would been soon tryin to reclaim boundaries. I viewed us as a couple of young kids walkin my girlfriend home to Pembroke Halls, feelin pretty fuckin good about just bein out an about of a night. Not to say that we didn't organize the odd outin to visit a rival gang – it was all still a game to us in 1978, before crack turned it all to casual murder an mayhem.

They leathered us good style, an I was the lucky one. They went for my mate first an I got a kickin as an afterthought from two of the black kids. Don't get me wrong, I got a few good shots in an managed to stay on my feet, swervin most of their blows, incitin them with my stubborn determination to resist a fall. Dirty tricks proceeded as a milk bottle was carelessly placed on my head, followed by a full crate of bottles crashin over my shoulders. Fuckin hell, what a commotion. The girls were screamin, the glass was smashin an tinklin everywhere an curtains were beginnin to twitch as people looked on to see the tail end of the attack. Brushin splinters from my kecks, I noticed the absence of my mate; he'd managed to do one away out of there, leavin me to get all the attention. My street cred ratin soared. I was that lone fuckin warrior out there defendin the patch an tellin the girls to stand back as it could get messy. Oh, yes the bravado poured out at every good story opportunity, of which I found many. Rougher than rough, tougher than tough, that's what I reckoned it was all about at fifteen. YEEEESSSSS!

Like I said, I was no angel an had been battlin up in Bolton only the week before. It was a tit-for-tat thing; first you dished it out, then you copped a load back, no hard feelins. In fact, as it goes, I ended up workin in a warehouse in Miles Plattin with two of the lads that I used to fight against back then. It provided somethin interestin to talk an laugh about durin the tea breaks.

So, back to the initial plot – I'm tellin a whoppin pack of lies to the old fella an gettin away with it. I'm finally allowed to get off to my room where I lay on my bed, re-enactin the scenes in my head, addin a bit of drama here an there for the benefit of the other lads tomorrow at school. Can't wait.

The next day it all went a bit fuckin sour on me. I'd managed to tell the story in full an was baskin in the glory when I got a shout to go to the head's office. Oh God, here we go, I thought. The CID had been on the phone askin me to call down the station after school. It turned out the other kid's mam had apparently gone ballistic on seein her son come in all black an blue with most of his front teeth kicked out. Shit! This means big trouble at home for me, I cringed. It's crap havin a policeman for a dad, he got to hear everythin first hand every time. There was definitely no hidin it now. He went fuckin bananas, threatenin to do me in a second time if I ever tried to follow anythin like that through again. Now I've never been a snake an wouldn't even consider standin back while a friend got battered. It was no mither to me that I just happened to get a kickin by tryin to help him out. I stood my ground an pleaded my innocence yet again, but the conclusions my old man had formed were set in concrete an nothin I could say would budge him from his preachin platform at this late stage.

The battles, however, continued to rage, especially at school dinnertimes when the local chippy became a bone of contention as it was situated on the boundaries of three schools: Wardley (my school), Moorside an Cromwell Road. All three would try to lay claim to the chippy, an absurd notion that quickly got completely out of hand with clashes occurrin nearly every day. One such day I was returnin to school with my girlfriend an her mates, havin bought our chips an eaten them. No one was around from our school an it all seemed quiet enough, but, as we turned the corner, a large gang was lyin in wait to pounce. It's a strange phenomenon I've noticed over the years that whenever you're about to get a good hidin, there's never a soul around to help save your bacon. I'm not sayin that all my friends were chickens who scarpered at the first hint of trouble, it's just that fate always sends me out on a limb an alone at such times. This was to be no exception. There was also a certain amount of pride at stake, what with my girlfriend an her mates standin by the action. There really was no option but to fly headfirst into the fray an keep my head down low to avoid undue damage. I swung around like a madman, tryin my hardest to fight my way out of the difficult situation. Presently, a dibble van flew round the corner, sirens blarin, sendin the hostile crowd scatterin in all directions, leavin just me to face the music. I half stood to dust myself down an realized they were about to move in to arrest me. Luckily, there were witnesses vouchin for my innocence but the bastards still bundled me into the van after bein told it was the Moorside lot who were to blame.

I couldn't believe it, they were only takin me down to Moorside School in the van to identify the gang who'd jumped me. That's it, I thought, I'm dead meat once they clock me gettin out of this van, doin the police's dirty work; they might as well have signed my death warrant. Now I know it doesn't pay to be a grass in any situation an I wasn't about to break ranks now. I told them nothin. Obviously the beatin had wiped my memory clean.

I returned to my own school only to be promptly sent home due to my battered an bruised condition. This was not an easy option to take as it was a precursor to yet more shit from my old fella. The double injustice of the whole affair was almost too much to take in one day.

Needless to say, I was a touch anxious on the way home from school, constantly lookin over my shoulder for a few weeks after the incident.

In truth, our school was findin it increasingly difficult to get the upper hand on the growin number of incidents that were occurrin in an around school. They simply didn't have the facilities to cope with the swell of delinquent boys that made up the fifth form in our year. How anyone ever managed to get a decent education with our disruptive behaviour goin on all around them, I just don't know. Classes were regularly disrupted by the antics of a handful of boys who would climb in through windows an sit smokin or throwin objects at a target on the blackboard in lessons they shouldn't even be attendin, often resultin in the teacher in question leavin the room in tears of sheer frustration. I'm sorry to say that I was often one of the gang.

In a desperate attempt to get me to do somethin constructive,

I was assigned to the woodwork an photographic classes to keep me busy an out of trouble, until such time that I could officially leave. Exams didn't even come into the picture.

All the excessive violence came to a head one day when a nasty confrontation in the shoppin precinct ended with a stabbin. A ripple of shock was felt throughout the local communities an the story was picked up by the national press, emphasizin the serious level to which the feuds had escalated. The kid pulled through, but the consequences of the episode were felt across the board an a truce of sorts came into effect. For a while.

Discontent at not havin the usual outlet of a good skirmish at dinnertime, we decided to vent our anger by aimin it at the authorities in the confines of our own school. The plan was thus: we would round up all the fifth form boys into the top common room, threatenin a sound thrashin for anyone not prepared to join in the proceedins. Not surprisingly, we amassed a fair gatherin of dissidents in a very short space of time. The next stage of the plan was to lead the throng down through the school in a defiant show of power by numbers. It worked a treat; the line of teachers lyin in wait for the onslaught broke instantly under the weight of our marchin army, partin like the Sea of Galilee as we strode on by. The route took us round the circumference of the school buildins an, fuelled by our success, we decided to go three more laps, just to make a point. The exact point we were makin wasn't really defined but it felt good all the same. It was certainly more effective than the occasional two finger salute, anyway.

As far as we were concerned, the education system had failed us badly, although whether that was the fault of the individual teachers or the Government's policy on education is a matter for debate. Personally I think the teachers had their hands tied due to a severe lack of resources an manpower to deal with the influx of rebels from the economically stunted surroundin communities in the appropriate way.

My poor long-sufferin parents were bearin the real brunt of my resistance to authority though, as I began to get more an more involved in greater acts of social misconduct. In short, I was turnin into a top thievin bastard, takin anythin from telephoto lens to the odd piece of transport here an there. The things we took were usually on the small scale, primarily to fund our nightly outins around the local towns. The items were never personal belongins though; they weren't acts of desperation to get a bag of brown or anythin of that sort, merely the misguided acts of a youth with a cloudy future, livin for the immediate moment. To my mam an dad I was a disgrace to the family name, probably still am come to think of it.

It was as if a fuse had been lit an was burnin slowly but surely towards an imminent explosion an nothin an no one could prevent it from happenin. They tried their best, puttin curfews on my leisure time an threatenin a lock out if I didn't make it home by a certain time. I took it as an invitation to stay out all weekend, partyin with my mates or, failin that, I'd pretend to adhere to the time limit set an climb in an out of my bedroom window via the front porch. One night, I'd done just that an set off on a furtive mission to meet my mates who were the proud possessors of a bunch of FS keys. We'd been advised that they would get us into any vehicle we wanted an we were itchin to try them out, just to see.

The local garage forecourt was targeted an we quickly began to test them out on car after car, startin with the best. We were down to just the one car left, an old banger of an Escort, a Mark I to be exact. Bingo, we were in. Not bein in the league of the professional car thief, once in, we were at a bit of a loss as to what to do next. In fact, we were a total bunch of wankers as far as hot wirin an actually takin a car was concerned. By some fluke, we managed to start the engine an promptly showed what a complete bunch of arses we were by smashin backwards an forwards, bodgin the gears up, forgettin to take the handbrake off, stallin an kangarooin forward; in fact, everythin possible to attract unwelcome attention to ourselves. It could quite easily have been the prelude to our first taste of borstal. But it wasn't. It was, instead, our first taste of drivin when we finally arrived on the Scan car park, Scan bein the local supermarket round our way at the time.

What a fuckin ball! After the initial gaffs at the forecourt, we came along in leaps an bounds, learnin some natty handbrake turn techniques, cornerin fast in reverse an generally screechin about, burnin rubber indiscriminately. Obviously this kind of behaviour lends itself to enquiry an not before too long we realized the dibble had been informed; a white Maria approached us headlong up the ramp we were descendin. We bailed out an ran like fuck, leavin the car, the keys, everythin. We were lucky bastards, escapin by the skin of our teeth. I stopped at the top of our road to get myself in order; my heart was doin somersaults an I was drenched in sweat from the bolt back home. About ten minutes passed as I sat reflectin on the night's adventure, steadyin my nerves before the careful, silent climb back in.

Feelin really chuffed with myself, I returned to the house an began my sneaky ascent up the porch to the open window, mission accomplished. How was I to know the fuckin porch would collapse on the very night that my mam was waitin vigilantly in my bedroom to collar me on re-entry?

After not too many more of these choice escapades, I was firmly asked to leave the family home, they could take the nightly heartache no more. That was it, I was on my own from that time on, no lookin back. I was sixteen, an it wasn't about to be an easy ride.

The summer passed quickly. I was relishin bein freed from the constraints of school. Every mornin, it was a gift to know I'd never have to go back to the stiflin regime an stinkin corridors of Wardley High School. I suspect the relief was on both sides.

I'd been stayin with a pal throughout that summer, while his mam an dad were away on an extended holiday. I couldn't believe they trusted him with the family home for such a long period of time. I mean, he could have had any old low life in off the street to stay over.

He did. He had me.

Not that I hadn't tried to go about things in a responsible an respectable manner. I had, in fact, decided it was time to go out an get a job as most of my mates had seemed to have managed to do without too much of a problem. I thought I'd better show willin an face real life full on. Some of my pals had got fixed up with a job in a warehouse an suggested that I should give it a try. I couldn't, in all honesty, expect for much more in light of my lack of qualifications an experience. I was also very skint at the time; even though I could sign on at sixteen back then, it was still tough tryin to party all weekend an feed myself.

One of the lads from the warehouse, who was off sick at the time with a sliced Achilles tendon (he'd been showin off in front of some girls, jumpin through an already broken window, daft bastard!) volunteered to take me down to the gaff in Cheetham Hill to introduce me to the boss. I was touched by his enthusiasm for gettin me in with the lads an was quite lookin forward to bein in the gang, havin a laugh an earnin money at last.

There was nothin doin; there was no job to be had an, worse still, we only had just enough money for the bus home when what I really needed was a swift pint to quell my disappointment. Dejected, we turned an idled aimlessly out into the street, kickin at thin air in a thinly disguised show of despair. Well I did. My mate, in his injured state, simply hobbled along beside me on his crutches, keepin quiet, acutely aware of my shattered hopes an the imminent onset of a bout of craziness.

The boss shouted us back in an my heart began to race a little faster with renewed hope. It was only a suggestion, but it was worth the try; their sister company over in Miles Platting might have a vacancy if I got over there pronto.

I set off like Linford Christie, eager to prove my worth an get that bastard job before anyone else did. Fuck, I'd forgotten about my mate's foot an our need of bus fare. Sod it, I'll carry the big daft bastard I decided, an began the trek over there. It's a fuckin long way from Cheetham Hill to Miles Platting with a cripple on your back, but I was so intent on makin a success of the outin that I crucified myself an got us both over there, nearly draggin the poor kid an his crutches along by the finishin line.

Yes! Result! I couldn't believe I'd landed a job on my first attempt – what a flash jammy bastard. My mate was double pissed off; I'd landed a better job than him with nearly double the wages an all he'd got out of the venture were two fuck-off blisters on the palms of his hands from haulin himself round the streets on sticks.

Life's a sadistic bastard sometimes but what can you do?

I slotted into my duties with ease, findin myself among the very lads I'd been fightin against at school, but it was cool now an we looked back on the battles with a bond of humour. I'd already passed the necessary initiation in their eyes an the transition from newcomer to one of the gang was smooth. It was fun to be workin alongside people of a like mind an I was comfortable sharin in their pleasures in the ska revival an funk, doin the obligatory soul moves an grooves in the back of the trucks to pass the time of day as we unloaded the imported goods into the bays, throwin the 'bollock bender' boxes from one place to another.

I began to hang around with my new found friends, goin out on the town to new places an gettin involved in different scenes. They played me Bob Marley tunes an taught me the importance of the lyrics of the Jamaican master of social comment. There were the unforgettable forays into clubland, such as the openin night of Legends, a club that would later be the settin for the 'Wrote for Luck' video with the Happy Mondays. It was a time of awakenins within myself, discoverin avenues of diverse musical tastes that had lain unexplored.

My new found respectability won me a place back in the fold at home. Things were, for once, goin really well. I found myself risin at the unearthly hour of six-thirty a.m. to be in work for seven-thirty so that I could collect a bonus on top of the £120 I was gettin weekly. At first, that seemed like plenty enough to be gettin by on, but by the time a few weekends had passed, I found I wasn't makin it past Sunday without beggin a sub from here an there. I hadn't bargained on how the girls take on a different attitude to the workin male an his dosh. They could fleece you in a trice if you weren't careful. Bein a bit green in the female department, I was initially well up for impressin the opposite sex an regularly took a good fleecin in a bid to get a shag. My success rate wasn't too good. I needed a method of uppin my income. Not surprisingly, the job didn't last too long.

I'd taken to havin a pint with the lads from work after the shift an got scared by what I observed. There were older geezers who'd been doin the same thing, day in, day out for years, their only supplement to the wage bein the odd lost bundle of towels an sheetin from the warehouse to sell on to friends. On this, they struggled to keep their house an kids tickin over, goin prematurely grey with the stress an degradation of not being able to cope with the pressure of keepin it all together on the meagre pay packets from the warehouse. It wasn't for me. I couldn't succumb to the dreariness of a life contenc surrounded by pyramids of soft furnishins an the occasional excitement of a stray batch for my extras in life.

I left the job an home again. This time I swung between stayin at my nana's in Liverpool an my nana's in Wigan, but none of it quite worked out. I didn't feel comfortable inflictin my lifestyle on either household an apart from that, all my pals, an therefore opportunities for earnin a bit of crust, were in Manchester.

I turned to my friend Maggi, whose mum, Mrs McGuire, had kindly offered to put me up, no questions asked. Mrs McGuire was a top woman, she turned me on to the Rolling Stones an the Beatles as they had been the favourite of her husband who had sadly passed away not too long before. They had a wicked record collection in their house an I spent many enjoyable nights just listenin to the tunes an appreciatin bein treated as an individual. I think her recent loss gave her a precious insight into the problems I was havin to face as a kid on the verge of adulthood. She took me in as one of her own. Perhaps she felt a need to care in the wake of her recent loss. I genuinely appreciated the trouble she went to. No one else would have tolerated the stunts I sometimes pulled – like the time I wandered into her bedroom in the middle of the night after a heavy session on the booze, lookin for the toilet. She found me standin by her bed, trousers down an pecker out, ready to commence bladder relief. She didn't even blink, but firmly steered me in the right direction an made nothin more of the incident. I was sorely embarrassed for weeks after. She had a respect for my needs, an even if she suspected my activities, she never grilled me or made me feel inferior. I respected her in return for understandin my troubles an givin me a safe haven, with time an space of my own to reflect on an come to terms with my new found independence.

One night, I bumped into a couple of old school friends of mine while out enjoyin a pint. They began tellin me about their recent escapades an how they'd been gettin a top raise from it all. They had one on that very night. I listened intently to their stories of bravado, followed by a run down of all the smart gear they'd amassed between them, not to mention the top birds they were now consortin with in the light of their new found riches. Call it greed, call it blind, naïve stupidity, I wanted in an told them so. My criminal career was about to take off.

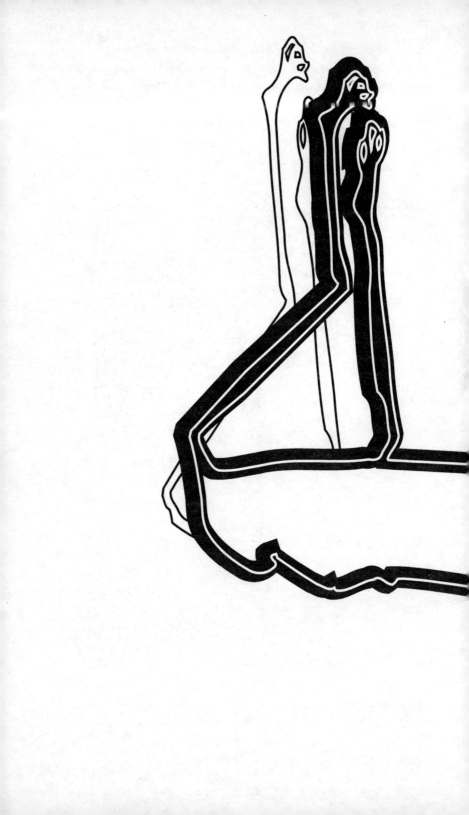

I waited for the first job with baited breath.

First things first though, I knew I couldn't take on the mantle of the underworld an keep my residence with Mrs McGuire. I tentatively enquired about turnin the shed at the bottom of the garden into my private little pad. I didn't in no way want my activities to have any reflection on the good name of her family. I respected the love an attention she'd poured on me durin my stay with them too much. Bein the sensitive an understandin person she was, she granted me permission to convert the shed into my own cosy dwellin. With the help of Maggi, I set to it right away, whitewashin the interior an puttin in a thick-pile carpet, followed by a raised platform bed, a TV, a stereo an a Calor gas heater. I even had my own facilities for makin the brews in the mornin. For a lad of sixteen, it was heaven. I was already makin some serious bird-baitin money within weeks of movin into the luxury pad. Okay, so it was a shed, but it didn't half come in useful as a conversation piece; an the girls just loved the novelty value.

For the first time in my life, I began to live the life I'd always suspected existed out there. I sat in my shed, gloatin about the birds, the clothes an the fact that I had the means to go drinkin or for a top scran whenever an wherever I wanted. I was the fuckin bees knees, oh yes, now I really was livin in the big world. I was now ready to take on the big job.

In the big world, however, a shed is always a shed an someone who lives in one is a bit on the suspect side, a bit of a target you might say. The police thought so, too, an just after my *pièce de résistance*, they decided a visit to my plot in the corner of the garden might pay dividends. Regrettably, they were right. At sixteen, it's all a cut an dried act. You take the risk an you reap the benefits. It's a shock when it happens, havin blocked out the inevitable, knowin it's right there behind you always, but never wantin to consider the full implications of the act.

The big job had gone without a hitch. There was a disused railway line that ran along the back of the houses where my mate an I could get from my shed all the way down to the golf clubhouse an back again without bein seen. Worsley Golf Club, we'd decided, was ripe for a turnover an was bound to be a guaranteed scoop if we could pull it off. What I didn't know at the time was that my accomplice had bungled the same job a few nights previously. I was confident enough but it didn't stop me from gettin the sweats as we raced down there at three a.m. on the chosen night, my heart beatin wildly with the rush of sudden adrenalin. We stole through the night silently, whisperin covertly, observin every shadow for signs of pryin eyes. We came to the edge of the golf course an surveyed the clubhouse from a distance. I could hardly breathe, my chest was so tight with the knowledge of the crime I was about to commit. The silence was deafenin. It felt like we'd been crouched there for an hour before my mate jumped to his feet an gave the signal to advance. It seemed so familiar, this game of hide an attack – only this time we weren't kids playin war an the target was a buildin with glass windows, locked doors an alarms that would alert the world to our endeavours. Time was of the essence.

I didn't suspect his previous failed attempt even when he cut round to the side of the buildin; he knew exactly where to go, headin for the boarded-up window where he'd done the damage a few nights before. He'd apparently got no further before bein chased off by the dibble.

The board was screwed on tight. We set to immediately removin the first board to find that they'd actually replaced the window, so then we had to get the glass out of four of the frames before sawin through the rest of the frame with a hacksaw. It was a long, laborious job an I stood back constantly, eyes dartin frantically into the surroundin blackness, ears alert for the slightest sound of approachin cars. Nothin came. With both layers off we were met with yet another obstacle. They'd put another fuckin board on the inside of the window. No time to waste now – it had to be a case of exertin brute force for the quickest solution. The board fell away with a startlinly loud clatter an we were in.

Once inside we got to work straight away makin a beeline for the till. Obviously, assured of the holdin power of the reinforced security, they had been confident enough to leave the takins in the till. What a fantastic mistake that was. There were a few thousand pounds just sittin there, an my fingers worked like fury as I stuffed the lovely lolly into every pocket I had. There was so much loot, it was a struggle to fit it all in, but I managed. My mate had been scannin the rest of the shop for the most desirable goods that we could easily carry back an get rid of quickly. He came dashin back to the counter, hissin under his breath, 'Dibble!'

I froze on the spot, notes drippin from every pocket, an sweat drippin from every pore. The sound of the engine drew nearer an the headlights blazed straight through the front windows, castin angular shadows around the shop's interior. The spell that was keepin us motionless broke in the realization that we would be spotted an we scrabbled for somewhere to hide. In the frenzy, I knocked over a basket of golf balls that went skiddin off, ping pongin in all directions an gettin underfoot. It was a proper cartoon moment of madness. We dived for cover behind the counter. I hardly dared to breathe. I felt drunk through lack of oxygen an deliriously giddy with apprehension. Seconds later, they pulled away, back down the lane; we were safe! I almost collapsed with relief, an then a childish frivolity took over our senses as we began to rampage about throwin Slazenger jumpers into golf bags with gay abandon. In my excitement, I began throwin golf clubs out of the gapin window.

'What the fuck are you doin?'

My mate thought I'd flipped, an started throwin them back in again.

'No, I want to take the clubs, they're fuckin smart an worth a mint.'

'You daft bastard, how are we going to carry all those, never mind sell 'em. We might as well 'ave, "we robbed the golf club" tattooed on our 'eads!'

The argument continued with golf clubs bein tossed back an forth; the job was turnin into a farce, only I was too blind with panic to see the humour or the logic in it all. I was adamant.

I finally conceded defeat on the subject an returned my attentions to the Slazzies. We cleared the place out of jumpers, gettin every size an every colour there was. We managed to get about twenty golf bags stuffed to the rim with the fuckin woollies an started to leg it back, the same route, to my shed.

A top night's graft. I sat in the safety of my bijou dwellin, huggin the grands before me an rollin around in the piles of quality clobber. Whooo hoooo! We'd done it alright, an now all we had to do was get rid of the booty. Easily done in a town like Walkden, where money is short but fashion labels are an essential part of the front.

Maggi called round to the shed early the next day an couldn't believe his eyes. The place was rammed to the rafters with golf bags that lay about four deep against the walls, each one stuffed with Slazzie jumpers. He took his pick of the best, as a landlord should, an wished me luck with the rest. I felt like a prince. As planned, the girls flocked round, soakin up the free dinners an cooin over my expensive wares. For a fleetin few weeks, life was fuckin ACE. I had the means to do exactly as I pleased, so please myself, I did.

Nothin lasts for ever. I was down the local boozer about three weeks later when I got the shout from my mate that the bizzies had been round his house with a search warrant, askin loads of ominous questions about my whereabouts. Fuck, this is it, I thought, an promptly legged it home to start the clear out in advance of a pull. They found me down the boozer a few days later. I was deep in the throes of an invigoratin game of Space Invaders; it was the highest level I'd ever got to an hardly pausin to listen, I requested that they wait till I'd finished my game. Amazingly, the copper stood back an watched my progress for a short while, engrossed like myself in the complexities of the game. However, after about five minutes of listenin to my protracted pleas to continue playin, he decided I was takin the piss an I was curtly escorted back to my shed for a search to commence.

I was convinced the place was clean but in my foolish haste, I'd thrown a few bags of the jumpers in the dustbin. There were also a few lyin around the shed that had escaped my attention in the big clean up. There was no denyin it, I'd been done for, good style. Someone had grassed me up, there was no doubt about it. I'd been givin the fuckin things out like toffees: the new Robin Hood sortin out the merry men of Walkden an Worsley. It was bound to happen, but in my naivety, I hadn't known any better. Generosity has always been my downfall. This though was no light trip, I was fallin hard an heavy an there was no runnin from takin the rap this time.

The spiral downwards gathered speed.

I was bailed to a probation hostel in Eccles with a ragbag bunch of other young offenders while I waited for the usual reports to be filed an processed. Fuck, this is a shit state of affairs to be in, I thought, as I listened to the long list of rules an regulations governin my every move. The bullshit bore into my skin like battery acid, makin me wince. The vice was gettin tighter, crampin my thoughts, condensin my life to the point where I felt on the verge of implodin under the stress of captivity. One false step an they'd have no qualms about arrestin me an takin me down to Strangeways to do the remand. There, I'd have to contend with the big-time boys; I should think myself lucky. They assured me of this fact continually, danglin the threat over my head, a glintin blade to sharpen my senses an keep me in line.

For the first week, I played the game by their rules. The mere thought of Strangeways sent a cold shiver down my spine an a heaviness hung like a solid clay ball in the pit of my stomach as I contemplated the horror of its reputation. I'd passed the place many a time on the bus up from town, tryin to imagine the desolation of the cells from the safety of my seat. It had a proper sinister look about it, like a throwback to the workhouses of a bygone era. Strangeways. On looks alone, it certainly lived up to its name. I didn't want to end up in any place with a name like that.

Second week into the remand, I began to get a bit cocky, findin ways of slippin round the dreariness of the routine. One night, I slipped right out of the window, confident in my ability to fool the staff. All went accordin to plan an I slipped quietly back in later the same night to resume my place in the stained an smelly bed to which I had been allocated.

By the third week, with my court case loomin up close, I decided the only option left was to run for it. There was no way I could bear goin through with the court appearance, knowin the inevitable would happen; that I'd be sentenced an go down for real.

I was cold, I was wet an I was starvin. I slept rough most of the time, occasionally gettin my head down at a mate's house here an there, but never more than for a night or two so that I wouldn't get them into trouble for harbourin me. Things were gettin worse by the minute. I thought back to the comfort an warmth of the set-up I'd had in my little shed. Bastard, I'd blown it an now I had nowhere to go, nothin to do but wander the streets, dodgin the marked cars an keepin my head low for fear of bein recognized. It was hell. I felt that I was already in purgatory.

One wet an rainy night, out of sheer desperation I broke into my old junior school in a bid to get my head down somewhere warm an dry. I found an scoffed a whole box of crisps. It was the first 'food' I'd had in days. I was fuckin starvin. The tension of keepin a constant watch over my shoulder was beginnin to break my spirit an I was literally exhausted from it all. I curled up by a radiator, wrapped in the rubber PE mats an slept fitfully till the early mornin, makin off before the first signs of life hit the streets.

Like a prick, I stayed around my own little patch, returnin time an time again to the same places, like a homin pigeon to its loft. Things were rapidly comin to a head. I couldn't expect the situation to lead anywhere but back to the slammer, an I knew it. Thankfully, I was to have one last bite of the apple before the final bell was struck, signallin the end to my freedom, if that's what you could call it.

By some stroke of luck, I managed to get some dough that was owed to me an splashed out on a big chunk of dope an a stash of booze for a forthcomin party. My pal's mam an dad had gone away for the weekend an the typical teenage party was in preparation. The party went with a bang an I even managed to cop for this bird who I'd had my eye on for some time. I'd summoned the courage to go for broke, knowin it could well be the last time I'd get to grips with any female flesh for a long time.

This was to be the calm before the storm.

I was now the proud owner of my own tent, complete with sleepin bag, so I no longer had to brave the elements every night. I pitched it on some waste ground, an shuffled around inside for a while, gettin my beddin in order, enjoyin a clandestine spliff to christen my new home. All was goin well. I emerged a short time later, zipped up my new front door, an set off down the path to see one of the lads. For the first time in a few weeks, I felt relaxed, vergin on happy almost; I had a warm an dry bed to return to, it was all I needed to know right now.

I'd got to virtually within spittin distance of my mate's house when two CID came grazin down the road, all eyes an ears, lookin for charge sheet fodder. They were the same two that had arrested me earlier an on spottin my familiar ganglin walk, they screeched to a halt, did a rapid U-turn an began instant pursuit.

I flew off the mark like a mad March hare, headin back down on to the Birch Road Estate. They were on my heels, thirsty for blood. One of them jumped out an continued the chase on foot thinkin he was within easy reach of catchin me. In your dreams fat copper. I had the distinct advantage of bein half his age an fit as fuck, flyin through the night, hurdlin fences an gates in my stride. I was on top form an he had no chance of catchin up with me. I heard him way behind me, shoutin up reinforcements in between gasps.

I ran deep into the heart of the estate, crouchin in dark corners of gardens, ears pricked an limbs primed to sprint off, alert to every snappin twig. A few times I got moved on as people demanded to know what the rogue divin through their privet was up to. Eventually, after a few crafty manoeuvres, I made it down to a pal's back garden. His sister came out, handin me a hat an a smother. I made the decision to move off just as a bus was pullin in at the nearby stop. I couldn't believe my good fortune an hopped on, grinnin broadly at the victory.

I alighted at my new girlfriend's house, still flushed from the success of the close escape. I stayed overnight, wallowin in the comfort an security of her bedroom, an enjoyin the female attention. I had to be off at the crack of dawn the followin mornin to take my mate his hat an coat. He worked on the local milk round, startin his days at some criminally early hour of the mornin. True to my word, I got it back in time, said goodbye an went off, back to the tent to get some more kip in; it *was* very early.

Some nosy twat had obviously notified the dibble about my new plot, as no sooner had I drifted off into slumber than two uniforms were pokin around, draggin me out of my hardly warmed pit. A body-search ensued. A sudden flash of panic energized my legs into a top sprint as I made one last dash for freedom. Again, I soon gained the upper hand, out-runnin the two uniforms with ease. They were takin no chances this time though an before too long, the whole estate was crawlin again with reinforcements. They couldn't let this little upstart take the piss a second time. I dived out of a garden an cut down the old railway embankment, straight through a thick patch of brambles. No way will he follow me through there, I sniggered. Hard bastard didn't even flinch at the hindrance. Well, at least he's gettin cut to ribbons just the same, I thought, an just to be defiantly sadistic, I raced back up the hill, leadin him straight through another lot.

I lost him on the next lot of gardens an managed to keep up the cat an mouse scenario for what felt like an hour. I was well an truly fucked by now though an committed myself to sittin it out in an old outside bog in a familiar garden. They either found me or they didn't, but it was a certainty there were no routes out of the place left unmarked. The dogs were brought in. It wasn't long before a party of them could be heard comin up the garden, the dogs right on the scent an yappin with excitement.

The hunt was over. There I was, standin on a dingy, stinkin bog in the middle of the estate, completely surrounded with dibble I'd taken the piss out of proper an now they'd be wantin my head on a stick, no fear. Fuck me, it's all over now, they're tellin me to come out an give myself up peacefully. Now why would I want to do that, I thought, an didn't move a muscle, waitin for the big kick off. There was nothin to lose, I might as well stand my ground an delay the inevitable beatin a bit longer, at least until I get my breath back an can go about things in a dignified manner, I reasoned to myself.

The door swung open an a snarlin wet snout came rushin in, its jaws fastenin tight round my calf. I automatically booted out in pain with my other foot an the beast backed out yelpin. I stood yelpin on the bog at my own wound. They prised me out with brute force as I lashed an wriggled about, resistant to the bitter end.

Boy, were they angry now!

They slapped on the handcuffs an laid into me straight away, but my mate's mam came out. Timing! One of them gave the warnin to lay off with witnesses about. The handcuffs were tightened behind my back as tight as they would go an they led me off to the waitin van, each gettin a sly kick in on the way. They took off the cuffs an put them back on with my hands to the front this time, squeezin them really tight again. They told me they were goin to drive back nice an slow so that my hands would be turnin blue by the time we got to the station. True to their word, the ten minute journey lasted for about half an hour, givin enough time for each of the dibble present to get a proper dig in. I'd taken the piss out of them for two whole days an they weren't about to let it drop quietly. They even stopped off along the way to allow the other uniforms who'd been involved in the chase a chance to take a swipe at me on the way past. One of them threw one at my jaw. A gut-curdlin crack sent me reelin sideways. My jaw was broken; even to this day, my face clicks an the bones make a loud crunchin sound when I'm eatin.

The abuse didn't stop at the station. I was thrown into a room where five more came marchin in. One of them tried to rip the jumper I was wearin. He was incensed that I'd had the gall to go an buy a round-necked jumper identical to the V-necked ones we'd taken from the clubhouse. It was like a red rag to a bull, an I was bein a smart arsed little twat in their eyes. They didn't like it one bit. In the scuffle, another snatched at the gold chain I was wearin an snapped it off. That was the last straw, I couldn't contain myself any longer an let fly at the young officer who'd gone too far. It was a raw scene of intense anger blazin off every man in the room. A senior officer was forced to enter to try an diffuse the situation before it got too out of hand. I wouldn't drop the issue. I wanted the one who'd snapped my chain back in the room, one on one. It was an impossible, no-win situation but I was beyond sense an reasonin by now. They let me be, recognizin the madness I was prepared to go to before I'd drop my defences.

A short while later, I was taken up to the interview room where I was told I'd be up in the court that day. Shit, that's that then I thought, I'm on my way down. Before that happened though, they tried to pin some more crimes on me. A CID officer walked smugly into the room, carryin a clear plastic bag containin an axe an a Dracula mask. I nearly fuckin choked as a laugh of incredulity stuck in my throat . . .

Someone had robbed the petrol station a few nights previously an was bein hailed as a mad axeman in the local press.

No fuckin way man! I laughed back in my chair, you can't put that one on me! Runnin round with an axe an a fuckin Dracula mask. Fuck off!

It was obvious I wasn't their man on this one.

I was taken to Eccles Court later the same day where I was sent down for six months to a place called Werrington House in Stoke. There was no time for contemplation, I was put straight in the van an we were off. I chain-smoked like a bastard on the way, on the advice of the two dibble who sat along side me. All belongins would be removed on arrival.

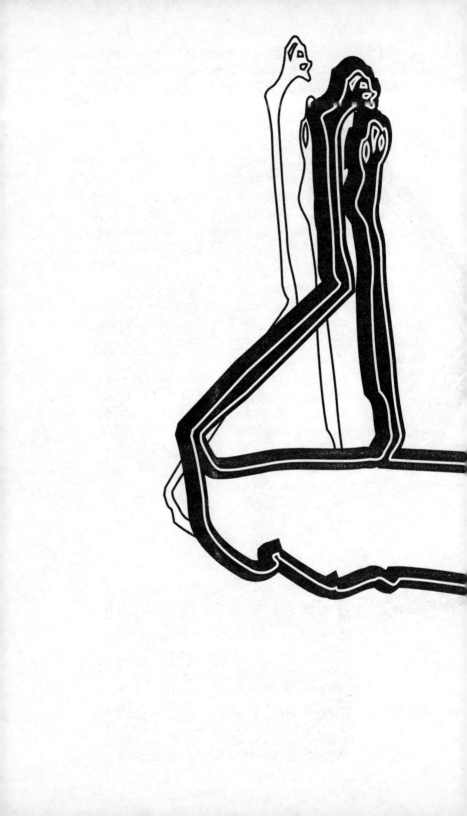

I was about to enter into the regime known as the short sharp shock, based on the idea of an army boot camp. The routine was peppered with petty rules an regulations, specially designed to get right up your nose an knock the insolent young offenders into shape, quick style. One of the rules was a complete ban on smokin.

On arrival there I was first greeted by a prison officer (PO) who immediately caught me off guard with a sharp punch to the abdomen, orderin me to take my hands out of my pockets an had me addressin him as sir before I'd even had a chance to get to grips with the situation in hand. He barked out the rules, leavin me in no doubt about the consequences of not adherin to them completely. Next, I was moved quickly along to the reception where I was issued with my kit bag an handed over what little possessions I had. I was now ready to go an meet the Governor.

After all the formal introductions were over an I'd been told what a little shit I was for just bein there, takin up their precious time, I was led off to the reception cell, where I sat on the bed flickin through the prison rule book. There was nothin else to do but go to sleep. At least it was better than the tent or the streets as in the previous few weeks. I felt no remorse, only a deep anger. I vowed to myself that if I should ever end up in such a place again, it would be for somethin worthwhile, not some stupid schoolboy job for a pile of jumpers an a bit of change.

The mornin shout came early. It was still dark outside an my mind reeled with the confusion of adjustin to the strange surroundins at such an ungodly hour of the day. After breakfast I was allocated to the cleanin duties as were all the reception inmates. I'd never cleaned so much in my fuckin life, reworkin time an time again areas that already appeared spotless. It was mind numbin. The evenin was spent learnin how to make a bed pack an how to lay out your kit for inspection. One wrong crease an you were done for.

I soon settled into prison life, there was no way round it. If the rules were broken, no matter how petty they seemed, the days were clocked on to the sentence, simple as that.

Every mornin, everyone had to have a wash an a shave. I stood there lookin at my reflection in the mirror, tufts of bum fluff wafted about on my chin; I'd never shaved in my life, there was no need for it, a five o'clock shadow would take me a month to cultivate. I got nicked on the spot for omittin the ritual shave. I couldn't believe it, surely they could see it wasn't necessary, what with my peachy delicate complexion. Extra cleanin duties were wopped on to my already full itinerary. The next mornin an every mornin after that saw me wieldin the blade cautiously across my already hairless chin.

Dirty boots were another bone of contention with the screws, one tiny spec an the book was thrown. It was a fuckin crap state of affairs to be in but we made the most of our time, playin for laughs constantly to keep the spirit intact as best we could. The no smokin rule was a constant source of amusement, the lads havin competitions to see who could get the most foolproof way of smugglin them in. I'd been put on admin cleanin duties an discovered *the* best way to get the contraband in. I was on to a winner; havin full access to the visitors' toilets meant I could get the cigs dropped off in the towel roll holder an simply collected the stash as I went about my day. Okay, so it's a bit of a sad form of entertainment for a lad of sixteen to be wastin his wakin hours on, but in a place like Werrington House, anythin to occupy yourself with, to break the monotony, was a blessin. Just the plannin of gettin the odd crafty puff on a bit of tobacco reminded the lads that they were alive an that the system hadn't browbeaten them into submission just yet. That quick, all-important blast on a dimp rolled from toilet paper might have been disgustin, but it provided an essential link to the outside world that our friends inhabited. Before this time, I'd never really given much credence to smokin tobacco. Now it had become an all-consumin matter of obsessional importance.

I soon realized that the best way to survive the ordeal was to keep busy an so I made damn well sure that I played on every team in every sport goin at the place. I did football, basketball, volleyball, the lot. This enabled me to get out of the confinin walls, goin on endless trips out to other gaffs with the various teams. I never felt so fuckin fit an it helped me to keep out of trouble. The screw in charge of the gym was a bastard, but for some reason I liked him for his odd little quirks. He'd make the reception lads call him a bastard straight in his face, as they filed out of the gym one by one. After issuin the insult each lad would receive a dig in the ribs for bein a cocky little cunt. The ones who didn't know the rules an tried to slip past silently got two digs for bein soft. I called him a bastard every fuckin day, with conviction.

Everybody knows a young lad can't be let back into society an survive if he doesn't know how to march in the correct way, an so we had to suffer the tedium of the drill, every day, mornin, noon an night. The screw that supervised this thrillin activity had the misfortune to be shaped like an egg on legs. His nickname was Egg White, an he knew it. Now to keep the lads in step, it was important for them to chant the left right rhythm out loud. This bein uncannily similar to the screw's nickname, it was too good an opportunity to miss; the shout would travel randomly up an down the line, just audible enough to be noticed but not so pronounced that he could decipher where it was comin from. Top fuckin laugh or what. Well I've had better, but as prison pastimes go, screw baitin an gettin away with it has to come out tops on a young offender's list.

On the whole, I coped with the sentence pretty well, even in spite of the tough regime that could easily send you insane if you let it by not learnin to play the game right. I didn't get into too much trouble durin my stay, with only a handful of fights to get the peckin order sorted out. I was also labelled a smoker, a vice I've never managed to shake off. As vices go though, I can think of worse.

It wasn't right until the end that I had a bit of a funny turn under the pressure of the system. It was letter time just after lunch. All the lads had to sit up straight, arms folded in front of them to await the ceremonial handin out of letters. The bubble of inner pain finally swelled to its optimum point an without warnin popped with a bang as I rose to my feet, turnin over the table an shoutin, 'I'm not fuckin sittin like a kid with my finger on my lips to wait for no fuckin letters any more. I don't want any fuckin letters anyway an I don't want to send any fucker a letter either. Fuck off the lot of you.'

I heard the words spillin out of my mouth but had no control over the outburst. It was very close to the end of my sentence, but not close enough. I'd been clockin people leavin who'd arrived after me an it was doin my fuckin nut in. I'd served my sentence well, keepin my head low an behavin to the best of my ability in a provocative environment that lends itself easily to violence if you are not careful. I'd also recently received a long an difficult letter from my mam. I felt bad an didn't know how to begin puttin the wrongs right. The sentence had only succeeded in removin me from the streets an integratin me with yet more criminals. It wasn't an effective system of reform, it was just a stark reminder of how young lads like myself, bored shitless by a stagnant society, were desperate enough to put their freedom on the line to get the things that would otherwise be denied them, probably for their entire lifetime.

I was taken from the dinin room to see the Governor. Incredibly, he took the time to chill me out; it was obvious the anger was a demonstration of somethin goin on far deeper in my mind than a deviant attempt to cause a scene. The compassion an understandin shown of the mental meltdown I was sufferin gave me a renewed strength to hang on in with dignity till the end of my stretch. As it neared the time for my release, I began to feel the light inside beginnin to burn brightly again.

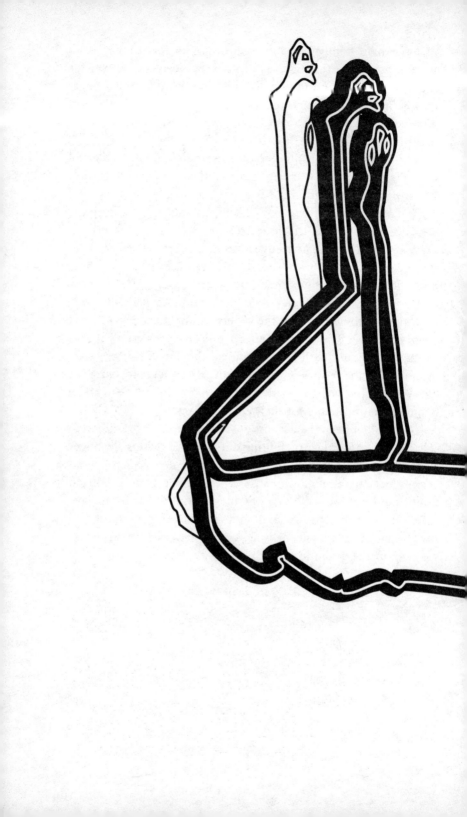

It was under a week to go to release day. I was havin wet dreams about women's thighs rubbin over my ears. OOOOOO! It really was gettin too much for a young man to bear. I was so excited at the prospect of seein my girlfriend again, but also dreadin it in case she didn't want to know me now I was about to become an ex-con.

On release, I was admitted to a halfway house in Crumpsall on Leicester Road. My newly appointed probation officer met me off the train an took me straight up there. It seemed okay. It was a luxury to be merely back in civilization an free to see my mates, so it didn't really concern me what the surroundins were like – as long as they were warm an dry an with a front door that opened freely when I turned the handle.

After gettin my stuff into the room an receivin my own front door key, I decided a visit to my mam should be the priority on my agenda. She blew my mind away; she was ACE. We had a long an emotional reunion. I told her I'd really try to change my ways. I wanted to do it for her an for myself an I fully believed myself at the time. It hit home on that occasion just how much I'd been lettin my family down an I felt a complete shit at what I'd just put them through. I vowed to try my best to behave from now on. She gave me some money to go an kit myself out in decent clothes; she'd always been a proud an well-presented woman herself an I think it was eatin away at her seein her boy in such a sorry state.

I burned off into town an bought myself some new clobber in which to celebrate my freedom that night. She'd given me enough to get some trainers, a pair of cords an a jumper an I was heart-wrenchinly grateful for her forgivin gesture.

Thank fuck I could go an see my bird lookin half decent, I thought, as I boarded the bus up to her place. The reception I got wasn't too bad – I was expectin worse – but that night

I couldn't quite figure out what was wrong with the set-up. We were in a club with all my pals, but I became aware that she wasn't respondin in the same way to my advances with everyone around. None the less, we went home together an I got to realize the fantasies I'd been dreamin of for the last few weeks inside.

The followin day, it all came out in the wash; all my mates had been shaggin her while I'd been away, the fuckin bitch. I was gutted, but not for long. Life's too short for tarts to be ruinin it. I had to back down with grace an accept the situation for what it was. It wasn't as if we'd been a definite item before I'd gone away, so nothin much had been lost.

It was an omen of things to come.

I'd only been out for a couple of weeks, Christmas was comin up an I had no money an no means of earnin, especially with a criminal record an the residues of a sentence still hangin round my personality. I'd started takin loads of whizz an had developed a strong affinity for smokin strong weed to counteract the depression of adjustin to bein back in the thick of it with no definin routine to keep me on the straight an narrow. The promises were slidin fast.

A few mornins later, I came down the stairs an met the sight of one of the girls, also on probation, bustin a gut, tryin to break into the office. It was an amusin sight, so I stood back an observed for a while, laughin to myself. She wasn't makin good progress an the suspense was killin me. I had to take her aside an offer assistance, which she willinly accepted in her desperation. The door popped open an she made for the strong box containin the money. This girl was wild with the need to get some dough. I was a bit short on the cash front myself an, seein the perfect opportunity, seized the chance to line my own pockets an get the hell out of there.

I turned up at my mate's not long after collectin my entire belongins – it doesn't take too long to pack a holdall – an I was buzzin with excitement over the possibilities of what I could achieve with my pile of cash. I achieved a few choice additions to my sparse wardrobe an promptly hit the town for a night out. After a few pints down his neck, my mate began to feel a bit on the charitable side an agreed to me stayin at his gaff over the Christmas period. Well in!

As it goes, we shared a common problem, in that he was skint an was busy devisin ways for gettin the Christmas readies in too. The conversation turned quickly to ideas for gettin a raise together for the forthcomin festive season. The more we drank, the more the schemes took on a darker hue, till eventually I found myself discussin doin the darkest, most dangerously lucrative of jobs on the list. I couldn't believe I was even contemplatin such a scam, it was what I'd only dreamed of in the past; bein in a position to pull off the big one. Suffice to say, it was a very ambitious scheme that needed a lot of forward plannin. The people I was with took me into their confidence an I felt pathetically privileged to be privvy to the homework they'd done over the last few weeks. They decided that the time was ripe to go for it. The routes had been planned, the vehicles had been acquired an I was goin to be in on the whole manoeuvre. Fuckin hell, this is it, I thought, Billy big time here we come.

The job was a disaster from the moment we set out. That mornin we'd woken to a world covered in the whitest blanket of thick, virginal snow. Unabashed, we tried to go ahead with the plans, crashin one of the vehicles almost immediately, skiddin about like the unprofessional twats we were in the fresh snow. That job was definitely off the cards. It was with a curious mixture of relief an regret that we trudged our way back to the house to revise the original plans. Plan B wasn't such a palatable option. In fact, it positively stank of the completely immoral behaviour of verminous scumbag ilk. It went against the grain of my thinkin an the codes of conduct that had been instilled in me from an early age. I was bad but I wasn't that bad, was I?

I held back, not wantin to take an active part in the conspiracy. I was cajoled into the position of lookout, which I still felt eerily uncomfortable with. The target was a house in which, it was rumoured, was a large wad of cash, just waitin for the likes of us to go an collect. This was someone's house for God's sake. It was too late, I'd already been party to the strategy they were goin to use. I was trapped by my own feelins of greed an crushed by the fact that I was involved in somethin that I had no means of stoppin. The momentum was already takin over, grabbin me by the collar an throwin me headlong into the biggest, most shameful mistake I ever have, an ever will, make in my life.

It was still snowin but it seemed a minor obstacle in their thirst to get to the goods on offer. We dodged about outside the house in question, weighin up the job an gettin psyched up for the pounce. A passin taxi driver clocked our strange behaviour an I got a gut feelin again that this was not goin to go as planned. I sat on the fence, wishin I was a hundred miles away from the scene. I'd been involved in a few dodgy escapades in my time but nothin so depraved as this. It was a Catch-22 situation; if I fucked off, I ran the chance of droppin the rest of them in deep shit, which they would never forgive or forget, but if I sat it out, I was an accomplice to a crime I didn't condone an could quite easily end up back inside for. I was still on probation, so this outcome was an absolute cert if it came on top. There was also the fact that I'd done a bunk from the halfway house with a pocket full of stolen dough gnawin at my conscience. It would all be taken into account in the final hour.

I heard one of the lads tryin to jemmy the window an I felt a rush of nausea as the realization set in that the job was definitely goin ahead.

The occupant of the house heard the shitty goins on an crept downstairs. A heavy object crashed through the window my pal was about to enter. It hit him squarely on the head, splittin his scalp wide open, the blood streamin down his face in rivers within seconds. We flew up the road in a blind panic. In the distance, the police were heard pullin up at the scene an we knew it was goin to be tough goin to break away from the search this time. The deep snow covered every surface with a smooth white icin. My trainers, with their brand new tread, made sharp patterns in the crunchy fresh snow as I raced along. It was fruitless tryin to escape, our tracks were easily identified, further enhanced by the steady trail of blood drippin from the wound on my mate's head. We ran for about two miles, criss crossin our paths in a desperate attempt to lose the law. The dogs weren't about to be put off the trail by a few tricky marks in the snow when they had the scent of fresh blood to follow. Great blackish-red streaks stained the lily-white route we'd taken, leavin handy visual markers everywhere. It was just a matter of time an stamina.

I felt sick with the knowledge that all those promises I'd made were about to be trashed an I would be once again proved to be the worthless little piece of filth I'd become. I'd let everyone down, includin myself. My head was poundin. I was distraught with the inevitability of the outcome of it all. What a fuckin prick. What a fuckin low life scumbag. I wanted to implode on the spot, erasin my blemished existence from the otherwise untarnished family I'd left behind to suffer my weaknesses. It struck me hard an clear that I wasn't the big man doin the big job for big money, I was a kid who didn't have a clue about how to go about livin a decent life. I was a failed criminal an I deserved everythin that was about to be thrown at me.

I was back on remand. The other lads, to their credit, tried to minimize the damage by vouchin for my innocence, knowin how I'd been against the idea from the word go. It was of no use though, I'd run from the scene like a guilty bastard an the police were convinced of my involvement.

I was immediately remanded to Strangeways to await sentencin. This was the moment I'd been dreadin an my spirit sank to an all-time low. When I'd been sent to DC I hadn't been too bothered about the issue of bein locked away, I'd managed to stay in fightin form, lettin my troubles run by like water off a duck's back. This time things were a bit different. I was goin down with the meanest of the mean in a dire place called Strangeways. I realized, the moment I set foot in the prison, that the life of a real criminal is pretty fuckin crap an I was a top twat for thinkin otherwise. All those plans for doin bigger an better crimes were quashed in an instant an I banged my head with my hands in shame at bein such a fuckin prick.

My confidence hit rock bottom.

That first week I made myself really ill. There used to be only one toilet on the landin in those days before the big riot on the roof, an as the whole wing fought to get their turn on it at slop-out time, there was no chance of me gettin anywhere near it at the crucial moment. I didn't shit for a week. There was a bucket in each cell for the inmates to use, but I just couldn't bring myself to use it while sharin the cell with another inmate. Then one night the shit hit the fan, or the bucket to be precise. I couldn't hold on any longer an the lot exploded in a spectacularly embarrassin moment of raw humanity. It was fucking horrible. I could imagine what it must have felt like to be in a concentration camp with no shred of dignity left to hold on to. All I can say is, they didn't riot in Strangeways for nothin. I soon learnt the ways of the inmates in the toilet department an by the second week I was pissin in the big bucket an linin the piss pot with newspaper. That way, my shits were properly parcelled up an ready to be disposed of in the medieval manner; they were thrown out of the window. Disgustin, but true. The prison system reduced grown men to livin like rats in a sewer. There's no way anyone can say that havin to resort to such base behaviour will have a beneficial effect on men who have to return to society after servin their sentence an behave in a normal an acceptable manner. Prison does not make a better person of you. It demoralizes the soul an turns previously relatively clean, petty criminals into dirty addicts with an even fuller understandin of the many vices in this world.

The men were shut in their cells, completely cut off from outside contact, for twenty-three hours every day. The boredom was cripplin. The only relief from this was the exercise period which turned out to be quite amusin as at the time there were about forty or so men of varyin ages from around our way. There had been a massive campaign in recent months in a bid to clean up the area. It was strangely comfortin to see so many familiar faces, even if some of them were vergin on the insane, literally.

There was the occasional relief of goin on a jaunt to the church on Sundays an the thrillin treat of a film once a month to look forward to. It wasn't so physically demandin as the DC had been but havin such a severe lack of activities was, possibly, even worse still. Basically, you could sleep the time by, play cards, read or sleep some more. I should have come out of that joint lookin like a prince with all the beauty sleep I was gettin in.

After about ten weeks of this, I let out a huge sigh of relief when I got the call one mornin to go to the Crown for sentencin.

I was shipped out to a closed borstal in Wigan called Hindley. The regime there was totally different to that of Werrington House. For one, you were allowed to smoke, which was a relief because I'd become an all-time smokin champion from doin all this bird in recent months. I also got straight into a fight. I'd been there less then an hour an was on my way down for dinner, lookin like the typical fresh-faced reception, holdin my knife, fork, spoon an cup. This Irish kid took one look at me an went to grab my fork as a ruse to see if he could get me at it or if I'd be an easy pushover. No chance, I'm not havin it, I thought an instantly poked him in the eye, lashed out with a headbutt an followed it up with a few good shots while he was off-balance. It had been a total surprise for him, he just hadn't expected such a rapid retaliation.

I was glad of the opportunity to get the facts straight at such an early point in the sentence; I was not about to be had over or bullied by anyone, no matter what their size or status. It really is a dog eat dog situation in these places an if you allow yourself to be bullied just the once, your life isn't worth living from that moment on. Unfortunately, the Irish kid had a bit of a reputation to uphold an I'd just blown his cover on my first day. He didn't give up easily, comin back about three or four times to redress the balance of things. Each time I stood my ground, even though he was a bit of a hard bastard. In the end, I had to play it tactfully an let him get a few good digs in to even up the score or it would have carried on for weeks. After that, we kept up a respectful truce. I even got to like him of sorts an we were involved in a few laughs together. In the main though, I made a promise to myself to keep my nose clean an get through the sentence with as little trouble as possible. I wanted to get out quickly so that I could go about rebuilding the ruins of my life. I wanted to play it straight this time. No more fuckin crap about leadin a life of crime to get by. There had to be somethin better on offer somewhere.

Once again, I managed to get on the football team to liven up my time in there. I got myself a job in the concrete shop, too, to keep my head low an out of trouble. It wasn't a popular choice of job an so people moved on to other things quickly, leavin me the opportunity to climb the ladder to the position of number one just by stickin it out. I was lookin for an easy life an didn't care if the tasks were menial an dull. I decided that countin concrete blocks, posts an pavin slabs wasn't too bad a way to pass the time if it kept me straight an out of harm's way. I quickly got to the top of the job ladder an found I could relax an take it easy, makin brews for the screws an generally just standin around outside, makin sure it all ran smoothly.

I apologize if it is all beginnin to sound a bit dull, but then prison is fuckin dull, so that's the way it goes. Just take my word for it.

There was the odd outburst of madness to break the routine though, an I was a lucky bastard for gettin away with some of the scrapes without gettin extra time. The best one was a mini riot that the lads in the TV room organized one night for a bit of light entertainment. The shout went around that at a given word the room would be barricaded an we would stage a sit-in. There was no clear reason why this should be, other than to wind the screws up to the maximum. It was just one of those moments that had been brewin for a few weeks. As the screw approached to turn off the TV an order the end of the recreation period, the word was issued an we started to sling tables an chairs up against the doors. The riot bells went off immediately an we sat listenin to the mayhem goin down in the rest of the prison as all the doors were shut, lockin the other prisoners secure in their cells so that all staff could report down to the TV room to tackle the supposed riot. No real riot commenced; the lads were content to sit around havin a laugh, watchin the telly an smokin their cigs.

Negotiations began but none were goin for it until they got through to the one lad in the room who was doin a six year detain. They had him by the short an curlies, tellin him not to make his already bad situation even worse by addin more unnecessary time on to his depressingly long sentence. It didn't take too long for the poor lad to crack. He wanted out an no one was goin to argue with the poor bastard when six years of his life was at stake. The door was opened an all hell broke loose as everyone made a mad dash for the stairs at once to get in their cell before the blame could be laid on their shoulders. The punishment for bein actively involved in a riot situation was an extra six months on the sentence. It was every man for himself as we bolted for it, heads down to avoid bein recognized. I got back to my cell an acted the innocent fellow.

The followin day we were ordered to write down the reason for the riot. Every man wrote that the reason for the riot was because we hadn't had enough trifle the previous Sunday. The next Sunday, there were extra big helpins of trifle for everyone to keep us happy. Fuckin ace! The things a lad has to do to get his fair share of trifle, it's astoundin!

As you can imagine, time drags by very slowly in a place like that. It's a constant battle of wits to keep on top of things an not slip into a deep depression. There were some nasty incidents of extreme violence that plagued the thoughts of every man in there. One kid got seriously slashed up in the toilets an another was held hostage in his cell by two nutters who'd flipped big-style after bein grassed up. They'd wedged the grass by his head, up against the door, an had broken glass pinnin his neck on the other side.

There were a good few lunatics in there, come to think of it, who wouldn't shy away from any form of violence; they'd lost pure time already an didn't give a flyin fuck about anythin. They were dangerous, unpredictable an best kept away from. Like I said, I kept myself quiet an busy most days in the concrete shop, countin concrete posts an the days to my release.

Ironically, it was my friends on the outside, who thought they'd do me the favour of a cheerful visit, that really did my head in an made me almost lose my grip on things. They'd arranged to come in an drop me a lump of draw on their way to Blackpool for the day. Three of them came on the visit an another twenty or so were sat waitin outside. It was fuckin torture. They stayed for all of ten minutes before announcin that they had to get off as everyone was waitin for them outside. I was gutted to say the least. Fuckin bastards, I'm sure they did it on purpose.

'Wait over that wall, I'll be over in twenty minutes.'

I tried to joke about it but the words left a dry, sour taste in my mouth, as I imagined the laughs they'd be havin, for sure, while I'd be sat in this stinkin pit of a place with nothin but a spliff to liven up the day. I lay there that night, smokin spliff after spliff in an attempt to obliterate my wanderin thoughts on the world outside, tryin desperately to hang on in.

My release day was comin round slowly. Eventually, the day came an I was taken up to the Governor's office to see about gettin off. There were a few of us up for release that day an we were treated to a heart-warmin, confidence-buildin talk about the statistics on reoffenders. Apparently, out of the ten of us standin there, it was a proven fact that only one would never be returnin for more of the same. I baulked at the thought of comin back for more fucked up institutional bollocks an made a promise to myself that I would be that one person who turned his back an walked free for ever. Bollocks to all that shit, I thought, life's for livin an livin this ain't.

There ended the worst, demoralizingly low eighteen-month period in my life. I kept my promise an never went back. There have been the odd occasions when I've slipped up an caught myself veerin towards that avenue again, but so far I've managed to recognize the patterns of behaviour an alter direction before bein sucked back in an gettin fully immersed in the stupid, mindless nonsense again.

I've skipped a lot of the gruesome details of life inside. I simply couldn't face goin into it all an openin up the can of worms that I've managed to keep shut tight for the last fifteen years. It makes me feel physically sick with depression just thinkin about that period of my life.

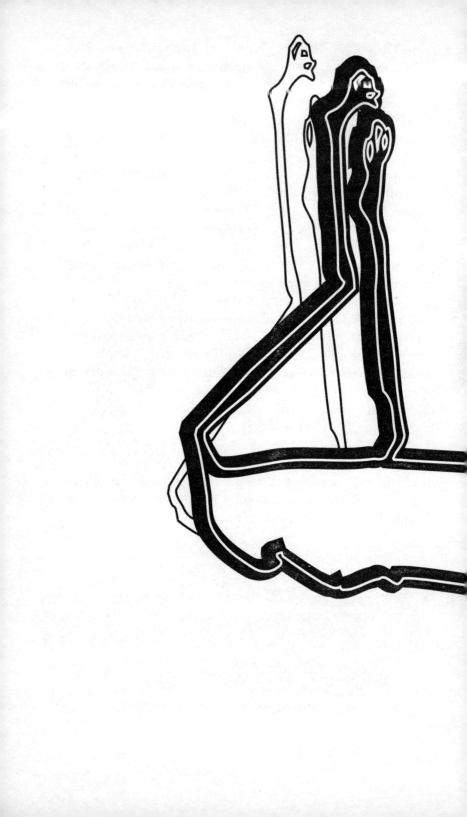

Time to move on. No lookin back.

Once more, I was released into a halfway house while I got my shit together. I was resolute in the fact that I wouldn't be goin back to a life of crime. This would definitely be the last time I'd find myself readjustin to a community life as I had no intention of ever leavin it to go inside no hell hole for any reason, ever again.

The first night back I went out to celebrate, feelin genuinely purged of all the shit an troubles that had tormented my existence in the last year an a half. I wanted a girl to complete the picture, an so we headed for a club called the Wishing Well in Swinton. I was full of optimism for coppin a shag, fuelled by the new knowledge that the club was frequented by a gang of girls who all lived together an apparently loved their orgies. Their place was known as the Chicken Ranch, after some well-known film in which Dolly Parton ran some gaff staffed with free an easy women. Even the taxi driver on the way down there knew of the place an the name it had acquired, such was their reputation around those parts. Whey hey! I rubbed my hands in anticipation.

I tried with all my might, but just couldn't manage a score on the bird front. My ego deflated, we set off to a mate's house for an impromptu party. All the chicken ranch girls had been taken. The rest of the lads sat glumly, makin do with watchin porno films in the front room. This was a particularly sad state of affairs to be in for a young lad on his first night back in the land of the livin. I sat there feelin mad horny an there wasn't a spare woman in sight.

When another two of my pals turned up out of the blue with a couple of girls from my old school, I began to cheer up an decided to give the old chat-up routine one last shot. I'd been fuckin up badly all night due to my cripplin shyness borne of a lack of practice from bein shut away in the prime of my youth when I should have been out every night perfectin the right manoeuvres. It had been a long time an I was rustier an less refined than an old farmyard tool at this game.

It was obvious that a full-on shag was not on the cards that night, so I lowered my sights an resigned myself to just bein in the company of a female. The gentle approach paid long-term dividends. We got to grips with a session of heavy pettin an cuddlin an it felt so good just to be holdin a girl close again that I found myself feelin totally smitten by her.

She became my girlfriend for the next twelve months or so, helpin me enormously with my reformation of character along the way.

Much to the annoyance of the social workers at the halfway house, I got myself a job as a painter an decorator. I'd been babysittin with my girlfriend for a young couple called Steve an Elaine who had two young daughters. Steve had been a bit of a rogue himself in the past, gettin into trouble with the law an stuff, so he was understandin of my plight an took me on in his business to get me back on my feet again. I started to play football again, too, gettin in two games a week an feelin double fit in the process.

With my first lot of money, I bought myself a bike. This was more like it, I was gettin back the confidence that the removal from society had stripped me of. I just couldn't understand the reactions of the staff at the halfway house to my new found independence though. It seemed to be gettin right up their noses for some reason I couldn't quite put my finger on. I mean, alright, I wasn't stayin there more than a couple of nights a week at this stage but, as I tried to explain, I was buildin a relationship with my new girlfriend an the eleven o'clock curfew wasn't exactly conducive to strengthenin that tie. They frowned on the fact that I'd got myself a bike. I argued that it was a justified move on the grounds that I needed transport to get to an from work.

Now, I was always under the impression that social workers were there to help you get your life back in order. That leads me to the assumption that they either thought I was a lyin little bastard, or they were peeved that I didn't want or need their help an guidance. Either way, they weren't doin their jobs properly in my eyes, an the pricks threw me back out on the streets. Now if they had thought I was lyin, this would have been a deliberately malicious act – not somethin you'd expect a carin social worker-type to do. Maybe it was just my face didn't fit, who knows. As it goes, Steve, my boss, had heard of my plight an offered to put me up in the spare room. Fuckin nice one Steve an Elaine! Their generosity touched me, an I can honestly say that I'll be forever grateful for the trust they gave me when everyone else was writin me off as a wrong un.

My drug input, however, was on the increase, which was seriously impedin the quality of my work, as you can imagine in a skilled job that needs a steady hand an a certain amount of concentration on the eye/hand co-ordination front. To be honest, I never was destined to be a painter an decorator. In short, I was fuckin crap at the job, even though I tried my hard-est to get it right for Steve's sake. In fact, I think he was losin more money than he was makin as he dashed around puttin all my mistakes right!

Elaine became pregnant with their third child an realizin that I'd overstayed my welcome, I did the honourable thing an left them to it. That night I was down the boozer drownin my sor-rows over a pint with a mate. I'd just upgraded my bike for a car an told him, at the end of the night, my intentions were to go an get my head down in the motor an I'd think about the next day when it arrived. I asked him to keep his ears open for any news on a place to stay. For the moment though, I was tired an pissed an the car seemed a perfectly reasonable option compared to the hardships I'd suffered in the recent past. I smoked my last cig an got out my sleeping bag in preparation for gettin my head down for the night. There came a tap on the window. It was my mate, Curly. He'd been home an told his mam about my predicament. She'd immediately told him to come an get me; I was welcome to go an live at their house if I wanted. Fuckin hell, did I. Good old Mrs Curlew, what an angel in the night. It never ceases to amaze me how charitable people can be, helpin out when the chips are down. I've never forgotten how grateful I was to these people, an all through my life, when I've had the means to help,

I've made sure I offer all I can to the ones that need it most. It doesn't hurt, an anyway it gives me the opportunity to repay my debts in some token way.

I'd developed a fixation along the way with needles, as I'd taken to injectin – anythin. There are many cults around the world that get their buzz solely from insertin needles or other sharp instruments through their skin – the rush from this alone is very addictive. Unfortunately, my needles were always hypodermic to enable various intoxicants to pass through into my bloodstream, as is the predominant practice in this sad country.

My drug habits were becomin a real problem now, although I hid it out of respect for the people who had offered me salvation. I was still tryin to keep on the straight an narrow, workin on an off in my mate's shop, where he was the manager. I also helped out on his dad's rounds, deliverin pies, but I was deceivin myself mostly as I slipped down the helter-skelter into the underworld of drugs, quickly developin the mentality that goes hand in hand with that kind of base situation.

I waded on relentlessly through each long day, sinkin deeper an deeper into the icy grip of a drug-infested lifestyle. On the surface I appeared to be alright, as if I was perfectly suited to the mould I had cast myself but, underneath, I was bitter an cold: I wanted a better life but the means to get it eluded me in the fog of toxic crap I was pourin into my already wasted physique. The slow drip of passin time drained me of the will to do anythin but consider the next lot of drugs, any drugs that would deliver me from this sorry existence to a different dimension where feelins could be put aside. I couldn't see a way out of the situation I'd cornered myself in. I had no money an no means of makin any without resortin to crime, which I desperately tried to avoid at all costs. There was no way I wanted to end up back inside, stuck in a never-endin, vicious cycle of bein a perpetual jailbird. I was merely tickin over, gettin drugs in for myself an sortin out the people around me to pay for my own. You couldn't even call it drug dealin; it was a closed circle of close associates gettin their daily fix together.

One such dreary night, I called round to a friend's house on my usual mission an found another pal sittin in the front room, smoking a draw. Fuck it, I'll stay here an get stoned, I thought. I was in need of some company to lighten my darkened mood The trips came out an my mind began to crystallize the vaporous thoughts that had been swimmin just out of reach in my depression. In the come down, ideas ricocheted around an shot to the surface in rapid succession as everyone in the room focused on ways we could propel ourselves out of this black hole. The other lads were in a very much similar frame of mind to me, with nothin of any significance goin on in their young lives.

Slowly, a positive vibe crept into the conversation an began to resonate around the room as we formed the plan for the big escape. One of the lads had been to Corfu the year before, to a place called Kavos, an was busy paintin a picture of paradise. He'd been offered work there, helpin out a local who was doin up his properties for rentin out. He still had the address.

Fuck, it sounded good to me, I'd never set foot out of Britain before an I knew that if I stayed around any longer, the only place I'd be headin would be back to the jailhouse.

It was a direction I'd never thought of takin before an the more I thought about it, the more I craved the adventure of travellin in a foreign land. I would have departed that very day had it not been for the small matter of passports an money.

It took about ten days in all to get everythin together an, in the meantime, I was busy doin the rounds, tryin to summon up recruits for the pilgrimage. No fucker was havin it; they didn't believe I was on my way out of there. No worries, you just stick to the routine you know an let your heart bleed when I send back the postcards, I sniffed. Borin bastards! See ya when I get back!

The mornin of departure, we lined our nostrils with a shit load of whizz, packed a half-ounce of draw an set off to catch the Magic Bus, destination Greece. Our method of transport was so-called because it was a miracle that we ever made it, bones intact, all the way to the end of the line. The price, £39 for a one-way ticket, reflected the bog-standard of the means of travel, but we didn't care about minor altercations such as lack of oxygen an loss of circulation, we were going on a fuck-off mission to far flung lands, an anyway a bit of discomfort was a small price to pay for seein every interestin inch of B road in Europe.

The crossin from Britain to France confirmed that maybe I was right throwin two fingers up at the Navy recruitin officer that time in school. I wasn't sailor material, that's for sure. I threw up the minute the ferry lurched against the first wall of waves an alighted a putrid pale green hue at the other side. I could hardly walk the short way back to the bus, my brain refusin to accept that the ground was solid an stationary.

I thought of the long journey ahead, takin in France, Germany, Austria, Yugoslavia an finally Greece. It was a fuckin mammoth trek to be contemplatin, but it was too late to be havin second thoughts an there was fuck all to go back to anyway. I focused on the destination, an told myself to get a grip; we were on our way an that's all there was to it.

Back on the bus a party scene was developing as we got out the tunes, the beers an the bong. Suddenly, we were the most popular lads on the trip; everyone, it seemed, wanted to be our friend. They should have had the balls to bring their own weed along, that's all I can say. Bunch of fuckin sycophants. Well, some of them were alright as it goes, an we let them join in our little shindig at the back.

Everythin was hunky dory for the first few days, then the drugs began to wear off an the come down began. By the fourth day in, I was sweatin, frothin at the mouth an howlin like a rabid dog, clawin to get off the cramped an stiflin coach. My arse was numb an my feet were swollen an stinkin worse than a week-old kipper, but then so were everyone else's. I like a good moan though now an again; it passes the day time of day when there's nothin left to smoke.

One of the lads, a seasoned traveller on the number 36 from Salford to the Manchester Arndale, reckoned there was only one way to travel a journey such as this, an that was by gettin blind drunk. Yeah right. When we got to Yugoslavia, he was nearly nicked for havin a slash up the side of the customs hut an by the time we'd got to Greece, he'd lost everythin: passport, wallet, luggage; the lot. Yeah, top way to travel.

Gettin off the coach at Athens, the first thing to hit me was the stench. Fuckin hell, I'd never smelled anythin like it! I remember thinkin to myself, God I hope the rest of the place doesn't smell as bad as this, it was knocking me fuckin sick. We went straight down from Athens to Petra where we had to wait overnight for the boat to Corfu. Not one to hang about waiting for things to happen, I set off into the night to find a draw. The kid I was with was like a bag of nerves, a top prick. I realized from the moment we arrived that he was going to be a complete nause all the way down the line. He was jumpin around like a cat on hot irons. I should have known from past experience what a twat he was. He wouldn't go anywhere with us at home unless he was in the boot of the car. What a fuckin paranoid nonce.

I ended up gettin a small bag of weed an smokin it on the beach in the dark, listenin to the waves poundin in from the Mediterranean Sea. I was itchin to get to the other side an see the island of Corfu for myself.

The followin day we woke up to glorious sunshine, even though it was only the middle of March. In a defiant salute to the miserable, damp weather we'd left behind, we immediately stripped off to our duds like typical English men abroad an felt the warm sun thawin our malnourished an milky-white bodies. We dashed into the surf like a bunch of nutters, splashin around an whoopin for joy with the locals lookin on in disbelief. It was fuckin fantastic. If they'd been where I'd just been for the last two years, they'd have known what all the fuss was about.

We boarded the boat, an headed straight for the bar. A couple of young American girls had the misfortune to catch our eye an we tried desperately to entice them to join us on our adventure. That would have been the icin on the cake, but in our over-exuberant state, we managed to frighten them off within hours of meetin. There'd be plenty more where we were headin, we reminded ourselves.

We stepped off the boat in Corfu to the sight of windswept, deserted streets, the bars were closed an it was pissin it down with rain. We were six weeks ahead of the start of the season an there wasn't a bikini in sight. We all turned to the lad who'd instigated the mission.

'You fuckin wanker! What the fuck 'ave you brought us 'ere for!'

The picture of paradise I'd held in my head to get me through the long an uncomfortable journey was ruined in an instant. We sat down on the nearest wall, huddled into our lightweight jackets against the drivin rain, wonderin what to do next. Five minutes later, our luck miraculously changed for the better as a car pulled up an out got this geezer called George Ruzzos. He asked us if we were lookin for work. I couldn't believe my ears; one minute we were destitute an ready to kick off royal at each other, the next we were fixed up with a job an dumpin our bags in a bar to go on a walkabout with big cheesy grins on our kippers.

We headed off on the road which led up into the hills an found a taverna full of local fishermen. No sooner had we sat down than the wine began to flow, an flow, an flow. Short of a bit of entertainment in the run-up to the holiday season, the fishermen took it upon themselves to get us blind, paralytic drunk an take great pleasure in watchin our rapid descent into oblivion. On the way back down, one of the fishermen mentioned that he wanted to get his boat back into the water an feelin gallant with a belly full of booze, we leapt to his aid with no hesitation.

What a fuckin palaver. Manhandlin boats into choppy seas had never been an occurrence in my life, an attemptin my first while blind drunk was nothing short of pathetic. We splashed about like the novices we were, gettin piss-wet through an snortin copious amounts of salty water in the process. At some point in the procedure, I managed to lose a trainer, which unaccountably turned up the next day in some place completely unconnected to the route we'd taken, or thought we'd taken.

We stumbled back to the bar to get our bags an, exhausted from all the drunken goins on, promptly collapsed out cold on the floor, where we remained for some hours, sleepin off the excess of alcohol. I woke to the sight of my mate screamin his head off an swingin a machete about like a madman. In the confusion of wakin up snoggin a cold marble floor, findin one foot numb in the draught from bein minus a shoe an havin severe difficulties focusin, I couldn't figure out what the fuck was goin on. Understandably, bein the first foreigners to arrive in town, the local lads had taken an instant aversion to the drunken English lads intrudin on their patch. It kicked off splendidly, an the war continued to rage the entire time of our stay. At least we made a lastin impression.

Work commenced the followin mornin, after we'd had a chance to replenish our energies an reach a temporary truce with the locals. George owned a few apartments that needed a bit of tidyin up along with a stretch of the beach. It was hard graft but it felt good. I was keen to throw myself into earnin an honest wage doin somethin legit an I was lookin forward to seein the sun an eyein the gorgeous girls – okay, so it was pissin it down for the first few days an the holiday season was a few weeks off, but I had all the time in the world. I was young an free an startin afresh on a clean an straight stretch, not a hard drug in sight.

The first few weeks went brilliantly well, workin hard up until the season got underway an gettin rat-arsed pissed every night. I was slowly buildin up a healthy tolerance for the local brews, until on my birthday, I went all out for England, drinkin myself stupid on retsina, the deadly Greek wine.

It was an embarrassin scene, or so I've been told, dancin round with tables in my mouth an offerin all the Greek lads out. Not surprisingly, it wasn't long before the locals surrounded me in force, threatenin to stab me in the armpits for bein a top nause. By some incredible stroke of luck, I managed to make it back to my hotel room in one piece, armpits intact. I'm not quite sure what happened next, but the followin mornin found me lyin in my room, hallucinatin like a bastard an feelin like I'd had my insides removed an replaced with specimens from a pickle jar. Everythin around me was unaccountably smashed to fuck; its evil stuff that retsina for obliteratin the memory cells. I had the serious DTs from all the hard drinkin I'd done since we arrived. I was seein dogs on my bed, had spent my last reserves of energy leapin around swottin flies on the wall an there had been a purple-headed man crouchin on the end of my bed all night. I'd been tellin him with a stern reverence that he was going to be very ill in the mornin.

George Ruzzos came into the room to try an rouse me from my pit.

'Marcus! Marcus! Come on, it's time for work!'

I was goin nowhere, especially not to work. I was ill.

The next day, word had got round about my escapades in the bar, an that, coupled with the decimation of the larger part of my room, was too much for George to contend with. I was sacked.

Most of my partyin had been in the company of the 18–30 gang, which happened to come in very handy as I found a vacancy with them immediately, stockin the bars an generally helpin out. This, I soon realized, was in fact a far more covetable job with much better prospects for coppin with the birds; it's what they came away for. Bein constantly around the bar, I was a veritable magnet round about their fourth or fifth cocktail. All I had to do was wait, easy.

About the second week into the new job, two tasty French girls came into town. I busted a move an got into one of them before they were taken by some Stavros or other. They were on an island hoppin trip an I decided to go with them. It was gettin on top around town after that incident on my birthday with the machete gang. Word had spread an there were rumours that the police would be makin a move to do us over. There had been a spate of crime in our little patch an the word was that we were to blame. Not true, but considerin the impact we were makin on the local community with the nightly stand offs, it wasn't surprisin that the finger was pointin in our direction.

I was gettin pissed off with the lads that I'd arrived with anyway, actin like top pricks all the time. Going away with your mates, it seems, is a sure-fire way to end a friendship. I was more than ready for a change of scenery.

The dibble turned up the very next mornin to bust us. Findin nothin of any interest, they resorted to requestin that we move on; they didn't need the hassle on their island so early in the season. I stood my ground out of sheer bloodymindedness.

'Fuck off, I'm not goin anywhere you pricks!'

I was on the next boat out.

The island hoppin with the French girls was a pleasant reprieve from the pressure of bein with the lads. I relaxed an enjoyed myself, takin in culture, copious amounts of sex an burnin to a crisp in the boilin hot sun. Not necessarily in that order. The time soon came for the girls to be headin off back home. They invited me to go with them but I was itchin to go further afield; the travel bug had me firmly in its grip. Nothin so good had ever happened in my life an I wasn't about to stop there, not even for an oooh-la-la tasty French chick. We made tentative arrangements to meet up in Lyon in six weeks' time but, as is usual in these kind of set-ups, it never came off.

I soon teamed up with another kid from Manchester who was graftin the place an we went off to Italy. We got into scrapes all along the way as my promises to quit the life of crime flew silently out of the window in my desperate need to survive.

Before too long, we hit the trail again, this time goin to Turkey to try an cross the Turkey/Iran border into India. We waited around for a few days, tryin to get it together to get across but you only had eleven days to get through to the other side due to the ceasefire in the Iran/Iraq war. Third World motherfuckers were doin our heads in. It didn't work out, so we headed back to Italy an on to France, spendin a month or so dossin about. Then it was back to Spain, on to Portugal, then back to France again, pickin the grapes.

Somewhere along the way, I parted company with the kid from Manchester an started trawlin around with a mad Australian. I called him Aus an he called me Manchester.

He was in a continual state of shock at the irregular way I had of goin about my business; I was turnin him into a full-on scally. Nearly every place we visited had to be quickly vacated as things got out of hand with dibble everywhere askin after a skinny young lad goin by the name of Manchester. Dickheads.

After we finished *travailler les vendanges* across the vineyards of France, we went off to Torremolinos for about a month with another group of English kids, but I wasn't satisfied with the way things were goin. It was all too fake an touristy for my likin. I wanted somethin more; workin the discos an gettin pissed up in bars with neon signs above their doors was not, I realized, what seein the world was about. I felt a strong urge to smoke top weed in its indigenous surroundins. I had my sights firmly fixed on Morocco.

I'd been gettin a first rate smoke off this Moroccan kid in Torremolinos who'd plied me with tales of his homeland an, most interestingly, the great valley of dope plants that his family cultivated. I listened in awe to his dazzlin accounts of forests of ganja coverin the entire valley floor as far as the eye could see an I knew that I must go an see it for myself, or I'd regret it for ever.

Aus had been talkin with the group of English kids who were due to be headin off back home an he'd decided, havin never been to England, that he would like to join them. Fuck that for a game of soldiers, I thought, an announced my own plans to follow my instincts an get on the serious dope trail. England held no wonder for me, but I tried not to sour his expectations before he'd had a chance to digest the culture for himself.

We parted company an I set off alone, clutchin my letter of introduction that the Moroccan kid had given me, on my journey of discovery. I travelled down the short distance along the coast from Torremolinos to Algeciras. I caught the boat from this southern-most tip of Spain, over to Morocco an went straight to Tituan as instructed, to the address on the letter.

Tituan was a funny, scruffy-lookin little town, full of narrow dark passageways with shifty-lookin geezers in traditional garb hanging around doorways, eyein me suspiciously as I went by. Most of the buildins were painted a strange green colour, not unlike the hospital green of old times in England. Beggars sat at street level on doorsteps, many with missin limbs, pullin at my clothes as I went about the business of findin the address I had in my hand. It was a barren place, stinkin of real poverty, a massive contrast to the European holiday playgrounds I'd just left.

It didn't take me too long to locate the pension an I introduced myself to the family, nervously handin the crumpled letter over. The member of the family who received me was the kid's brother, Mohammed. He took me in without hesitation, handin me a spliff as a means of welcome. I wasn't sure what the letter had said but it was certain that in it, he'd outlined my deep interest in the family's sideline in crop cultivation.

Nothin in this world could have prepared me for that first spliff. It was the strongest dope I'd ever come across in my short but varied life. I was instantly stoned, meltin into the furniture in the pension in a deliciously myopic mist. It caught me completely unawares. I liked it. I liked it a lot an decided it could be of great benefit to my psyche if I stuck around here for a while. It wasn't like gettin stoned in Walkden with all the outside filth descendin on your thoughts constantly, this was a much cleaner feelin. It wasn't about escapin, it was about knowin, an now I definitely knew.

I settled down into a routine of day trips, eatin the local dishes of cous cous with everythin an swiggin mint tea. I went to the local pictures an watched films in a foreign language with foreign subtitles, it was *ace*. I floated around in a surreal haze of hashish heaven, lettin the culture wash over me, enchanted by the lifestyle that was a million miles away from the stressful isolation of the big-city-style drug culture that I'd known in Walkden.

I occasionally dropped heavy hints into the stilted conversations about the valley of weed an how I'd love to go an see it for myself. The subject was subtly shelved on each occasion; they were waitin for someone to arrive. I got the feelin that they hadn't finished vettin my character enough to be divulgin such sensitive information just yet an so after a while I let the issue drop. I was enjoyin myself anyway, what with the unlimited supplies of top quality weed an a cheap, cosy room at the family pension to retire to when the THC levels got a little too high. I also bought, on the advice of my friend, a traditional Moroccan rig out, complete with hood so that I could go about the town without gettin any mither from the locals. It worked a treat, even though I felt like I was permanently actin out a role in a Christmas play.

I'd been there for about two weeks when the atmosphere in the pension began to change. It was charged with a new tension, an due to the language barrier I couldn't quite figure out what all the conspiratorial whisperins were all about. The family had taken to talkin covertly in hushed tones in quiet corners, but it wasn't a feelin of grim forebodin that emanated from them, rather, it seemed like they were preparin for some great secret celebration. Their eyes shone with excitement at the plans they were makin. I knew that look, I'd seen it a hundred times on the faces of the boys back home in the run-up to doin a big job; it is a look that transcends any language barrier an can mean only one thing – money! At length, I was told of the big deal that was about to be pulled off – the long-awaited arrival of the Dutch contingent was imminent. I would be allowed to travel with them to see the crops at last. This was the moment I'd been waitin for, my sole reason for travellin all that way in the first place. I was as excited as the family at the prospect of trekkin up into the mountains to witness first-hand where the lumps of dope that had kept me goin through the rough times at home had started their journey from.

There was only one way up there an that was by donkey. It was a long an slow procession, givin me plenty of time to take in the stunnin scenery along the way. Eventually we came to a small valley an I didn't realize at first what the towerin plants all around me were. Slowly it dawned on me that these were all fuck-off ganja bushes, laden with the pungent sticky buds that I'd been smokin incessantly for the last two weeks. It was a fuckin amazin sight. The crops stretched off into the distance as far as the eye could see, swampin the entire valley with the sweet an intoxicatin aroma of pure fresh kaif.

We came to a hut in the midst of a small village an Mohammed glowed with pride as he filled his long pipe an offered it to me to sample his wares. I smoked myself into an ecstatic oblivion. Each time the pipe finished I motioned to him for a refill. After a while, he began to look on me with puzzled concern. 'You got a problem, you smoke too much!'

'No, no problem, just keep loadin up that pipe an I'll be fine!'

He couldn't have been further from the truth. For once in my life, I had not the slightest problem to contend with. I had found my personal nirvana an all my past troubles dissolved away to a mere distant memory, totally unconnected with this sweetest of moments.

I spent three days with them as they harvested an packed the goods ready for the descent. The Dutch were waitin somewhere down in the town, keepin a low profile, preparin the boat for the smuggle back to Spain. There was some nervousness about runnin into a possible road block on the way back down but in the event we had no trouble an the journey back passed without incident. I managed to get on the fact that they were slightly pissed off at not takin the risk of bringin back more in the light of such an easy passage. The deal went smoothly. The boat was loaded up an cast away, leavin everyone involved with a big smile of relief an joy, includin me. I got off to my room, still flyin from my encounter with nature an promptly fell into a satisfied coma on my bed.

I awoke late the next day to find that all my stuff, includin the trainers I was wearin when I'd fallen asleep, had been stolen, leavin me the proud owner of just a flick knife an a huge, hundred-gramme lump of zero-zero. Tryin to barter with the Moroccans with a lump of draw is like sellin ice to the Eskimos. In short, I was fucked.

Apparently, it had been the work of a cousin of Mohammed's who'd just returned from university in Spain an Mohammed was furious. I think he was more furious because he'd been covetin my trainers for himself with my departure drawin nearer.

The family rallied around, fixin me up with clothes. Mohammed even went down to the local market to replace my footwear with a pair of smelly cheap trainers in his embarrassment of the situation. Again, I was struck dumb by the way that people, less fortunate than myself in the overall picture of things, came to my rescue, offerin all the help they could to get me by.

It was decided that I could stay on an help his family in the various businesses they ran around the town. This involved going down to the border at Sitar to entice the Europeans arrivin off the boats from Spain to share a taxi ride with me back up to the pension an into the souvenir shops. All were owned by some branch of the family; they had the place completely sewn up an consequently were doin alright for themselves. I was seen as an asset to the family as I became quite adept at my job, so good in fact, that I did myself out of a room as the pension became booked up with payin guests. I was moved up on to the roof along with other members of the family to make way for the customers, who were unaware of the fact that it was an elaborate con goin down by all the members of the same family. They were fleeced from the moment they accepted the taxi ride into town.

I didn't complain about the demotion from honoured guest to lackey, they made sure I was fed an well-looked-after an the rooftop set-up wasn't as bad as it sounds in the sultry Moroccan weather. I was beginnin to feel as if it was time to move on though, I'd done all there was to do in this quiet corner of the world, an was happy to leave it at that.

I said my thank you's to the family who, not surprisingly, did not want me to leave; I'd been makin them a pile of dough in my short stay there but that was of no long-term use to me. I made my way down to Sitar an made an impassioned plea to my nana an grandad Berry, askin them to send me the return fare home. I had seen enough for now an bein penniless in this strange country, I knew it was time to go back. I survived the time waitin for the money to arrive by stealin food an skulkin around the port, sleepin down there at nights, takin advantage of the constant influx of Europeans. There's one thing you don't do in a place like that an that is to steal to survive. The locals were on to me in a flash an I was constantly chased an hounded as I dodged around waitin for the money to arrive. I was fuckin starvin an livin on my wits, in constant fear of bein caught by the police who would have no mercy for my plight.

I'd been skulkin, as usual, around the port one afternoon, lookin for somewhere comfortable to sit an watch the goins on when I came across a kid about the same age as me, hot-footin it along the quay to the boats. He'd obviously been travellin in these parts an looked anxious to get back home, much like myself. Somethin didn't quite add up about his appearance though an I found myself scrutinizing him to see what it could be. He had a fair bit of beard an his hair was pretty long, tied back in a ponytail an he had the same wasted frame as myself. Suddenly it dawned on me. He was too white to be a traveller! Even if you only glanced at the sun once a day, the lilliest of white skins would be sportin a tan in this climate.

He noticed me weighin him up an came over to ask if I was English. Recognizin the desperate glare in my eye of one in dire need of food an a ticket home, he sat down to offer me some unsolicited pearls of wisdom, so that I wouldn't make the same mistakes as him.

It turned out that he had come to Morocco to seek the freshest of smokes in its indigenous surroundins, just like me. Unfortunately, the combination of the highly hallucinogenic local greenery, a sad lack of proper nutrition an the bakin hot sun had culminated in a slight detour from his usually balanced mental state. That's what he told me anyway. This psychosocial development that had built up gradually over a period of about a month had led him to believe in the fuckin bizarre theory that the colour green, when present in certain situations, indicated that it was okay to make a move, be that to take or do somethin that might otherwise be considered not on. Conversely, if the colour red was at all evident, it was a no go situation on all counts.

He'd been testin this theory out for some time an was completely taken with his own success rate in applyin this method of assessin potentially tricky decisions, comin up trumps every time.

At this point, I'm thinkin this bloke is completely fuckin ga ga, but it was an interestin story so far an I had nothin of pressin importance goin on, so I let him continue.

His theory was about to crash in a big way. He'd been up in the hills all day, relaxin with a good smoke an ponderin his next move when on strollin down to the bottom, he came across a donkey tied to a post. He'd been thinkin how tired he felt in the hot sun an how far the trek was back into the town. This four-legged vehicle seemed like a gift from God an – wait for it – the donkey was tethered with a green rope. AH HAR! he thought, green for GO! Quick as a flash, he was on its back an off down the dirt track into town. An angry mob of Moroccans came hurtlin from over the brow of a hill, cryin thief an pullin him to the ground for a good flip floppin. It didn't stop there. They take such issues very seriously out in those parts of the world where it would be the equivalent of being a car thief in this country. He was tried an banged up for a full three months in the darkest, most grim cell full of cockroaches, with a hole in the ground for a bog an three stones for wipin his arse.

I looked him over once again. Poor bastard, he looked completely shell shocked. Mad fucker. The world's full of 'em. I patted him on the back an wished him well for the journey home, assurin him that I'd taken heed of his tale an that I'd tread very carefully around this town.

The letter arrived after about five days of hell. I opened it with a huge sigh of relief only to find that the money was not there. Either it had been stolen in transit or my nana had accidentally omitted to put it in in the first place. Either way, I was up shit creek without a ticket an had to contact them a second time to ask for another letter to be sent. I'm sure that they didn't believe my assurances that the money had never arrived. I felt like a complete fraud, a real shit of a grandson, even though it was the truth.

I was beginnin to feel really ill by now with the lack of proper nourishment an the pressure of leadin a Faginesque existence in such a dangerous atmosphere; I wanted to go home.

As luck would have it, on one of my forays into town to sneak some food, I came across an English geezer who saw my problem an offered to take me to his hideout in the hills out of harm's way; I was sure to be lynched if the locals caught up with me.

He was a psychiatrist who had analysed himself to the point where he had lost the plot an had taken to livin in a cave, deep in the cover of the mountain. He had a proper set-up goin with fur rugs an brightly coloured woven blankets draped an scattered around the place, it looked quite homely. There was a little stove for cookin on close to the entrance an further back he had his music set up on a natural shelf in the wall of the cave. It was quite a tidy place as far as caves go an I welcomed the peace an seclusion in my exhausted state. The bare stone walls that reached back into the belly of the hillside kept the cave at a very comfortable, near-constant temperature an, of course, it was always dry. I admired his small corner of the world for its simplistic practicalities. Here was a man who'd been completely fucked off by society. He'd had his fill of all the troubles in the modern world, which other people would bring to his office day in an day out. He'd run to the furthest, quietest corner he could think of an here he sat, happy as Larry, mindin his own business an listenin to his music with his pipe. Good man.

I'd drunk some dodgy water at some point on my rounds of the town an now I was safely within the confines of the cave, I relaxed to the point where my body yielded to the effects of the poison in my system. I took to my makeshift bed of hastily arranged fur rugs with a fever, oblivious to the stony surroundins.

I remained incarcerated in this prehistoric pit for quite a few days as the fever plunged me into a deep unconsciousness. In my illness, strange visions came to me in my dreams. These were not the ordinary dreamscapes of a person who is merely tired, they were vivid an scary fantasies in which I saw whole cities of ordinary people from back home, dancin in weird an wonderful ways while goin about their everyday tasks. The information crowded my mind with images jostlin for position, an sounds overlappin each other in unison. The people I saw twisted an writhed to this incessant soundtrack of loud an crazy, mesmerizin music. Their arms waved in rhythmic union with the beats as they bobbed an weaved about the streets an shops.

The sweats an dreams eventually subsided an I realized that it was time to check out the post office for any signs of my letter. I somehow made my way down into the town without bein seized an made straight for the post office. My spirits lifted; the money was in the envelope this time an I made immediate arrangements to get the boat over to Spain where I caught the train up through to France. I was still very ill an the journey sapped any remainin ounce of energy I had left. I was on autodrive by now, allowin my homin instincts to take over in a desperate struggle to make it back in one piece, without havin to incur any medical fees on foreign soil that I would not be able to cover.

I can't begin to tell you the relief I felt as I stepped off the train on English soil an was met by the friendly an familiar face of my uncle at his local train station down in Kent. I'd phoned my nana ahead to tell her that I'd received the money an that I was on my way home. She arranged for him to pick me up an give me some rest at their house before I made my way back up the country. I really appreciated the break in the route, I don't think I could have travelled another mile without collapsin from exhaustion. On reachin my uncle's house, I made straight for the bed an slept solidly for a good few days, only wakin for the occasional meal. I must have looked a proper state when I arrived, havin lost so much weight an with purple rings under each eye as a testament to my severe lack of vitamins on the last leg of the adventure.

Finally, I arrived back at my nana's in Wigan with its tidy little room at the back an the overall good feelin of bein surrounded by safe, normal people, day an night. I needed some time out to mull over the adventures I'd encountered on my travels an to generally readjust to bein back in the land of dole queues an pints down the local. I hadn't realized how much I'd missed the food of my youth an heartily tucked into every nourishin meal that was laid lovinly before me. Slowly, I began to regain my strength an tune into the rhythm of life in a Northern town.

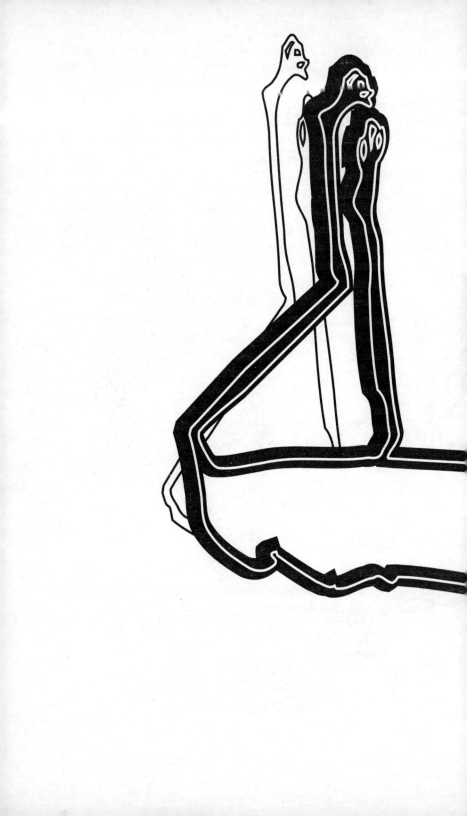

I left my nana's house in Wigan bright an early that mornin – well it was carefully timed to be before noon an after the rush hour anyway – feeling well enough at last after my period of convalescence to venture out on a weekend of pure hedonistic debauchery. I was taking the train into Manchester.

I felt a tinge of guilt as I quietly dropped the latch; the time was rapidly approaching when I would leave the safe haven they had provided, no questions asked, when I had returned from Morocco, a starvin an ailin shadow of my former self. Now, I felt good an was restless to pick up the threads of the life I'd left behind; I was missin the company of my mates. I reckoned I was ready to stride out an brave the harsh reality of life in Walkden an, more importantly, strong enough to resist being sucked back into the drug-infested hole that I'd climbed out of twelve months earlier.

I was deluding myself; the force that was driving me was a desire to share the spoils from my travels in Morocco; a tasty lump of zero-zero, the best dope that Morocco has to offer, an the equipment with which to enjoy it – an authentic Moroccan long pipe, beautifully crafted to do the job properly by a tribesman wise to the life-enhancin properties of a fuckin first-rate smoke.

I'd taken the precaution of phoning my mate to make sure he'd be there, although the likelihood of him being anywhere but his bedroom was slim, unless of course he was runnin out of supplies, in which case he would be in someone else's bedroom; the exhaustiveness of the pace of life in Walkden can kill you. We'd agreed the rendezvous an I was anticipatin an enjoyable session; I was curious to find out what he'd been up to since we parted company in Greece six months ago.

As I stepped on to the bleak, litter-strewn platform of Walkden Station, a sense of foreboding preceded an involuntary shudder. Clips from my own life in this shit-hole flickered through my mind an I froze on the spot questionin the sanity of returnin to the scene of such desperation. The decay was evident in every crevice, amplified by the stench of piss an puke. As a nervous reaction I felt for the hash an pipe, then remembered the mission; to see my friend, share my pipe an get pleasantly stoned, now where's the harm in that? I put all the sordid past behind me an began to feel a rush of adrenalin as I took the path that leads to his house.

The ring of the bell was replaced by the thump of my mate's footsteps comin down the stairs an my pulse quickened at the sight of his familiar silhouette through the frosted glass door, a sight I'd seen a thousand times, an it felt just like yesterday seein it again. There was a warm exchange of greetings before we made a furtive dash to the seclusion of his room to sample the wares I'd saved for this moment.

As he opened the door, I was met with the odour of a freshly smoked joint. 'Awww, yu've just missed Shaun!' he says, puttin' another 45 on the turntable. The tone in his voice indicated that I should be feeling disappointed, but who the fuck was he talking about?

'Shaun who?'

'Shaun Ryder, wait till yer meet im, wot a character, wot a geezer. I know you'll get on like a house on fire.' He seemed pretty excited about this possibility, like this Shaun was a part of me I'd lost at birth an I wouldn't be a whole person ever again unless I met him! I wasn't impressed, I had more important things on my mind. The contents of my pocket seemed infinitely more interesting at this moment; thoughts of this Shaun Ryder character were put aside as I reached for the diminishing lump of hash an lit the first of many pipes.

The tunes we'd forged a friendship to came out along with all the latest gossip. The afternoon passed slowly in a contented haze of camaraderie as we took turns to get thoroughly wasted on the calumet.

Some fifty pipes later, we decided a visit to the kid up the road was in order; a change of bedroom scenery an a fresh slant on the gossip front was needed as we began to reach that semicomatose, uncommunicative state where the stories begin to get recycled.

It was then that I remembered this kid's success at copping the bird I'd been coveting to take as a companion on my travels. She used to be a really sexy, good-lookin bitch an I was pissed off that this dickhead had pipped me to the post an all down to the fact that I'd exercised the misjudgement of taking her friend on a few dates. I should have taken the more direct route, but when I came to realize this it was already too late; she'd shacked up with this dickhead an my last-ditch attempt to get her to leave this cesspit of a town with me fell on deaf ears; he'd already given her a taste for the brown powder from the east an her fate was sealed.

My perception of their futures proved to be correct – a few years later I saw them lookin like the ravaged smackheads that they were, their teeth falling out an stinking worse than old cabbage an boiled potatoes. The lowest of the low, their ultimate nemesis was to end up on Witness Protection, branded outcasts an a grass for life.

As you might have guessed, I wasn't overly keen on making this particular visit but in my amicable frame of mind, I didn't protest; I resolved to let the day run its own course to see what would turn up. We entered his house via the back door, waving a cursory hello to his mam who was absorbed in some crappy soap opera on TV in the front room, oblivious to the corruption that was going on up her stairs. Once in his room, the scenario that had met me earlier that day was relived again.

'Awww, yu've just missed Shaun!' The strains of 'I'll see you on the dark side of the moon' drifted around the room – spooky!

Here it came a second time, how I would get on with this Shaun character, how we were a match made in heaven! For fuck's sake, they were going on as if I should be shaggin this geezer. I must admit, as the day wore on an I met with the same response everywhere I went, I began to wonder just who this kid could be an why they all seemed so adamant that we should meet.

It gradually came to light, as fragments of information were offered at pitstops throughout that weekend, that this Shaun had got together with a bunch of kids from my old school to form a band. They went by the name of Happy Mondays. What did they sound like? – nobody knew an the subject was shelved for the time being as I got on with the serious business of gettin loaded an satisfyin my libido as is the wont of a lad on returnin to his patch.

The feelin of doom that I felt on arriving in Walkden – you know the one, someone's walkin over your grave an a big chilly shudder takes you by surprise – well, it turned out that this was no misplaced feelin. A perfectly good weekend of homecomin celebrations, rounded off with a bonus shag with one of my ex-girlfriends, was completely ruined upon my return to Wigan. The police had been on the phone; CID at little Hulton wanted a word with me about some money that had gone missin over the weekend.

FUCK ME! I can't believe it, I've been back for one weekend an already it's on top. The worst of it was seein the look of dis-appointment in my grandparents' eyes – the activities over the last few days had taken their toll an a come-down of epic pro-portions was evident, but this, this was totally crushin; seein the people who cared for me hurtin an takin my show of indignation to be yet another delinquent outburst. It was at this point that everythin went ballistic with my nana screaming at me, 'I told you not to go back there, you wouldn't listen an now you're back in trouble. Mark, get some sense!'

Of course, I protested my innocence, but like I said, it was taken to be the pleadin of a guilty man, trapped an squirmin to get out of a particularly sticky situation. What could I do? If my own grandparents weren't havin it, what chance did I have with the dibble. I was ragin, there's no words to describe the injustice I was feelin at being hit on for somethin I genuinely didn't do. I pulled myself together an phoned the dibble shop to make arrangements to go an sort the mess out. That evenin I went over an over what money they could have been talkin about, I was totally confused. No way could I come up with anythin an none of my pals had mentioned anythin either about coppin a wedge; I certainly knew that I hadn't.

After a sleepless night, I made my way to the station, vowin to myself on the journey that this would be the last time I would visit this place, for sure. As usual they made me wait an eternity before sendin someone down to do the interview. The explanation for my summons almost floored me! Some morally retarded bastard had robbed me mate's mam's an nabbed all her bill money, an ironic comment comin from me I hear you say, but there is a code of conduct even among thieves an vagabonds that says you don't rob your own. My friend had put my name in but I couldn't blame him in the circumstances – I mean your mam is your mam when all's said an done, the lad must have been seethin for some fucker's blood. Still I felt like twattin the slimy git for suspectin me!

It turned out, he'd put in the names of all his mates, so it wasn't just me that felt like a leper an, after a nasty confrontation, I pledged to personally help him slaughter the vermin that had nearly severed a perfectly good friendship.

I've thrown this little scenario in here to highlight just how easy it can be to totally fuck up without any discernible effort at all when you just happen to be in the right place at the wrong time, as lads often are, especially this one.

Things were goin from bad to worse at an alarming rate. I knew I was facin a top crisis when I spent the followin two weeks holed up in my room in Wigan obsessively readin *The Hobbit*. My fuckin pressures; Giddeon was gettin to me, it was all too much to bear. Not even a boss tune an a heavily loaded spliff could deliver me from this one.

In a moment of sheer desperation, I enrolled on a shoddily designed course for the unemployed, thought up by some fat-arsed civil servant in a bid to juggle the four million dole figures down to a politically appeasin number. A joke of massive proportions saw me embarkin on a path of blue-collar hell, taking in the basic skills of bricklayin, plumbin, decoratin, machine toolin an an oh so interesting foray into the world of the sparky, all in one eight-week trip. The penultimate aim of these courses was to equip the remedial elements of society, that is me, with the skills an enthusiasm to get on their bikes an peddle themselves up an down the country in a vain attempt to secure some nice little low paid number in some other Godforsaken hole. Who did the pricks think they were kiddin, the only thing I can honestly say it equipped me with was the resoundin knowledge that this was not for me, ever.

All said, I gave it my best shot, taking the real nine to fivers' route of havin a pint of an evenin with some of the local lads. I even went so far as to arrange a nearby weed score so that I didn't have to visit the old haunts an invite unnecessary heartache back into my life. It still did my head in; I just could not cut it. I felt like a trapped animal, endurin a slow an painful death. Of course, it would all come to a head at some point an unfortunately the head it came to belonged to some big, daft, droolin six foot three Wiganite; a pure psycho who dreamed of women bending metal bars with their bare thighs an could punch the biggest thunder-boltin brain shakers I've ever felt to this day. It was a long fight but, boy, it was the best I'd felt in ages; I was finally purged of all the anger that had been wellin up.

My grandparents took it all surprisinly well, or perhaps they were thankful that someone had managed what they could not: to give me a proper licking after all the trouble an anguish I had caused them. Anyway, I spent the whole weekend with my head immersed in a bowl of iced water to try an minimize the damage so that I could face the throng with some dignity come Monday mornin. Imagine my surprise when I found the kid an his dad screamin blue murder about the state of his son's kipper as I returned to work. In my mind the fight had been fought fair an square – he punched the fuck out of me an I had broken his nose an kicked him in the head, enough said. But no! I was to receive a week's suspension for this misdemeanour. Fuck that, I thought, an walked off thinkin every shinin bruise was worth it; I could live with my pain.

Now I dearly love my nana an grandad, but, seein the grief I was inadvertently causin them what with the weed smokin an wot not, I realized it was time to move on. The vow I had made earlier about keepin out of Walkden was conveniently forgotten in my haste to move nearer the hub of things. In fact, my friend had secured himself a house in Salford. The property was ripe for some vitalizin input, an I reckoned I could be that missin ingredient. I installed myself double quick before the offic became redundant I rapidly adjusted to the life of a young bachelor; out on the tiles in various states of intoxication every night.

As we all know, a Giro is not the best means of supporting oneself when a bender of longer than a week's duration is embarked upon. At some point, usually very early in the proceedins it is necessary to determine a method of prolonging the fun. It is therefore with an air of expediency that the suggestions take on a criminal bent. This is by no means a thing to be proud of, in fact it is extremely sad that a disproportionate number of my generation see this path as their only salvation from poverty.

The answer came to me in a blindin flash one night in the middle of a hot-knife session – like answers often do, only maybe not the right ones – the way forward had already been offered to me in the form of a lay-on by some very generous, unsuspectin kid. In no time at all we had our sticky little mitts on a large quantity of free intoxicants. Let's party! A glorious stupor descended on our senses like a favourite blanket, protectin us from that harsh reality called life.

After two weeks of indulgence our smiles were beginnin to wane; a king-sized comedown was loomin on the horizon. We sat around in a foggy disarray, contemplatin our irrevocable fate. This time we had blown it big style, literally, with a hell of a bill an no means of payin it. SHIT!

The lads huddled together deep in discussions that lasted as long as our comedown, mullin over ideas for comin up with a fast buck. A funny thing about takin vast quantities of illegal stimulants over a prolonged period of time, is that it quashes any inklin of sense an maturity digresses in direct relation to the intensity of the binge. In other words, the most immature ideas kept comin up as all other suggestions of a slightly saner disposition were tossed aside.

Yes I'd well an truly got myself stuck in a corner; from my very twisted angle it appeared the only way out of this self dug chasm was to employ some direct action. It had reached that time of twist or bust an I sincerely hoped it would be the former. I dared barely to think of the consequences; in the middle of the night I woke with sweat oozin out of every pore, my heart thumped loudly in my emaciated frame, an I couldn't control my twitchin feet as a great rush of adrenalin swept through my veins. I thought about backin out but remembered the huge debt we'd run up. My mind was swamped with chaotic deliberations; what I was about to participate in could so easily cost me my freedom, but then my freedom wouldn't be worth havin if I didn't have any means of sortin out this mess I was in. These thoughts ricocheted round my head all night till finally I had to accept that I could go down an, if I was, I was goin to go down fightin. I'd yet to learn that to fight the system was to fight yourself in the long run, but youthful spirit an optimism mixed with a hefty dose of juvenile ignorance is a dangerous recipe for trouble.

It is with a great deal of shame that I recall the events that took place. I was tryin so hard to stick to a fairly straight path, but it was just too easy to get caught up in the buzz of it all; that rush of adrenalin is as powerful an addictive as any drug, as is the money that comes as the end result. As with any drug though, there is a price to pay. It fills you with a self-loathin as you realize just what a shitty little cretin you really are to have stooped so low.

So, it was with a great deal of anguish that we set off for the venue feelin like the scum we were an wishin there was some other way to go about life.

I must admit, the followin week we returned to our manor buzzin our socks off; we'd managed to pull it off by the skin of our teeth havin been chased nearly all the way home – this minor hiccup had been written into our plans; we were ready for it an managed without too much ado to lose the dibble before touchin home base. But what we weren't countin on was the likelihood of some other daft cunt bein there already waitin to get on the same enterprise – what on earth was going on? What had actually gone on was an aborted attempt by the same team the month previously when they had chickened out, an now they were back to try again.

A quiet word in their ears reaffirmed the peckin order an our plans went ahead.

Back in the confines of my own room, I decided to drop a couple of acid tabs to round off the day in style. I couldn't have made a bigger mistake – every bush, every car, every lamp-post took on the guise of the babylon. They were swarmin everywhere. I heard full battalions of riot vans screechin to a halt by the front door followed by military processions beatin a two step up the garden path. It was a livin nightmare. I sat vigilantly by the window on the landin in readiness to flee an when it really felt like it was comin on top, I positioned myself SAS fashion at the foot of the garden beneath the cover of the undergrowth. Paranoia had set in big-style; my eyes bulged at the sight of the most mundane objects as they took on a terrifyin likeness to the boys in blue. Luckily, the trip gradually intensified to the point where I actually forgot about the matter in hand an began to enjoy myself, whilin away a good few hours watchin wondrous sights such as the grass growin an meltin simultaneously then weavin itself into the most intricate of patterns that trailed in iridescent, neon zig-zags like a busy night-time scene in a speeded up film.

To combat the shock of what I'd done, I spent the rest of that week trippin like a bastard or speedin like a hundred-mile-an-hour hurricane an all the while smokin as many spliffs as I possibly could. I'd heard that Bob Marley smoked at least a hundred a day an I was desperate to beat his record.

The guilt was, it has to be said, unbearable. I had promised myself an all my family that I would stay out of trouble an not even all the new clobber from my new found wealth could assuage the pain I felt inside at lettin everyone down again; in short, I felt a total twat. I punished myself for the entirety of the next month, knowin how if I'd not been such a lucky git, I could have completely naused my whole life, an that of those closest to me, by one stupid act of greed. What a dickhead I was!

I finally snapped out of my morose frame of mind an got on with tryin to find somethin worthwhile to do with my time. Nothin too conventional, mind you, just somethin that wasn't anythin to do with the criminal underworld. Convention isn't an easy bedfellow for me, as you may have guessed.

I came up with the crackin idea of hirin a tranny van an doin the Glastonbury thing. We did have a little trouble decidin who was straight enough to drive, or even qualified to drive for that matter, but eventually we set off with high hopes, lookin for adventure. It should have been straightforward enough, except we took a detour via Wales pickin up hitch-hikers an gettin them stoned in an attempt to demonstrate our charitable nature in top hippie fashion. We had the van decked out with blankets an cushions in various states of lumpy deterioration, an the obligatory ghetto blaster for that impromptu party vibe.

We were on to a winner; most people loved it, apart from a French couple who thought we were completely bonkers. They were justified in thinkin this because it wasn't too long before, in our disorientated state of mind, we were travellin in the totally wrong direction an in fact, dropped them ninety miles further up the road than where we had picked them up. Hey man, *c'est la vie!*

In our haste to get on the hippie trail, we arrived three weeks too early; like I said, we were keen. Undeterred, we set off in search of the hippies; they had to be around here someplace! It was midnight when we finally tracked them down. They were camped out at a disused petrol station an all across the field opposite. We pulled up an piled out of the van, to be greeted by the sight of all these hippies leggin it in all directions. Strange behaviour I thought an I went runnin after them where they'd disappeared into this field. The camp was massive; hundreds of coaches an vehicles of all shapes an sizes in various states of dilapidation. There were people roughin it in teepees an one geezer was sat in a chair watchin a telly stuck in a bush, oblivious to the fine drizzle comin down.

Yeah! This is it, this is trip paradise. Should be a doddle gettin sorted out here I thought an went in search of some booty, any kind, I wasn't fussed. I started divin in all these smelly coaches, happy as you like, confident of a quick score. No one twitched a muscle; am I invisible or what, I began to wonder after about the third attempt. The stony silence was startin to freak me out. Bunch of fuckin weird arseholes, talk about the slaughtered lamb. I deduced it was best to leave it till the mornin an report back to our van that the mission had been terminated due to a distinct lack of response.

The tunes went on an the pipe came out; the van began to fill with smoke as we settled back in our own smelly surroundins to await the next day. Then a peculiar thing happened. One by one, they began to approach the van. Anybody would think we'd just dropped in from outer space, I mean for Christ's sakes we were here courtesy of Salford Van Hire; you don't get many aliens drivin about in bright orange vans now, do you? Then again, this could account for a lot of strange goins on in Salford, but, I'm wandering off the mark here – so back to the point in hand. When they'd finished checkin out who we were an what we were about, they deemed us fit to join their posse an the trips came out. Yes! Full blown hippie mode, here we come. Some of the sights that met our eyes that night had us fair splittin our sides. The petrol station had an old house attached to it which was bein used as a squat, so we all headed in that direction. We thought we were pretty off it, but these people just take the biscuit, they didn't give a flyin fuck. What's more, it was doin my head in how some of them were really well educated an they had chosen to live this way, daft bastards. Hippie-revolution talk resounded throughout the night; they'd been in a full-on riot with the police a few days before, tryin to get a free festival goin at Stonehenge. This accounted for the sheer number of them; they had been travellin round in convoy for days lookin for a plot. Apparently, when we'd turned up in our brand new, bright orange van, they all thought it was a secret deployment of army officers, what with our skinheads, tryin to infiltrate their camp an not quite hittin the mark. Funny as fuck man, I nearly cried – no wonder we got such an icy reception.

During the night our lot had tripped off in all directions, so at sunrise I decided to make my way back to the van to get some kip. Everyone was there, smokin an chillin after the night's activities – all except one lad who just couldn't hack the lifestyle. In my altered state of perception, he seemed to possess all the attributes of a turtle, divin into his shell for cover, completely freaked out by it all. He'd gone under an was goin home, poor kid, only he didn't realize what a worse nightmare trip was in store for him tryin to hitch-hike off his trolley an without a carrot. I mean, just who would pick him up, I ask you? Well, one down an four to go. We decided to stay another night in hippie city, it had seemed like a good laugh so we thought we'd give it another shot.

Our real reason for stayin though, was a promise of a few hundred trips an a cheap pound of Leb. All we had to do was find the man with the silver elephants on the toes of his boots – sorted.

Another night of mayhem ensued burnin round the gaff with all these crusty hippies. In short, havin a ball. The pace began to take its toll an before dawn I started to feel well an truly fucked. I lurched off in the direction of our van, slippin past this old water dowser tellin stories of how he'd escaped jail by findin a cup of water in the courtroom blindfolded – who was I to argue. I politely turned down a cup of tea made from puddle water by some woman who looked like she'd been plucked from a Victorian horror movie an got my head down in our gleamin orange van.

I must have slept for about three hours when I awoke to the sounds of low-flyin choppers an orders shouted from a loud hailer. Jesus! That acid was powerful stuff, I felt like I was in Vietnam for a moment, the noise was incredible. I bolted upright, rubbin my eyes an it became clear this was no trip. Stumblin out of the van, I came across scenes of carnage an chaos; police were everywhere, in vans, cars an helicopters, some of them in full riot gear. Everyone proceeded to stash their spoils in a mad panic, wherever they could. We all crapped our pants, figuratively speakin, of course.

In one direction, a group of hippies were locked in a heated argument with an officer holdin a cane topped with a silver ball; the chief constable. Meanwhile, his men could be observed sittin uncomfortably confined to their car as a child belongin to the hippie entourage was gleefully pissin up the side of it. A deal was quickly struck an word got around that we had to move off before noon or they were stormin the camp in a no-holds-barred, heavy-handed fashion. That was all the promptin we needed, you couldn't see our little orange van for dust – we were the first out of there.

As none of us had eaten for days, the first port of call had to be a food stop. A small tourist-type café, sellin cream teas an the like to passin trade, was pounced on a few miles down the road. In the lead was my pal, covered from head to foot in tattoos an sportin a savage-lookin skinhead atop skeletal features, he must have been a proper scary sight to these little old dears.

This frail lady of considerably advanced years looked us over in horror. 'You're not with those hippies are you?'

'No!' we all chorused in unison, tryin to sound mortally offended. Amazinly, that was her only concern, an a hearty breakfast was served up without further ado. Refuelled, we set off on a jaunt to Torquay for the day. An a day it was as we reached the unanimous decision that it was fuckin shite. We headed back up North.

I arrived home to find the busies had been round at the house followin a complaint from a neighbour about excessive noise in the early hours of the mornin. The kid I was stayin with had apparently been tryin to cut open a peter usin an angle grinder! Oblivious to the job in hand, the police had told him to keep the noise down as people were tryin to sleep. The first chance I got I installed myself in a flat of my own; that kind of trouble, I didn't need.

The flat was in Eccles, it felt ACE havin my own space at last: I didn't have any dickheads around me doin their best to land me in jail. After movin some of my stuff into the flat, I went for a quiet pint an a spliff in the late, glorious afternoon sunshine with my pal. Life felt good again. My mate was excitedly tellin me about his planned trip, leavin that evenin for the Dam. He was goin with Shaun for a five day break. 'You should hold on an meet him.'

This time curiosity got the better of me; at last. I was goin to meet this elusive Shaun character I'd been hearin so much about for a good few months – I couldn't believe our paths had never crossed even though we'd been mixing about in the same circles for years.

Whey hey! Here they were an into the car park pulled the brightest canary-yellow Escort – which they'd endearinly named The Egg – with the windows rolled down an the tunes blarin at full volume. In the driver's seat sat Horse with his head just poppin over the steerin wheel, his eyes dark an hooded an wearin a grin from ear to ear. Next to him sat a similar-lookin kid with the same funny goatee-beard an pin-head crew cut. This was obviously Shaun; he was hangin out of the window, a king-sized spliff danglin from his grinnin kipper, shoutin a greetin an jumpin out of the car almost before it stopped. He came boundin over in a half runnin, half walkin fashion with a hint of a swagger, fixin his jacket with a shrug of the left shoulder an adjustin his tackle in the process. Straight away he handed over the spliff an introduced himself, 'Alright, I'm X.'

'Alright, I'm Bez.' Simple as that. We shook hands an he enquired what everyone was drinkin an immediately set off for the bar to get the booze in. You know what they say, first impressions count a lot an I couldn't help but think that here was a man after my own heart; a spliff an booze. I liked him already.

While Shaun was at the bar, Horse began tellin us about how they were buzzin their tits off about gettin the first copies of their first ever single that very day. No mean achievement; I'll drink to that one I thought – the lads doin somethin really worthwhile. With that, Shaun returned from the bar an the next few hours were spent enthusiastically toastin their first taste of success.

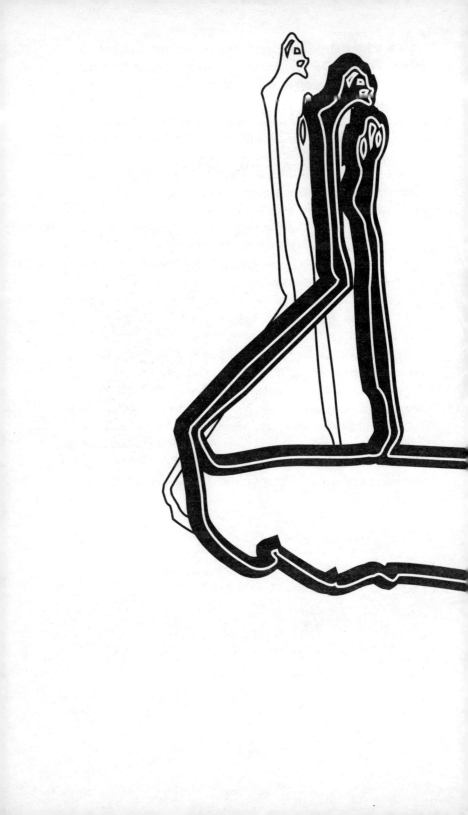

The single was on Factory Records, the legendary label owned by that universally unpopular impresario of the underground scene in Manchester – the entrepreneur formerly known as Tony Wilson, now to be known as Mr Anthony Wilson. A lot of people have said a lot of things about Mr Wilson an he has been heard to say a lot of things about the Mondays but, whatever has gone down in history, I would just like to say that he tries what others would not even consider, goin out on a limb to conquer new ground; a fearless explorer, the Chris Bonnington of pop. Sometimes he fails because of his ambitiousness, but then he bounces back an tries again. God loves a tryer an so do I.

This maverick music mogul also had the massively acclaimed New Order, aka Joy Division, on his label – one of my all-time favourites, right up there at the top of my list. So you can imagine how I was seriously knocked sideways to hear, after about the third pint, Shaun bangin on about a gig they'd just done with the said band. I was as giddy as a kid at Christmas hearin this news; somethin special was about to happen round our way at last. You could virtually taste the sweet vibes of good fortune minglin in with the smoke settlin over our little social settin.

This wasn't the only reason for Shaun to be largin it up in the boozer, although it was a perfectly good enough reason in itself. In fact it was a double celebration as he'd just sold his house after a recent divorce, an the dough that had consequently come his way was burnin a big, scorchin hole in his pocket. No wonder he thought he was the dog's bollocks, sharin the spotlight with the big names, cuttin his own disc an havin a few quid to blow as a newly reinstated bachelor – I felt pretty fuckin excited about it all myself an I was just havin a pint or two with the lucky bastard, such was the infectious nature of his heightened spirits. To top it all, as I mentioned earlier, he was off to the Dam that very evenin to toast this streak of good fortune in the proper fashion.

I soon found out that Shaun loves an audience an once he found out that we were attentive listeners, the anecdotes came hurtlin along thick an fast, delivered with a menacinly wicked grin to emphasize the sordid bits in his tales – the bits he obviously liked the best. His talk was pure tabloid, he could fill the *News of the World* with stories to spare; the press would love him an, indubitably, in time they did.

When we eventually parted company, it was with an invite to go down to his pad when they returned, to look over any souvenirs they might bring back with them. I gave an appreciative nod to the suggestion an made my way back to the house to move the last of my belongins into the new flat.

I was in fact completely tanked up, an no way was I organizin anythin so complicated an time-consumin as transferrin a set of matchin Tesco carrier bags from one address to another. An alternative presented itself in the form of some female company, an the fool I am, I went along with the proposal of neckin a trip an havin a quiet night in. The flat wasn't ready to move into anyway, I reasoned to myself, an succumbed to the prospect of a night of fornication. These mistakes do happen every now an then; my intuition yells one thing at me an for some strange reason known only to God an my mam, I end up doin the exact opposite, like some invisible force is pullin my thoughts along a strange trajectory in that spacious void called my mind. I blame the planetary line-up at the time of my birth, myself.

Mistake number one:

I should have gone with my intuition on this one. She began paintin my face, reassurin me it would be harmless fun.

Mistake number two:

Before you could say I don't quite think that shade of lipstick is really me, she had me dressed in the most hideously crap kex complete with braces an full face paint, lookin like some fuckin poncy new age hippy crossed with a Salford skinhead; rainbows an flowers daubed across my perturbed mug – Not my style, *not* my style at all!

Now, lookin a total twat in the security of your own home is bad enough, but to look out of the window at nine a.m. to see your mate pullin up in a car with three other geezers is somethin else. My mate was waving theatrically at me from the back seat of the car; his companions were three CID. All I could think of at that moment was what a prick he looked an that he'd better shut it, 'cos whatever trouble he was in, I wanted nothin to do with it. Then I realized what a prize prick I looked myself an legged it up the stairs to try an get the slap off my face, pronto.

As they entered the house, I could hear the panic risin in his voice as he tried desperately to deny the crime they suspected he'd done – a gold chain an sovereign had been snatched from a girl's neck the night before. Why is it always at the end of some trip, when the strychnine is settin in, an yer skin doesn't quite seem to fit properly, that some blatherin bastard tries to tangle yer up in his problems?

This blatherin bastard was askin me to vouch for his good character. I'd had Mary fuckin Quant on my case all night, my eyes were still rollin an I was wearin stupid trousers; the last thing I needed was to try an look sincere in my opinion of his honesty. I made my excuses, grabbed my bags an got the hell out of there as fast as I could without seemin too shady myself. I grabbed the girl on the way, so as not to leave any debris lyin around that I might have to go back for later.

Once out in the fresh air, the panic of the scene I'd just left began to subside; a quiet sense of relief oiled my stiff limbs an a buoyancy came back into my step. I was thankin God that I'd managed to escape from a potentially dangerous acquaintance without apparent incident an was just about to vocalize this point when – *swoosh* – the CID pulled up alongside an called me over. I handed my bags to the girl, tellin her to take them home to my new flat, where I would meet her later. I walked over to the car an in an instant they were upon me, grabbin my arms an leadin me round to the boot. I mean, for fuck's sake, I wasn't about to be goin anywhere now was I? After all I was an innocent man, or so I thought! With smug, shiny, fat smirkin faces they opened the boot in a dramatic fashion as if they'd discovered I was a secret arms dealer or somethin. There wavin back at me were four puny seedlins, the result of a stoned experiment that I'd abandoned, forgotten in the back of the kitchen. The seeds I'd thrown in the pot weren't even from a quality smoke. I was gutted; to be pulled for somethin so stupidly small, somethin that grows naturally in abundance all over the world, somethin that I hadn't even intended to cultivate. Fuckin weeds, why do they grow so easily.

To add insult to injury, the kid I'd been stayin with was sat in the back of the car squealin like a stuck pig about how he was prepared to take any rap but not for drugs. I couldn't believe it, all I wanted was a quiet life in the seclusion of my new pad an now I was bein hailed as the Percy fuckin Thrower of cannabis land – I hate gardenin, I hate tendin plants; why hadn't they shrivelled up an withered with neglect like any other plant I ever owned?

Within minutes, I found myself locked up in some dingy, urine-soaked cell with misery an anguish written all over the walls. A seatless bog in the corner, a thin, blue plastic-coated mattress an a smelly, itchy grey blanket were my only source of comfort. In short, any dibble shop, in any town. I began to march around in circles, pullin on these daft braces, shoutin, 'I always shop at Burtons!'

At the time it seemed the only sensible way to deal with the trauma, considerin the events of the previous twenty-four hours. The dibble obviously believed I was completely bonkers an in their wisdom, locked me in the cell for the rest of the day to sleep off whatever it was in my system that was causin this temporary bout of insanity.

The next day found us both in court, shufflin about nervously as the judge granted us bail to await the results of the forensic tests in a few months' time, when we would be kindly invited back to face more petty persecution at the hands of the law. I was really chompin at the bit over what this fuckin prick of a kid had landed us both in. Not only had he blatantly grassed me up, but he'd gone an done exactly what he'd intended not to do which was to get us both a charge sheet. He'd been cleared of the muggin as he'd been on an ID parade durin the day while I'd been asleep, an some other kid had been picked out. If he'd kept his cool about the barely recognizable seedlins we'd have both skipped the bastard cultivatin charges too. It was all too ludicrous to comprehend; here I was tryin my best to walk away from the mayhem an some crazy warp in time lands me right back in the thick of it. All the same, I considered myself lucky; the episode had served as a sharp reminder of why I had to leave all that nonsense behind me if life was goin to be worth livin. I had a strong conviction that somebody up there was tryin to correct the error of my ways an I'd better start takin notice – or else!

The next few days I tried settlin into my new flat, wanderin around arrangin my few possessions in as many cupboards as possible an reflectin on the turmoil of the last few months, my train of thought enhanced by the addition of a spliff or two. It was really quite a comfortable pad I'd copped for an I found I managed to wind down to the point of bein practical enough to get a few healthy groceries in; the process of self-healin was at last underway.

After the third day in, lookin at the pristine paintwork an perfectly plumbed kitchen, I began to get REALLY BORED – domestic bliss was not on the agenda just yet in my young an impatient state of bein. The doorbell rang. My heart leapt with joy. Salvation was here at last; someone had finally found the sense to come an save me from my self-inflicted penance before a deep, black depression slipped a shroud over my life, put me on a production line in some fuck-off factory, an committed me to readin Argos catalogues at bedtime.

I opened the door to the greetin of a large, billowin cloud of smoke smellin unmistakably of the sweetest Dutch weed: it was my mate back from the Dam, grinnin insanely on my doorstep. My spirit soared, the tunes went on, an suddenly life was miraculously transformed back to normal as I listened to the antics of their journey. I was soon completely engrossed, jumpin around the room in an unself-conscious fashion, to the sound of Talking Heads – well it's what young lads do to demonstrate a euphoric state of mind, isn't it?

This was too good a story to miss; it needed the pair of them to tell it with style, so we headed off to check it out with the main man down at his pad – we went via a scenic route, callin off first at Ladywell flats: a really run-down, rat-infested tenement block, adorned with graffiti an the foul-smellin excrement of various types of mammals. The air really was fuckin horribly rancid, especially around the ever-present glue sniffers' convention on the stairs. Single mums with lank hair an full of tomazis leaned on the rails of the balconies smokin an gossipin as their children played on the burnt-out remains of the joy riders' weekend haul in the street below, occasionally barkin at the 'little soddin bastards' to fetch them a couple more fags an a loaf from the shop. Even the dogs hung around in twos or more.

The people who lived here never got to half fill their trolleys in the local supermarket – they were all barred for shopliftin to eat. This place was riddled with abject poverty; poignantly illustrated by the signs in nearby shops listin the prices for single eggs, fags an nappies, in fact, all the basic necessities, most of them comin in a 'MY MUM'S' wrapper. Incidentally, instead of takin stock of the situation an improvin it, the place was sold off to a housin association, with some of the flats bein sold off privately – another prime example of the carin government providin a decent home for the lower workin classes – I think not! Nevertheless back then the place was servin the local drug community well if nothing else an we soon found what we were lookin for, then bid a hasty retreat in case we got inadvertently sucked into the ghetto. The offy was the next port of call to pick up the obligatory four-pack, an finally, fully equipped, we arrived at Shaun's flat.

We were greeted at the door by a good-lookin chick of exotic origins – I know, completely politically incorrect of me to say so but that's the way it was, an with a nice arse too! I followed as it wiggled up the stairs, transfixed by the shapely curviness just on my eye level. I wondered if there was any more of the same in store. Now, that would have rounded the day off nicely.

Windin down from his recent brush with the Dover Customs an Excise, whiskey in hand, surrounded by booty from the duty free an lookin slightly disgruntled but none the less content, there sat Shaun. By the look on his grinnin kipper, I could tell he was pleased to see us an was itchin to tell the tales of his travels to an attentive audience. With a large whiskey each an a dash of the wicked lady ticklin our nasal passages, we settled down with a heavily loaded spliff an the story began to unfold.

It all boiled down to that well-known dilemma suffered by anyone who has visited the Dam an indulged in the novelty of bein able to buy a top-class weed along with their coffee. The potency of the smelly green stuff always gets underestimated – you buy far more than you actually need, which results in the need for a big decision as the last few hours are drawin in. You desperately try to smoke all the weed you have left, knowin full well you're not goin to manage it by the deadline. This leaves you faced with one of two possibilities:

a) accept with grace that you're not goin to manage it on time an leave your weed on the table for the next lucky punter, or

b) cringe like the tight bastard you are at havin to throw money well spent down the drain an devise a plan to smuggle the contraband home with you.

Obviously, the latter option appealed more to my pal an Mr Ryder on this occasion, an they decided the lads back home would appreciate a top souvenir of their travels. True. Unfortunately, after passin through Passport Control without a hitch, they boarded the coach with Shaun burnin straight for his stash to announce his triumph, only to be witnessed by a couple of Customs men who had infiltrated the passengers in the hope that this would happen. He was immediately hauled off with a few other hapless hopefuls. The search was conducted by some big, fat-tittied dyke. It wasn't long before Shaun's newly acquired porn mags came to light an another offence was marked up, under the Obscene Publications Act. To make her point, the customs officer began to draw circles around erect penises entering women's vaginas, attemptin to make Shaun feel embarrassed an ashamed of his heterosexual feelins.

'What do you intend to do with these Mr Ryder?'

'WANK!' came the cheeky reply.

She'd unintentionally played, slap, bang, into his hands: talkin dirty an lookin at porn mags – right up Shaun's street.

An evenin of pleasant congeniality passed with a succession of sleazy tales from the Dam followin one after the other; a back-drop of classic tunes infusin our souls an a plentiful supply of duty free ensurin that the night didn't burn out till we were spent. I left the next mornin, my lips still stretched in a tight grin from ear to ear at the thought that I'd just found a top soul mate, a proper psycho bastard, or to put it another way, a bit fuckin insane, but a unique character with a dangerously astute insight into the darker side of life. I couldn't possibly have foreseen at that moment in time just what twists an turns that friendship was goin to bring to my life in the very near future.

Stood at the bus stop that next mornin was one of my pals, so bein the decent lads we were, we pulled over to give him a lift. He'd just got out of the nick from a nine-month stretch for possession an intent to supply some narcotic or other – a frequent hazard of livin in an around Walkden if you are young an male with a poor education. It turned out he was stayin with his mam an things were gettin a bit too claustrophobic under her carin an watchful eye. He needed some space to breathe an inhale smoke, an I needed a housemate after livin alone for all of three days; I was, unbelievable as it may sound, tirin of my own company. A deal was struck an that afternoon was passed installin this pal into my gaff. Not too bad a move as it turned out. He proved to be a valuable asset around the house, bein pretty well-trained in the art of housework an cookin. I'd never found much time for any of that sissy shit, like I've said it was all done for me at home by my mam; I just wasn't equipped with the knowledge or the experience to get to grips with it. Now, I realize, it's basically a matter of movin your arms an legs in a certain fashion an engagin the old grey matter to co-ordinate it all but, as you can imagine, this was a really scary thought back then.

An agreeable few days passed by as I acquainted myself with this new flatmate's record collection: his taste in music wasn't too bad at all, an the food kept appearin at regular intervals to add to the overall feelin of well-bein. It was a good decision lettin him stay, I thought, as my energy levels began to be restored in readiness for the next explosion of activity, which I didn't realize at the time was gonna lead to the start of my savin grace.

With my belly full an not a care in the world, I got up to answer the door. In comes my friend wearin a smile that would outshine the Blackpool Illuminations.

'I've just copped for some boss black micro dots.'

No kiddin, it's written all over your face mate, I mused.

'Mmm, let's have a look.'

In it goes, an eyesdown for a lucky trip. BAM, BOOM, FUCK, the lot went instantly pear shaped. There was a poster on the wall of a naked woman wearin just a cannabis leaf to cover her modesty. She stripped it off, revealin a perfect pulsatin pussy an began to writhe about all over, rubbin herself passionately. The rest of the room began to move around to the same undulatin rhythm. Fuck me, this was some heavy shit to be contendin with all of a sudden; I fell back marvellin at the awesome sight. My mate astounds us both at that very moment by findin that the hi-fi can play two tapes at the same time. What a bearin this has on the trip; there was Penguin Café an Frank Zappa blastin out at the same time. My physical existence in time an space was facin an unreasonable multitude of questionin; I had to give in an accept that reality was goin to be evadin me for the time bein. The lot had gone, in a big way.

A few hours later, with a full-on riot ragin in my head still, we decided to force the padlock on a door in the hallway that had been doin my head in since I'd moved in. No one had gone in or out of it the whole time I'd been there an curiosity had got the better of me. Armed with a screwdriver an superhuman strength, we managed to pop it open to reveal a dark stairwell goin down into the cellar. Tiptoein an gigglin nervously, we inched our way down by the light of our Zippos. Wow, a proper party room had been discovered right there in our very own basement – we laid a claim to it, bein the only intrepid adventurers down there in years, it looked like. We bumped around in the darkness an found another door. With one good shove it opened up into a garden an we were off into the big outdoors – there's no describin the lure of nature to lose yourself in with a black micro dot swimmin around in your veins. Every leaf an petal is a book to read an there were volumes out there. Unaccountably, some undefinable time later, we found ourselves back in the flat, chillin with a smoke an agreein that was some crazy shit we'd just experienced. We began to laugh again at some of the snippets of madness that rebounded back in flashes through out spaghettied thought patterns.

There went the bell again; in marched X, Horse an Ronnie,

clutchin cans of Special Brew an crackin a succession of jokes as a form of high-spirited greetin. Life was rushin at them fast an furious an I was just a pit-stop on their way to the rented rehearsal room under the Boardwalk, where they practised. I was made up that they'd thought to call for a quick beer an a spliff as I hadn't seen Ronnie for some time, the last bein in a local dive called the Wishing Well, a sad place by any standards.

We recalled the evenin. It was a typical night down the club, aided by a healthy dose of LSD which resulted in copious amounts of side-splittin laughter at the motley crew of punters that prefer to party close to home 'cos it's what they know an it saves on the taxi fare. Never mind that the beer tastes like piss, the women stink of piss an the bog floor is immersed in it due to the slack-bladdered pissheads relievin themselves indiscriminately. We remembered that we had nearly relieved ourselves on the dance floor at the point when the laughter had started to hurt an snot an spit an tears had erupted from our orifices across our achin, purple facial muscles. Ahh yes! Amusin memories.

It didn't take long for the conversation to get round to the powerful potency of the black micro dots as sampled the previous day. Not much arm bendin was required to get them to agree to a session after practice. Fuckin too right they'll be back, I thought. I closed the door an went to get some kip in readiness of the forthcomin recreation period.

As anticipated, they returned later that evenin an double doses were handed out all round. BAM BOOM FUCCCCCK-KKK MEEEEE! Here we go again – the chick on the wall was at it again, rubbin herself invitinly, the man found the wizardry to make the two tapes play simultaneously an the whole fuckin lot went bollocks to sanity. In between delirious fits of giggles, with his head bobbin in agreement with himself, Horse put a plan out for the trip an proceeded to pull out his bass an plug it in. Ronnie quickly got on the buzz an got the drum machine goin. Before we knew what was happenin, we'd built the biggest, baddest wall of sound imaginable an it sounded fuckin *ACE*. It all made perfect sense; the chaotic cacophony of notes an rhythms echoin the dissemination of our cumulative thoughts. WOW!

We paid another visit to the cellar; a light had been installed since the last romp in forward plannin for just such an occasion. Everyone agreed it was the perfect settin for our nocturnal activities: tucked safely away from the throes of the public gaze – an the neighbours.

By the followin day we had pared the tunes down to just one at a time, accompanied by a civilized cup of tea along with our smokes. A harmonious consciousness hovered above the room, about ceilin level, as the remainin bunch of party people languished in the certainty of enjoyable company. The lads were bidin their time before gettin off to practise for a forthcomin gig at Corbieres; it struck me that I had no direction to focus on an I was yet again skint. I'd made arrangements for a night out with X but didn't have the readies to even pay a visit to the papershop to get a packet of fags. Life was suddenly a major pain in the arse again. I began to get that hopeless feelin, diggin about for lose change in an empty pocket an fightin the impulse to resort to employin the guise of the criminal. It's fuckin bollocks runnin out of everythin: I felt that it just should not happen an bein good at nothin but partyin, I was in no position to do anythin about it. I just could not comprehend it at all.

A crisis of mega proportions was loomin as I set off out in search of I didn't know what.

Desperate ideas began to seep through the post-acid fog inside my head; the sudden onset of a serious quandary froze my limbs, makin my gait that of a man knee-deep in a quagmire of his own shit. I stepped off the curb, lost in the expansiveness of my dilemma. Immediately, I heard the anxious beepin of a car horn an turnin, ready to give a heartfelt fuck-you two-finger salute an a gobful of abuse, I realized it was a pal of mine in a Bedford tranny van.

Ace: a lift, an even better when you've got no destination in mind, because goin nowhere can be fuckin tirin on foot. I jumped in laughin at his choice of transport; mainly to alleviate the pain of havin nothin in my own life to laugh at, 'cos to be right, at least he had transport with a tank full of petrol. What did I have? – a pair of size nines an no energy.

Still, I couldn't help wonderin what he was doin in a Bedford tranny when the last time I'd seen him, he was drivin round in a Granada. Granted, it was a few years old but well luxurious for the lads to go jibbin about in. We all used to look pretty fuckin comical drivin about in it, five little undernourished skinheads, speedin inside an out, faces twitchin everywhere, lookin out for anythin to pass the time of day. No small wonder we were always gettin a pull from the dibble; it just can't have rung true at a glance, especially as the driver was midget-size too.

Luckily, my mate didn't take offence at the mockery I was makin of his mode of transport. He laughed along with me – or was it at me? – as he explained that the van had already paid for itself through his new enterprisin scheme. Oh yes, we were certainly the children of the Thatcher era – entrepreneurs every one of us – fuckin brilliant. I listened keenly as he described the 'job' he had created for himself; he made it sound almost bona fide. The van had been named PISPIT – pallets I see, pallets I take. Fuckin ACE idea, the boy's a genius I thought, an immediately recruited myself as second in command.

It was a nice little earner as it goes, entailin little effort an a decent return with no qualms about officer fuckin dibble turnin up at the front door of an evenin. We'd spend the days trawlin various sites, our beady, trained eyes zoomin in on any unsuspectin redundant pallets an then it was simply a case of backin up, throwin them in, up to sixteen at a time, an off down to the pallet yard to collect our wages. A piece of piss. The PISPIT saved my bacon good style over the followin few months on an off, when a quick route to a few bucks was needed.

I'd weathered the storm beautifully an felt quite chuffed with myself for keepin my head above the surface in the face of a twat of a personal crisis. Now all I needed was a fresh image to express my new found *joie de vivre*, so, like all good workin-class lads do, I set off to get some new clobber an a fist full of the life-changin black micro dots with some white ones thrown in, just for the yin-yang of it – a night on the town was imminent.

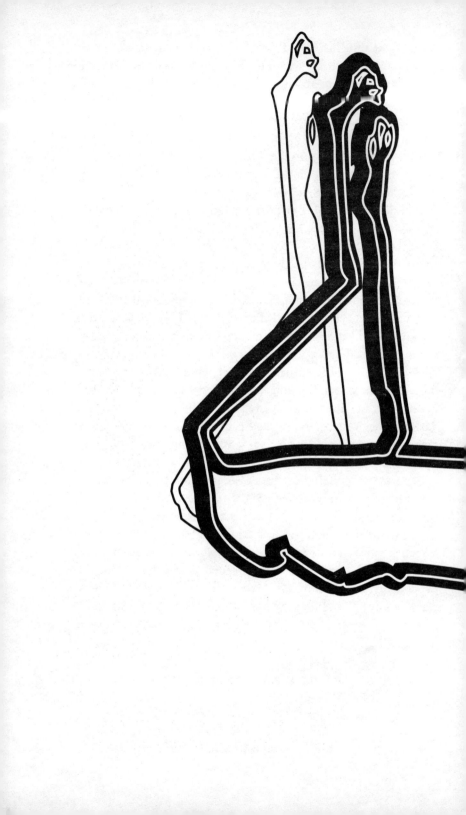

MORE OF THE SAME, PLEASE

By the time the weekend arrived, I'd amassed enough readies to get together with the rest of the lads in the local boozer an could confidently shout up a good few rounds without losin face. I was also feelin pretty fuckin fly in my new clobber . . .

The troops were amassed an ready for action; all those heavy trainin sessions of recent weeks were about to pay off. The lads were already sinkin pints like well-seasoned navvies, warmin up nicely for a full on session on the town, smokes bein rolled an rerolled in the corner as the alcohol began to affect basic judgement skills – was that the shiny side or is it just wet from the spills on the table?

'Watch yer drink – oi – yer gerrin a bit excited – sit down – that's it, the whole fuckin packet's fucked now, useless! Fuckin baboon, gerra grip.'

One of the crowd had forgotten in his excitement to remove his pint while animatedly recountin a recent violent encounter from which he'd departed completely unscathed, of course. My Rizlas were not so lucky. The spliff-building ceremony came to a swift end. I felt like twattin him but instead returned to my pint an lit a Benson, there was plenty of time for it all to happen later.

I cast a glance round the assembled mob of skinny fuckin motley scumbags, takin in five animated conversations at once. The sounds of a menagerie of sycophantic mental cases adjourned to review the collective image in terms of pullability an acceptability crashed through the general football an birds tabloid talk.

'Top pants', 'smart top', 'boss shoes – Clarks eh? – killer-style man'. Such simple things, such an important issue.

We all passed with a resoundin first class honours; it was agreed that everyone was lookin just fine an dandy an so, comfortable in this certain knowledge, we were ready to set out on the test of takin the town by storm. The adrenalin was coursin through our veins in the light of a mass invasion on the female population of the city an our intended takeover of that bastion of design an cool – The Haçienda. No fear that we were in reality the biggest bunch of nonsensical twats in town, in our view we were the only bunch of twats in town that mattered; attitude accounts for a lot an we were goin for gold on this occasion.

The local boozer suddenly began to feel too flat cap an whippets for our progressive mood. It was time to get offmans. A quick confer resulted in a unanimous vote for the good ole bus – taxis are an extravagant waste, too much beer money goin down the wrong drain – an so it came to be that we boarded the nearest double-decker that was headin in our intended direction, takin up our position on the top deck an at the back, naturally. Schoolboy habits die hard!

Unbelievably for these enlightened times of passive smokin awareness championed by the right-on health-conscious brigade an a near public floggin if you so much as sniff a Marlboro Light, you were actually permitted to make the decision 'to smoke or not to smoke' to your heart's demise at the back of the top deck – an so we did, heartily. I know it's harmful to my health an I have collected many errors in my lifetime that are strengthened to a mighty force by habit, smokin bein the major, collectin lighters in my pockets, a complementary habit to the former, bein a minor. So there we go, a slight streak of kleptomania to add to my many flaws, to boot.

Meanwhile, in between the spliffs, the black micro dots made their welcome appearance, passed around like toffees on a Bank Holiday outin, an the trip commenced.

There was to be no let-up in the constant boyish banter for the duration of the journey. I sat back an tuned in; it was akin to listenin to the radio dial bein whizzed backwards an forwards erratically an catchin momentarily on various obscure foreign broadcasts as I got caught up in the crossfire of a mêlée of dialogue an jokes aimed at the innocent fellow passengers an their unfortunate foibles, each more ludicrous an encoded than the last, with Ronnie fieldin the best observations from the back. This was a private party an the entry was strictly formal black micro dot an no tie, no doubts there.

We were that annoyin bunch of misguided, bad mannered bastards at the back of the bus; obscenities, profanities an dimps bein tossed around like a tennis tournament, teasin the girls into submission amid their fits of embarrassed giggles. They were tryin desperately to ignore us; they'd been freshly warned by their parents before leavin the house about lads like us, the rough types, who swear an smoke an take drugs an seduce young virginal girls. They loved it. That naughty an nasty element seems to work like a magnet every time. It's been tried an tested over the centuries an written into the history books. Little Johnny boffin bonce didn't stand a fuckin cat in hell's chance, the ladies had already lost it to the lads.

The rabble became louder an the air became smokier as the bus jolted an swayed its way through Salfordonia, that great yawnin chasm that lies between the suburbs an the city. We're well on our way to the promised land of Manc central. The descent from the Irlam Heights is a sight to behold from the top deck in the throes of a loomin micro dot madness; the neon lights of the city illuminate the backdrop of grime-blackened, derelict mills, their silhouettes scattered like majestic mansions of a bygone era amid the modern towers of the CIS an Piccadilly. From this elevated vantage point, the lights take on the guise of beacons guidin you into the Manc Metropolis, a welcome an familiar sight that never failed to rouse the spirits as we closed in on our destination.

The bus shuddered to a halt dischargin a final sulphurous smellin cloud of carbon monoxide an a small gang of equally obnoxious, polluted males outside the dismal catacomb of the underground bus station in the Arndale. The journey had taken a lifetime an the trip was comin on fast, turnin the lights into glorious high-pressure sodium streaks of orange an the cars into Meccano models. Slidin through the traffic without standin on it is no mean feat when your feet are feelin mean.

I had, in fact, lost all feelin in my feet an the ground appeared alarmingly close, resemblin a continuously movin conveyor belt of cracked slabs. Time to cut out an hit the bar, any bar.

We hit on a bar within a few hundred difficult yards an promptly hit the nearest chairs, concentratin hard on tryin to convey that expression which says it's not your turn to shout the beers in. Confusion reigned as every last one of us, completely shell-shocked from the fuck off first rush of acid vision, began to argue the toss of who should fetch the pints. The bar swarmed an heaved with ties an handbags, packed in so tight that asphyxia was almost certain in the event of tryin to order up a round of ten pints an change for the cig machine all in one go. The problem was not gettin resolved. We had to face facts; either sit it out pintless until the feelin became bearable an the hand mouth co-ordination thing returned or move on to a more comfortable environment that didn't entail the duress of surplus lamps an the nine-to-five sardines talkin office an salaries.

'Fuck it!' came the decisive announcement from X, 'let's get straight down The Haçienda an stop pissin about.'

It was agreed in unison. The Haçienda was surely the best place to park our minds in this communal state of delirium; the present company an surroundins were doin our collective trip no favours at all.

It has to be said that up until this point, I'd never actually set foot in the much revered Haçienda. I'd heard various accounts of its size an style as tales of debauched nights out were regaled to the lads over a recovery pint in the boozer of a Sunday afternoon. It sounded in the main like my kinda gaff; vast, dark, loud an funky as fuck an, most important of all, I'd heard from geezers not usually known for their prowess, that it had excellent odds on coppin a shag. This last thought occupied my mind for the duration of the walk down past the G-Mex an over the road to The Hac.

I foolishly enquired how much the entrance fee would be. I was shot down in a furnace of flames by an indignant X.

'Fuck that man, we don't pay, we're on Factory now, we gerrin for nothin. Just tell the doorman yer with us, yer in our band, you'll gerrin all right.'

Shit, I wanted to puke. This was all I needed, off my fuckin potatoes, flyin to the hilt an I've got to try an blag Attila the Hun on the door that I'm somethin I'm not. Oh well here goes, I thought, in for a penny, in for a pound – or rather in for nothin as the case may be. It seemed a strong matter of principle that under no circumstances was the offer of money to be made. As initiation ceremonies go it wasn't the worst I'd ever heard of, an so I dutifully followed their cue, which incidentally wasn't the one formln round the side of the buildin that I'd tried to join like the nice polite lad I am.

X moves confidently forward past the punters an flashes his membership card in a carefully understated, nonchalant manner an I follow in his slipstream, feelin mighty sheepish in my present frame of fuzziness.

'OI!'

I looked down, concentratin on my feet, tryin with all my might to pretend the 'oi' wasn't directed at me. Feignin ignorance on acid with a fifteen stone bouncer breathin down your scrawny, ill-nourished neck is not an easy task.

'Oi, I said you, where do you think you're goin?'

My tongue stuck to the roof of my mouth as it appeared to swell to twice its normal size in a matter of seconds. To make up for this sudden loss of speech, I began to gesture in a way that made my body bend an bow an my arms flap wildly at my sides like a young chick attemptin its first flight. I was rooted to the spot in the middle of the foyer an all eyes were trained in my direction. Bedlam raged in waves of noise all around me as X, on a rescue mission, was tryin to convince 'God' the doorman of my acceptability. My bodily mannerisms screamed drunk as a skunk or utterly insane, either way he was havin none of it. X needled his way into the head of the undeviatin doorman an somehow located his sense of humour an a spec of humanity.

'He's in our band, he's not fuckin drunk man, he's off his fuckin head, trippin. We all are. He just needs to get in an listen to some tunes, it'll be sorted, don't worry about it!' This is not verbatim but close enough; you get the gist.

To be honest, it all turned a bit fuckin wah wah as the music emanatin from the dance floor mashed into the conversation an diverted my attention completely. The bouncer eventually melted enough to X's magical, impish charm an the moment slipped by as we wandered off to find the source of the thuddin beat an quench our thirst at an empty bar.

On a benda in The Haçienda . . .

WHOOOO! What a gaff. It feels like enterin a cavernous, cold storage room at the meat factory. I'm half expectin to see rows of headless animal corpses hangin from massive hooks above the dance floor – an yes, it was that cold back then in pre-ecstasy days. There are twenty-foot ribbons of heavy duty clear plastic hangin from a girder at the entrance; it's a fuckin giant refrigerated cabinet in an alien supermarket, I'm convinced. I stop short of the plastic strips, not sure whether to go through or detour round them. I decide to lunge forward an go for it, feelin like Mr Benn as I emerge, a pupated version of my former self, on the other side. The club is virtually devoid of any discernible colour, except for the lights which rain down in prisms of colour an melt into glitterin puddles on the shiny blue floor. I'm transfixed by the notion of slip slidin my way through the light storm to get to the bar. I'm distracted from this per-plexion on spyin two enormous elevated screens lookin across the dance floor, displayin all manner of disjointed images to complement the ambience. I love it, an decide to test the boards for bounciness.

Bodily movements feel at first as if they are bein dwarfed by the sheer vastness of the vault that is the main dance floor. Then I begin to unfurl my limbs; they've been cramped by too many years dancin in tight circles in depressin, dingy little discos with no space an a strict 'dance like a square or you're out' policy. At last I've found the feet I've been lookin for all night an realize the place is just perfect for trippin. The sound echoes, bouncin in an out of the dark alcoves an up from the concrete an industrial rubber floorin, blastin my emaciated form from every angle. I am a human shock absorber. It's so loud, so fuckin all-consumin, it makes my scalp tingle an my hair hurt. I begin to stomp around feelin ten foot tall an full on one; no sickly furniture to get stuck on or closed in tables to get stuck round, just space to mooooove an grooooove. I warm very quickly to the layout of The Haçienda an wallow in the unfamiliar but pleasant feelin of bein able to stretch out, limber up an dance on down to my heart's content in whatever way I choose. Fuckin *ACE* place.

I catch up with X on the other side of the dance floor an we begin to weave about, bobbin up an down like two men possessed, out on a day pass from the local asylum. Two tripped out skinheaded fuckers, bold as brass, just marchin all over the gaff like it is our party.

I feel like takin my hat off – but of course I'm not wearin one – to Factory for havin the commendable sagacity to build The Haçienda. They simply – knew. There's no trace of ritzy crushed velour or claret carpets. Dolly disco it ain't.

An epiphany flashes into the recess normally occupied by my mind: the pursuit of happiness means nothin when you've finally found joy. All those years of trailin round the wrong interiors have been wiped out in an instant. From now on it doesn't matter because I will be comin here, knowin it will always be a great night out without doubt.

I'm bustin moves I never even knew I had in me, uncoilin my limbs an exorcizin all of that pent up anger an frustration that is borne of an obligatory need to be 'sane' an well behaved in the outside world. I've finally found my special haven, my heavenly sanctuary in which to let it all spill messily out. I'm spillin everywhere.

The rest of the lads stand huddled over the balcony above the dance floor, overcome with hysterics an too far gone to come over. They remain at a safe distance for the duration of the night, watchin the stunts that X an myself are pullin. Fuck, we're havin fun – oh yes. Our small but perfectly malformed audience offer encouragement as we skirt the dance floor on the pull. The girls, it seems, have more sense an in the main take themselves to quieter, hassle-free zones, leavin X an myself with a very large expanse of dance floor all to ourselves.

Reality, without warnin, suddenly takes a serious side-step when through the lights an smoke emerges a figure that bears the distinct likeness of Hooky. It could be a *Stars in Their Eyes* moment, it is that surreal! He's stridin over to us, laughin his bollocks off.

'What the fuck are you two cunts on?'

'Fuckin hell, what are you on with those fuck-off motorbike boots?' retorts X without missin a beat.

I set off laughin, big bubble-snotted bent-double laughin. I'm so out of it that even Matthew Kelly would be funny at this moment in time, but Hooky is especially so 'cos he seems like a gynormous caricature of his stage persona from the position I've adopted, which is dangerously close to the vibratin wooden dance floor. I can't get my head round the fact that Hooky has chosen of his own accord to come over an talk to the two biggest tripped out motherfuckers in the gaff. His reply is suitably cool considerin the slaggin his footwear has just received, 'Fuck off, what yer drinkin yer cheeky cunts?'

What can I say. What a night to be out, I don't give a flyin fuck about toss all an Hooky is laughin all the way to the bar to get the drinks in. Miraculous. I begin to think that maybe it is our party after all an I've somehow missed some major change in my life's direction. Perhaps this is the major change in my life's direction an I'm too wrapped up in it all to see clearly. LSD, what a cracker of an invention.

X loudly verifies the moment by proclaimin over an over while bobbin up an down in manic circles around me, 'Bez, we can do anythin we want.'

He means, I'm sure, within the boundaries of the club but my altered state of perception takes me much further afield to encompass the whole fuckin screenplay, with us planted firmly in the leadin roles. I ponder the prophecy a while, it sounds good to me. It also sounds like we know somethin that all the other suckers don't know. No problem, we'll just have to convince them. I throw my head round the subject for a while then drift slowly back down off this higher plane realizin that what X is sayin could have great benefits in the immediate surroundins an promptly skin up with a smilin kipper. I light the joint an turn to face X, 'Oh yeah?'

'Yeah!' – he seems sold on the idea himself.

I'm not sure whether to be convinced by this monosyllabic

reply but decide to go along with the scam anyway. Whichever way you look at it, life is turnin into a big fat cherry pie, with double whipped cream.

At this point, there is no such thing as time, only the very moment that I'm livin in, an in this moment I can do anythin I want. An so I do. X is right, the cryptic bastard – or else I'm just trippin, but then isn't everyone in their isolated perception of it all? God, I wish I could stop thinkin so fuckin BIG.

Groovin back out on to the dance floor, I spot a tasty little number with long sexy legs an a cute face lookin in my direction. This is it, I tell myself, an the chase is on. The music stops. No it's not one of those fallin in love moments, it's the end of the night. The glass collectors pour on to the scene in droves to augment the futility of my endeavours, clangin, clashin an clinkin the empties to emphasize the end of the freebie frolics, signallin the inevitable time up on the scorin front. The noise of the employed tryin to get home to their bedsits. They are causin my trip irreparable damage. I realize it's not their problem an we resolve to leave quietly.

Outside. We are alone in the confusion of the moment, our friends long gone on a mission to get the good few miles back to normal land. I honestly can't remember the departure of our fellow funsters an, even worse, we've no place to go. All my attempts at coppin off with that bird at the eleventh hour ended in a bizarre peacock of a routine with a spectacularly top blow out to end all blow outs; she collected her coat an legged it into the first taxi. You can't be a super stud every day of the week. What the fuck, the night is young, we reason, maybe we can cadge a lift from some long forgotten friend up town. Along the way, we comfort each other's egos with glib remarks about fat ankles that aren't so sexy after all, shruggin it off casually like lads do in the face of yet another rejection of their testosterone – laden loins, an clumsy masculine charm.

Town has the cold, deserted look of Morecambe seafront in the dead of winter, but I'm already sweatin like a bastard at the thought of the long slog home. Tryin to make the best of a bad situation, we grab a family-size bag of wheels, which if you remember are cheap corn puff affairs in the shape of cart wheels, drown them in thin acetic ketchup an set off on the trek. A continuous monologue of happy gibberish garnished with smatterins of the masticated corn starch an sauce aids our precarious an slow progress through the streets of Salford back to home base.

Goodnight.

Yeah – it was. By mid-mornin, the bacon butties were well under way, the coughin had subsided an copious amounts of coffee had been poured down our dehydrated gullets.

By noon, the feel-good factor was creepin back into my battered psyche, the remnants of the previous night's foray into groove city still vibratin in my cortex but on a manageable scale now.

By one in the afternoon, a wave of euphoric reminiscence had washed us back into town for some more of the same, the main aim of the day bein to procure some new gear to facilitate another stylish swoop on the town that very night. A few more micro dots found their way into our already adulterated bloodstreams to add a further dimension to the excursion.

First stop was that legendary urban urinal known to the world an its grandma as the Arndale. We meandered deep into its fathomless depths tryin to fathom our next move. The method of movin transpired to be a variation on the marchin, bobbin an weavin perfected just the night before; it seemed the most natural option for gettin from A to B at the time. The shops provided a myriad of entertainin diversions such as racks of shoes that looked great, smelled fantastically of newly stitched, fresh leather an felt even fuckin better. In fact, we concluded, they were the best fuckin shoes we'd ever felt in our lives. Sniffin an strokin shoes, as you can imagine, soon gets plenty of unwelcome attention an our quality control checks weren't goin unchecked – it was comin on top rapido style so we headed off to seek salvation with Phil Saxe in his little shop, tucked away from the furore in the underground market.

Phil's little empire was a mecca for bargains on the casual cords, jeans, sweats an shirt front. In fact, you name it, he had it, or somethin very similar along the lines of. Phil happened to be the Mondays' manager at the time, a very convenient asset for the lads on the outfittin side of things. Bein a geezer with his ear to the ground, busy scoutin the city for new talent, he would see first hand where the trends in street fashion were goin before the mainstream high street shops could pick up on it. One such line he really smashed it in was the semi an fuck-off flare explosion. Now this had been goin on in Phil's shop for quite a few years an was just about reachin the end of its credibility as a cool item to be wearin on the streets, when it was regurgitated an mulched into a high fashion item available from any outlet with a glass front door an a taggin system.

I remember well the so-called rebirth of the flare, it made me laugh my bollocks off. The whole thing got totally out of hand an ended up as a semi-intellectual debate in a prominent, glossy monthly style bible about a bunch of blokes goin under the banner of 'Baldricks'. I ask you, what a load of nob head nonsense. Mentionin no names here but – remove ya-selves!

Phil Saxe – Jewish humour, lots to say, says it all. An affable fellow by all accounts with a head as round as Frank Sidebottom an talks with an endearin slight lisp – I like him, there's nothin to dislike really. He had complete faith an a foresight for the Monday's success that propelled the band head an neck out in front of the other bands around at the time. He knew the circuit an the people that mattered, an that's all that mattered. The top an bottom of it was that the Mondays were desperate to get on Factory Records, full stop. There was no thought of any other label, Factory it had to be. Phil was the key to the infiltration process that was goin down, an a damn fine job he was makin of it too. He was as excited about the whole set-up as the band, enthusin endlessly about the future possibilities, bestowin an enormous credence on the abilities of the biggest bunch of scruffy scallies in Salford – an that takes a lot of neck to promote.

This particular afternoon we sat politely listenin to Phil's career bustin moves, watchin him pounce on the phone every time it rang in the hope that the all-important call from London was comin through. We tactfully ignored his apparent disappointment when the calls turned out to be just another order, we knew he was on the ball anyway. I wandered around the racks of clothes, pullin the occasional shirt or pair of pants out to inspect, hopin for the offer of a hefty discount to come forth. Phil turned a blind eye to my antics, wise to the rules of my game, returnin the conversation deftly to the topic of music. I carried on relentlessly. The clothes felt good, the acid had put me in a positively tactile mood. I stopped abruptly at a pair of killer cords, the look, the colour an the feel was me an I was havin 'em or fuck me, I wasn't goin out that night. X dug into his pockets an kindly proffered a tenner for mine then proceeded to purchase his own.

We were definitely goin out on the town again. The decision had been considered an met without any verbal interaction, it was just known; all the right moves were goin down an we were still only into the early afternoon.

Bein the ruthless ruffians that we were, we prepared for a quick exit after our needs had been met, that is, some new clobber had been craftily wrangled out of Phil for that evenin's adventures. Apart from that, Phil was seriously takin the edge off our acid with all his talk of business. The only business we had in mind was attendin an open meetin in a certain city-centre basement bar frequented by the 'lads' an a one-time haunt of the grafters.

Liquid refreshment beckoned, givin rise to a momentous moment of confusion as we stepped up to the bar.

'Shaun!' a voice shot across from the corner by the pool room.

X turned towards the greetin an bellowed, 'Bez!'

'Wot!' came my startled reply. Why on earth was he shoutin at me an lookin in the other direction when he knows I'm right here. It was almost farcical. Puzzled, I took an involuntary step backwards an tried to rationalize the situation in hand. All became clear a few moments later. The Bez in question was the infamous Andrew Berry, preferred hairdresser to the yet to be stars. He had his own barber's in Tib Street an his own band called The Weeds who were, coincidentally, playin the Corbieres gig the same night as the Mondays the followin week.

We joined him for a pint. As I sat down, the lad sittin by him caught my eye. Fuck me sideways, if it wasn't the same kid, Gringo, from Wythenshaw who I'd met in Greece just as I was about to get off to Italy.

What a small world.

What a top day.

What a coincidence.

What a trip – both of them, past an present.

He'd only saved my bacon big-style, pickin me up off my arse, metaphorically speakin of course, when I'd only had about £40 quid to my name an was about to leave on the ferry for Italy. I was in a bit of a dilemma to say the least. Bein a grafter by trade, it was of no trouble to him to get me kitted out in fine style, fed with exquisite food an entertained in the best places in town for a good few days. I was, at the time, starvin an ill-equipped to do anythin but graciously accept Gringo for what he was an his way of gettin about life. I was really fuckin thankful that someone was there to lend a helpin hand, no matter how dubious the circumstances were. I couldn't believe he had popped up again out of the blue an was sittin in the pub with me in Manchester that afternoon. What a day already.

The pub was gettin busy; the afternoon trade had just begun an I don't mean at the bar. The grafters were busy plyin their wares that had been freshly plucked from the various quality fashion outlets on the surroundin St Anne's Square. It was a casual affair, not too obvious as items of clothin were exhibited an passed around for inspection. The whole scenario was conducted informally over a good few pints, stints of pool an a low key smoke or two. The 'customers' were as ruthless as any fashion-house buyer in their quest for quality an style but the grafters knew their trade inside out an the beauty lay in the affordable prices they quoted. Bargain was not the term to describe it. Bein in the right place at the right time secured you the best outfit in town for the princely sum of two micro dots an the promise of a pint. Well the lads had to look the part if nothin else, didn't they?

As it goes, my offer of four black micro dots bought us two handsome Marco Polo T-shirts; just the ticket. You can't beat the black market for a bit of bang-up-to-date fashion savvy.

With that bit of business wrapped up for the day, we headed off back to Bez's barber's shop, takin up the offer of a free hair-cut an a friendly spliff, a move I think he probably regrets to this day as, for years after, every six weeks or so saw us turnin up in his shop, houndin for the obligatory freeby haircut an a chance to get stoned in comfort. Nice one Bez!

His shop was pretty goddam cool as it goes; the music suited the boys down to the ground an on this occasion Gringo added the nice touch of droppin a large bag of whizz on the table, which got passed around like sherbet dip in the school playground. Needless to say, the conversation got very busy among the assembled crowd, enthusin between boozin about anythin an everythin; talkin a shitload of shite. My chance reunion with Gringo that afternoon turned into a real fruit-bearin acquaintance as thereafter we would all rendezvous at Tib Street to talk shop. Poor Bez; a gentleman if ever there was one.

We eventually prised ourselves away from the throng late that afternoon, well pleased with the booty we'd managed to amass for ourselves along the way. It wasn't a bad cache at all: two tops, two pairs of pants, a ball of pure, free haircuts an flyin off our barnets all the way along. We couldn't have got it better if we'd planned it. We hit a local club that night with relish, dancin to all the crap records, anythin in fact that the DJ decided to assault our ears with. We didn't give a toss. We were still happy from the euphoric forays into the city that the previous twenty-four-hour stint had beheld. To be honest, I don't think we could have managed another hike home in the dead of the night, wheels or no wheels, not even with quality ketchup. To my complete an utter amazement, I actually ended up coppin for some bird without even tryin, in fact the thought hadn't even entered my mind, I'd been so involved with my own shenanigans. I know for a fact that my eyes were poppin from the bender I'd been on an my mouth was frothin worse than a rabid dog lookin for a bitch on heat. It didn't seem to put her off. I agreed to the suggestion in hand; she looked perfect in my frazzled state of mind an I hadn't had a shag in weeks – oh yes, the stars were shinin on me tonight.

I felt a pang of guilt at leavin my new found lunatic of a friend but he assured me it was sweet; his bird was at home waitin for him, so he reckoned he was on for a bit of slap an tickle anyway. We parted company, plannin to meet up the next day.

The followin week passed by in a whir an a blur, travellin backwards an forwards but mostly backwards it felt, between town an X's flat, swappin stories about our past endeavours an generally gettin to know each other's idiosyncrasies. I found X to be full of them, each more eccentrically diverse than the last, an most were concerned with indulgences of one sort or another.

One story that struck me as genuinely funny without bein too engineered was the one about the Mondays wantin to get on Factory an devisin a plan to facilitate the jib. The main reason seemed to be down to the basic fact that New Order were on the label an their roots or rather Bernard an Hooky's roots were Salford through an through, much like ourselves, an like I said, early New Order, to us, were the dog's bollocks. We also believed that Tony Wilson, for all his Oxford education, could cut the mustard when it came to promotin a new music genre.

Anyway, the scheme went somethin like this: Horse would join some health club that he had seen Hooky comin out of on his post rounds. The plan was formed that Horse would get inside by some means an at the first chance would nab the membership book containin all the details of the members includin the address of Hooky's gaff. With the task completed, X, Horse, Ronnie an PD all turned up at his house an knocked at the door.

'What do you lot want?' was the startled reply. 'I ain't got no money.'

'We don't want yer money, we just want to give yer this tape. We should be on Factory Records!' The lads liked to keep it simple an to the point. They were adamant, to say the least.

Hooky took the tape an promised he would listen to it. On the follow up they were told to go away an keep tryin other words. Obviously X's style of lyrics were difficult to come to terms with at the first airin. Now it came to light that although the response had seemed somewhat negative at the time, it was in fact one of Ronnie's proudest moments some time later when he heard his drum pattern copied by Steve of New Order on the intro to one of their songs, signallin that perhaps they really were on to somethin an all was not lost. Maybe some day he would get his chance to pull them over it, or perhaps it would be just laid to rest, but it was a compliment of the highest order; it was a compliment from New Order.

The Corbiere gig was rapidly approachin, the very next evenin to be precise, an me an my mate had managed to cop for a mixed bag of temple ball, cashmere chares an a full bar of clustered finger, yeah a beautiful sight for sore eyes if ever I saw one. A couple of grammes of the old chaz was also acquired somehow along the way, to ensure that the night really went off with a bang, a slap an a fuck-off fizz. I even cleaned up the Moroccan long pipe especially for the occasion; you can't have the finest to hand an leave it to the accompaniment of a few flimsy Rizlas to do the trick, now can you. Such discernin tastes deserve to be treated to the best possible smokin tackle, purloined in the very culture from whence the goodies came. Let's be right here, we're talkin quality smokes for quality blokes out on the razzle. I can't kid myself, I was as excited about the followin night's escapades as the band themselves. It was a strange feelin knowin that I was about to witness a turnin point in my mates' careers an I knew, as sure as eggs are eggs, that they would almost certainly knock the socks off anyone that cared to turn up for the evenin's recreation.

I stumbled off home to my pit in the early hours of the mornin, mad for a woman, an decided to phone an old girlfriend, talkin dirty in the vain hope of a frolicsome shag. I was sussed immediately; she knew I was off my nut an was after any cheap fumble in the heat of an exasperated moment of amphetamine avarice. Not tonight Bezzy boy came the message, loud an clear. I reluctantly cocooned myself in the warmth of my comfortingly smelly covers, lit one last spliff an floated off, dreamin contentedly of the day to come.

It was already well into the afternoon when I awoke out of a deep coma to the strains of The The blastin on the turntable.

TURNTABLE!

Now there's a word you don't encounter any more in this day of DAT this an CD that! A slight aside here: my little boy, in all his worldly technical knowledge, asked me what the large black CD in the corner of the loft was. I was at great pains to inform him that the large black CD was in fact a vinyl record, something that we dinosaurs refer to as an LP. The concept was completely lost on his tender years. He is six years old as I write this epic tale of my youthful discoveries of the world of popular music. Oh well, times move on I suppose.

Back to the matter in hand. The laughter comin from the front room roused me from my REM phase of sleep. That's 'rapid eye movement', not to be confused with the band, whom I most certainly was not dreamin about. I rolled over an prised one sticky eye open to seek a better view of the alarm clock. I was alarmed. It couldn't be that time already! I stumbled into the nearest pair of grumps an sauntered, yawnin an scratchin into the livin room to be greeted by the sight of my two pals already into their second course of dinner – there were fat, daddy lines of the man from Peru out on the kitchen mirror an a smoulderin pipe on the boil. I was unhesitant in my collaboration in the moment of chemical pursuit of happiness. I snorted my breakfast with relish then ate a bacon buttie with HP in one undignified gulp; a shit start to the day if ever there was one.

Feelin fully prepared for whatever the outcome we set off to town, callin in at the Yates Wine Lodge on the way to warm the cockles with a hot blob or two. Yuk. I don't know quite what it's made of, it always does somethin weird to my digestive system that shit but it sure as hell beats a cup of PG Tips on a chilly winter's day.

We arrived at Corbieres to find X bobbin about on the door tryin to wangle the last bit of draw off some poor, unsuspectin punter. No way did the kid want to part with his hard-won booty but, under extreme duress, he was about to give in to X's not so gentle persuasion. X spotted us comin round the corner an backed off – much to the kid's relief. He had been saved by the bell as it were an we scuttled down the stairs an into the back room to unfold our wares to a gaspin collective audience of artistes in waitin.

We were about the first ones there but still we crammed into the tiny cupboard room out back to retain that all-important air of exclusiveness, the way that the really important people do in times of extreme stress an nervousness to separate themselves from the common packs of payin punters.

The makeshift stage was a cleared corner near the cupboard to the left of the bar with the band's equipment squeezed in so tight it was touch an go whether Ronnie would be able to get to his drum kit without doin permanent damage to his manhood.

Yeah man, this was rock an roll; back stage, okay, side stage, in a cupboard gettin drunk an stoned, greetin each new arrival with a beer an a pipe. After a while, scores of beautiful girls began to drift in an out bein flirtatious an sexy. Well, you have to make some bits up don't you. Actually there were some lookers in the audience but they were keepin their distance, weighin up who would be the safe bet to put their money on to make it to the big time. Obviously they didn't hold out much hope of our gang makin much of a mark on the old clapometer that night.

By this time, the cupboard was rammed to the rafters with family an friends, spillin out into the bar area where the manager was fightin a losin battle to keep the ganga smoke confined to the ridiculously tiny room that we had been assigned to. I could see him glancin nervously this way an that with each fresh surge of fragrant fog that wafted past the nostrils of his customers at the bar. The situation had clearly snowballed completely beyond his control but at least his bar was heavin with a buzzin crowd. The feelin that we were all in for a real treat was unanimous as the pre-gig chatter turned up a notch or two at the rumour that The Smiths were in the buildin.

Now for those of you who can remember, Corbieres is not that big a buildin to fail to notice someone in, especially someone as famous as Johnny Marr. I did three full circuits of the gaff an could not see anyone that looked even remotely like him. I'm shit at recognizin people, it's one of my weak points, or I recognize them an can't remember their names. Either way it can lead to some embarrassin moments that leave me lookin the token ignoramus twat of the night. I must admit, the various intoxicants I'd consumed up to this point could have had a major bearin on my lack of awareness. In short, I don't think I would have recognized my own mother to be honest.

I gave up the search just in time to settle down to listen to The Weeds, Andrew Berry's band, that had sauntered on stage. They got off to what I thought was a wickedly cool start with just funky Si on drums an dreadlock Micky on bass while my name-sake, Bez, skinned up a massively big fat spliff. The audience were revvin up with the band; the purposely simple drum an bass intro was gettin them at it, ensuring that when Bez kicked in with his guitar an vocals, they were already groovin along nicely. The heat rose noticeably by a few degrees in those first few minutes. Yeah man I thought, it was goin to be a fuckin stormer of a night. By the time they had finished their set, the crowd were gaspin for more of the same; it definitely wasn't goin to be a cold reception tonight.

The Mondays took their positions in the cramped an sweaty corner, vacated minutes before by an exhilarated Bez an his gang. X emerged from his cupboard hide-out, fully loaded an ready for take off. I'd been in there with him, tryin to quell my own butterflies an I was only a voyeur of the goins on. The panic of the moment had sobered me up a few degrees an so I'd indulged a little more of the mind alterin tackle along with X to get me in a more appreciative mood to listen to the music. A half bottle of whiskey had been hastily passed around the band to quell the tension an lungs were stretched to burstin as the last pipe had done its rounds. Man, you could have cut the tension with a knife in there, it was so thick with last-minute nerves.

There were about 150 people in there, which is no mean number in a small gaff like that, an they were all impatient to hear the first chords of music to give their tormented, tappin feet somethin to work on.

Fuck me man, the first number ripped the place apart, the crowd went berserk an I thought my head would split in two, it blew my mind so much. It was funky as fuck but unlike anythin I'd ever heard before. Chaotic but together; strange but familiar. I looked around an realized that the entire gatherin was awestruck, with mouths an eyes wide open like they were tryin to ingest the band whole, en masse. A peculiar sensation could be felt in the air as the lads in the crowd recognized the raw epit-ome of their lives encapsulated in this motley bunch of hooligans an processed into music that could, quite feasibly, soundtrack their lives. This wasn't pop or punk or rock, it was a little bit of everythin they wanted to hear an more; a lads' band for the lads, a band they could get into without bein ribbed down the boozer for showin their enthusiasm or accused of bein anythin less than a real geezer.

X looked cool as fuck on stage with his prix-a-mar sweatshirt with the subtle ganga leaf symbol. They all looked cool as fuck on stage, let's be right. It had to be one of the most refreshin gigs that the small-time circuit had seen in a long while. What more can I say, I was impressed an so were the rest, an don't let anyone tell you any different.

The next day we made our way down to see X to listen to the tape of the previous night's performance. It was late afternoon when we finally arrived an X an Horse were still in bed, with the carnage of the post-gig romp scattered all around; a stray bra was strewn casually over the back of the settee like a trophy to mark the night's success. Go on lads!

Everyone moved in a slow, liquid mercury kind of way, pourin themselves out of their beds an makin signs as if we were all deaf that a cup of somethin hot containin large amounts of caffeine an sugar was needed on board, now. A succession of brews an a round of the old smelly sulphate did the trick an soon everyone was back on form, chattin merrily about the gig. All the usual accounts were thrown into the circle of gathered friends; lots of piss-takin an send ups goin down as the night was analysed an mulled over time an time again. It was a good way to spend yet another day of unencumbered unemployment; all fast talk an slack movements.

The day proceeded along these lines: listenin to the tape from Corbieres umpteen times, smokin pipes an reachin a resoundin unanimous agreement that the tunes were fuckin heavy shit an Moose had played a blinder on guitar that could not be surpassed. Back slap an slap back, all afternoon. The lads were buzzin their nuts off.

Weeks passed by all in the same vein, sinkin pints down the boozer an tryin our luck at coppin for a bit of skirt with little victory, with intermittent visits to X's mam, Linda, to be fed with corned beef an tomato butties an, if we were really lucky, a full

Sunday dinner. An angel if ever there was one. Without Linda I don't think we would have eaten at all in those days, there was no time set aside to be thinkin of gettin shit like food together. The visits were usually rounded off with a raid on his grandad's booze cupboard, the likes of which I'd never seen before; crammed to the hilt with every kind of spirit ever distilled on this planet. *ACE.*

Special missions were occasionally planned to go on a jaunt to the Cat in Swinton, when we were really brassic, to purloin some poor unsuspectin girls' lager an lime money. The method of extraction, performed by a deft X, is almost legendary now, involving a shoe removin foot twiddlin routine to riffle a purse an then puttin some back quickly as he always got the horrors at the last minute but had to finish the filch anyway once he'd started. Shit, I'm as guilty of such nasty shite myself. Believe me when I say that the crap tactics we used to stay alive on the streets make me wince to the core; it's fuckin hard to write about somethin you've been tryin so hard to keep locked out of your personality in the present. Ironically, it goes against all the rules I try to instil in my own children; we live an learn, I hope.

Branaghans, Pierros, Corbieres, Haçienda. It was a familiar routine to many. There was a distinct underground network of boys from all areas of the city doin the same rounds, some known through their reputations that preceded them, some remembered from my little sojourn in the nick an the rest formin an army of unemployed petty criminals, strengthened by swellin ranks over the last two generations; a piteous result of the steady decline in the economy. The Government made an paid for these people with their mindless righteousness, knowin what's best for the masses. Lies lies lies an then some laws to suit their own, leavin the rest out in the cold to suffer an God forbid lest we shouldn't smile about our misfortunes.

We didn't smile about our misfortune, but some of us couldn't help the cravin for somethin to smile about. Strength in unity – the subculture is forever bubblin under the surface of any proletarian class.

The subculture is here, with its own laws on the street an its own standards set without reference to the establishment – it's survive or die, literally or metaphorically, they are one an the same. A more immoral stance is to be found at the top of every hierarchy, seen each an every day as the rulers flaunt their ruthless double standards in our faces in communications across the board.

Xmas was fast approachin an the Mondays had to get a support slot with New Order who were playin The Haçienda, a one-off gig for the *Tube*. They got it of course, no bother. The set-up was to be two numbers for the *Tube* an then a full-on gig later the same evenin when the club threw open its doors to Joe Public.

Yeah, everyone was buzzin to the max as we'd all been invited to attend as VIPs by the Mondays. I was pretty fuckin excited at the prospect of seein with my own eyes exactly what goes on behind the scenes in a pre-gig environment of this size. I wanted to know what the real carry on was all about, if it was worth the hours of speculation by every kid who's ever been to a gig or if we were all labouring our thoughts under some giant misconception.

A load of us met early that evenin in a boozer called the City, right across the road from The Haçienda. On the way into town, in my excitement, I'd necked a full trip, like you do, an was already flyin by the time we'd reached our destination. X an the rest of the lads were already in there havin a pint to quell their nerves, so I duly enquired what everyone was drinkin an went to the bar to get them in. I came back about three minutes later tryin hard to remember the mission in hand – I was sussed immediately. It was plain to see that I was deep in the throes of an LSD moment of madness, happily potterin about in a dimension all of my own. X, straight away, requested some of the magic potion that had put me in poco loco land. This didn't go down too well with the rest of the band who frantically begged him to hold back in the face of such an important gig. Personally, I'm glad now that he didn't as the consequences of his intoxication that night led to a critical turnin point in my life; I was about to get thrown into the entertainment business at the deep end an have never lived the moment down to this day.

'Give us one!' came the bedeviled request.

'X, wait till later will yer, we've got a gig tonight, just have a draw, a bit of whizz an chill out yer mad man,' came Horse's impassioned plea for reservin a modicum of sanity an professionalism on the front line.

'Fuck that, I'll have a trip, Bez sling one over.'

What could I say, I wasn't his keeper; I slung him a trip an the cheese pie in the sky was cast forth. Out of control an off at a tangent, we sat gigglin, contemplatin the moment of truth an the bag of lies that was about to rip open before our eyes.

Foolishly, sensin the unacceptable heights I'd launched my brain to, I asked a friend to talk me down to a more comprehensible level. I'd asked the wrong person. He took me off down a maze of ponderous paths, deeper an deeper, till there was no chance of turnin the corner an findin an oasis of normality; the whole fuckin world had gone west by now. Top one! I ended up in double fits by the time I disembarked at his particular station. What a cunt, how could he do that to a friend?

In the corner Maureen, Doreen an Soreen were hubblin, bubblin, toilin an troublin their way through some natty hits from the pub circuit, circa 1945 on the battered old Joanna. Some geezer with a flat cap, big ears an no teeth was accompanyin them with his spoons that he had apparently whipped out from his fly region. A right royal knees up was goin down as the old-time music hall tunes worked a treat. Unaccountably, we found ourselves drawn into the hubbub, with much thigh slappin an pint swiggin addin to the general festive scene.

Suddenly, someone noticed that the small portable on the bar was showin familiar shots of our hallowed Haçienda; the *Tube* was broadcastin from within. The time had come for New Order to make their appearance an X had already legged it over the road to get a live view of the proceedins. I tried to take in what was happenin, squintin at the tiny screen; a blur of movin colours an shapes tormented my already flickerin eyes an the noise from the pub drowned out all but a slightly decipherable sound. We jostled to get a closer plot but by the time we'd got it all together, it was celluloid history.

X came boundin over from The Hac as soon as it was finished, seekin sanctuary in the company of some like-minded people; his trip had hit full force durin the set an it was evident that any coherent communication with mussos an camera crews was on top an out of the question.

One pint later, we were wavin our new found friends good-bye, disengagin ourselves from one more round of 'Roll out the Barrel' an rollin our crew over the short distance to The Hac. The real foot tappin an knee slappin session was about to begin.

Once safely entombed inside, we headed straight for the bowels of the club, where the changin rooms were located, gettin lost in a web of corridors an stairs, passin crates of various types of booze an old props, givin the illusion of bein in the back wings of a disused theatre. I was beginnin to feel guilty, creepin about like a burglar with a distasteful fetish for dusty stage memorabilia when X located the right door an we were in.

I'd never been backstage before at any gigs an I wasn't disappointed by the sight that met my eyes. It was just as I had imagined it to be. There were rows of mirrors surrounded by bulbs, large square sinks lookin like pervy unisex urinals, a couple of overstocked fridges an about a hundred people millin about, all generally havin as good a time as one can get in a basement full of free booze an imported powders. We settled in our allocated corner an watched the scene unfold before us. There was Bernard standin in the middle of the commotion, lookin the handsome, clean-cut smug bastard that he is, smilin benignly to himself an getting loads of attention from three attractive young girls, scantily dressed for the occasion. Tony Wilson was busy bustlin around bein a token luvvie, callin everyone darling. It was *ACE*, I was lovin every momentous minute, really enjoyin myself an even relaxin enough to be crackin jokes between each champagne refill of my plastic picnic cup.

Phil came over to the corner,

'Right lads, you're on in fifteen minutes.'

The words cut through the conversation with the precision of a surgeon's scalpel. A cloak of shriekin silence fell heavily on the amassed crowd in our corner. I unzipped my special pocket an pulled out the pipe; the time had come to forget the freakish surroundins an retreat into a comfortin haze of never mind land. The job fell to me to instigate the much needed replenishment of remove ya mind substances as all around the band began to clam up, showin obvious signs of stress. For Christ's sakes, my palms were wetter than a weekend in Manchester an I didn't even have to face the crowd full on.

I glanced at X sat next to me, he was trippin his nuts off an lookin perplexed about how he was goin to handle the next half hour of his life.

'Bez!'

'What?'

'Get on stage with us tonight!'

He'd thrown the ball into my court, knowin that I was in the same state as himself. A bit of a 'I will if you will' kind of situation was developin here.

'FUCK OFF!'

'No, seriously, you got to get on stage with us, I mean it man!'

'NO WAY!'

The conversation went on like this for some time, then the ultimate challenge was cast down on the deck, a dare to beat all dares, 'Bez, if you don't get on stage tonight you're a fuckin soft cunt!'

Fuckin hell, what am I supposed to do now, I thought. If I do I'm a twat in front of a packed house, an if I don't I'm a soft cunt. I held my ground in the hope that he would back off, 'No, I'm not doin it, you'll be alright.'

'You soft twat!'

'Na man!'

'Just do it, jump on an do yer mad dance an, er, play this maraca.'

It was a ball-achin moment of adrenalin an fear in a potent mixture. I feared that I might really find myself stuck with this bizarre dare an have to go through with it to save face, an then have to face the flack afterwards as well. Shit, I wished I'd never given X that acid, I could really have done without the pressure of provin myself at that particular moment but I was torn between lookin like a wussey or doin the dare.

Next thing I knew, the band were bein called up on stage an there was no more time to argue the toss, I wasn't doin it, it was a fuckin stupid suggestion an that was that. The band an their entourage made their way up the steps to the side door. The walls of the flight of stairs had been spray painted with arty graf-fiti an surreal images, givin the impression of bein in a New York subway, but, on our transcendental passage from human to vir-tual, they appeared to be alive an movin in digital Technicolor.

The band walked straight out on to the stage an we all took our positions at the side to watch from the cover of the shadows. I looked out at the crowd an was flabbergasted at the sight before me; it resembled a congregation of zealous worshippers that ran to a number close to 100,000 – or so it seemed. They stared back from all levels; hangin from balconies an swayin on elevated platforms that zoomed backwards out of sight into darkened, distant alcoves where yet more eyes shone through the darkness. It was a cartoon moment straight out of *Scooby Doo*.

Wow, was I flyin by this time. The band struck up as X came stridin over to the corner an struck a maraca in my hand with a sideways sneer, then ambled lopsidedly back to his mic. He began to call my name, the twat! I knew then I had no other choice, the gauntlet had been laid down an the challenge set in front of everyone. Fuck that for a lark, I thought, I'm no soft cunt an jumped out on to the front of the stage with my maraca gripped firmly in my sweatin palm. I began to dance like a man possessed by the devil, shakin my maraca like my life depended on it.

I caught sight of X givin me a sideways glance an laughin with a wicked glint in his eye. By the time the first tune was over, I was laughin insanely at myself too. The almost nauseatin swell of adrenalin pumpin round my spindly form had me chasin the lights around an comin up against walls of pure sound from all angles convincin me that a major neuro blast was about to split my head open into several segments, from the nape of my neck to my crown like a tap-it-an-unwrap-it chocolate orange. I was blowin like a volcano, rushin like a bastard an dancin myself out of my body. I've never felt such a surge of gargantuan spiritual upheaval in my life; every fibre in my torso resonated an hummed a million different notes of pure pleasure at once. I was fuckin blissfully happy in a whole new dimension of my own creation an didn't give a toss who was watchin, or what they thought.

Funny as fuck.

We stumbled off stage about twenty minutes later, exhausted an sweatin like pigs. I couldn't get this silly grin off my kipper. Yeah man, I would say if you are goin to go in front of a shit-load of people for the first time ever, the best way to do it is flyin on a micro dot. Or maybe not. It worked for me, that's all I can say, but then again I can't advocate it for everyone; altruism was never my forte in matters of public riskiness. It was an accident for me, at the time. I had a fuckin ball though.

The first person that started talkin any sense to me was Mike Pickering; he handed me a bottle of beer laughin his head off.

'Nice one Bez, that was really funny.'

At that precise moment, I noticed I had a seerin pain comin from my right hand; I had worn a hole in it the size of a ten bob bit from shakin the maraca like fuck.

'Thanks Mike, I'm really glad you thought it was funny but look at my fuckin hand man, I suffered for my art out there you know!'

Everyone came pourin back in, buzzin their socks off, grab-bin beers an proceedin to down them in one, lightin spliffs an throwin themselves at the deck in a state of happy confusion, wearin 'what the fuck happened out there just then?' expres-sions. Much backslappin an many tokes on the old weed later, it was agreed that a shuffle out front was in order to secure a favourable pitch from which to view the New Order boys, an let us not forget Gillian, on the keyboard. By now we were all strut-tin about on cloud nine, gettin increasingly rowdy; our feathers well plumped from all the praise an adulation comin from all sides.

Out front it all became a completely different ball game with the full effects of the acid comin back in luminescent waves of sound an vision. People were comin up to me to shake my hand like I'd just done them a massive favour or somethin, sayin 'nice one' over an over again. Fuckin hell, for one mad minute I felt like a pop star; all I'd done was get on stage an rattle like fuck but, at the time, I'd meant every last swivel.

New Order came on to a thunderous reception an gave a fuck-off blindin performance which completely blew us away an put us right back in our amateur league place, showin us all what it was really all about when you have the professional know how an poise polished to the max.

I went to bed that night still feelin the tremor of the rush coursin through my knackered limbs. I fell asleep laughin at myself, with visions of a fifty foot maraca wavin frantically at a sea of multicoloured eyeballs adrift in the vast expanse of perpetually risin inky-black water.

Seven days to Christmas.

Time was slippin by too fuckin fast for my likin. I hate Christmas, all that false joviality an spendin money you ain't got on people you don't see all year. Don't get me wrong, I'm no Scrooge but the commercialism of it all has just gone too far these days an anyway, back then, family reunions were not my style.

I sat crossed-legged in my untidy room, surrounded by discarded clothes that I couldn't afford to get washed an dirty dishes that I couldn't be bothered to clean up. Depressed wasn't even close to describin the low I'd slumped into. I stared into the milkless cup of tea I was cradlin in my hands an tried not to focus on anythin in particular, hopin the moment of gloom would pass. A few minutes passed but not the gloom, an my tea had gone cold. I leaned forward an pulled the ashtray over to search for any reasonably rehashable joint dimps. It tasted disgustin but relieved the cravin for a minute or two at least. All my recent highs had culminated in this almighty crash an, to tell the truth, I was even sick of the sight of those micro dots by now, they were startin to become the bane of my life, posin questions rather than providin the answers. Time to cut out of that scenario then – well almost. Better not jump to any hasty decisions just yet, I decided, anythin might turn up with the post.

As it happened, my mate turned up with the post in his hand an an almighty grin all over his kipper that inappropriately screamed he'd been shaggin all night – how could he be so impervious to my delicate disposition in the season of goodwill to all men? He passed me the mornin post; nothin but ugly brown envelopes tellin me how much I owed for havin the audacity to be alive an residin within four walls. I dismissively slung them into the corner an got on with the real scorchin issue, the question that I needed answerin the most, 'Have yer got a draw on yer?'

'Yeah!'

Top one, whey hey, things were lookin up a bit. I managed to straighten out my crumpled form as he handed me the tackle to skin up: a full packet of cigs, king-size papers an a hefty lump of draw. I felt my facial muscles contract, pullin my mouth into half a smile at least.

'Fancy a brew an a bacon buttie?' he called from the kitchen.

'Fuck, do I!'

My spirits were liftin by the second, aided by a few deep lungs full of the spliff in my hand. A brew, complete with milk, appeared by my side, with a fragrant pig-flesh buttie on soft white bread. Luxury. I felt ready to take on the brown envelopes. Electric first: shit news; gas next: more shit, an the biggest envelope, a long, brown, very official-lookin affair, fat with papers from the dole office. I wasn't sure if I was ready to handle more forms to fill in but, in for a penny in for a pound, I reckoned. Wait a minute, I thought, no forms in here, just reams of letters an, YES! JACKPOT! – a cheque for £1,500. It was my deposit, returned with an extra three months' rent!

MERRY CHRISTMAS an HALLELUJAH, thank you Santa.

My miserable Christmas week had just taken a dramatic U-turn for the better; I couldn't wait to get out an join the world again an stop bein a pissed-off peasant.

The usual plan in the light of a windfall was swiftly put into action that very afternoon. I set off for town to rig myself out in clothes to befit a *nouveau riche* workin-class lad such as myself. Next, I scored some of my favourite pipe filler an then, an only then, was I fully ready to hit the town circuit in style. I was on a bit of a roll from that point on, joined for the most part by my new accomplice, X. The Christmas parties just kept on rollin an the success rate with the birds just kept on soarin; it must have been the festive spirit or somethin 'cos we couldn't put a foot wrong for tryin. Of course, we were double confident in our conquests, bein armed to the teeth with an overload of stimulants an filthy lucre spillin out of our pockets – never fails in the turn-on stakes.

An invitation came wingin our way one such night from Bernard. It was for a party at Jacko's, one of the New Order roadies who is now, as it goes, doin the stage monitors for Oasis. Top lad, likes to party hard an is funny with it.

A convoy of cars was quickly arranged. Horse, Ronnie, PD an Moose were in The Egg, X an myself were in a car with these two birds we'd managed to cop for – for whom we had two wickedly funny nicknames, but I've since forgotten them – an Bernard was leadin the way with his then wife, in his swanky brand new Mazda RX7. Flash bastard!

The party was to be a small push up the path of our learnin curve of what bein involved in the music business was all about. Rob Gretton an Tony talked incessantly to us of glitterin, bright futures an mega riches. The picture they were paintin was a romantic one of the press courtin the band, the band becomin a prized possession givin birth to many major albums an no sign of a divorce or court involvement on the horizon at all. It was a fairy tale affair they portrayed an the band were sucked into the sweet talk, hook, line an sinker. I sat there ponderin the possibility of it all happenin the way they said it could. Fuck man, it almost sounded too good to be true, but then again I had complete faith in the sway the band already had with the press an the public that had encountered them in the raw. I had felt the energy pourin out of the music an listenin to the way things seemed to be developin, I couldn't help feelin that I would like a bit of that action in my life too.

Was this not the very career I would be perfectly suited to, I kept findin myself thinkin; loads of travellin, loads of girls, loads of drugs an all revolvin around the best music I'd encountered, first hand, in my life. What more could a young lad ask for? Oh yeah, a shitload of money. Unfortunately, the latter never materialized, but I can't deny it was a top laugh trying for it along the way.

I really enjoyed meetin the people at that party, it put a new outlook on life's possibilities into my head. The talk wasn't phoney, as you might imagine, it was gutsy an positive with a strong input of business savvy; the kind of music talk I hadn't come across before. Till that point, all the talk I'd ever heard about music was from the artists themselves talkin subjectively about their work. Here were the people who oiled the mechanisms for generatin the music in a business sense, takin the talk over to an objective level an in doin so, soundin a hell of a lot more convincin to my layman's ears: sales talk. It was fascinatin stuff to take in.

The end of the party brought a big plus for Ronnie who, seein the openin at this relaxed point in the proceedins, pushed for the confession from Steve that it had been his drum pattern that he'd nicked. Steve happily confessed an Ronnie left a flattered an contented fellow.

Christmas Eve was imminent, the followin day in fact. Myself an a pal of mine had decided to take the festive frolics into our own hands an had arranged a party for Christmas Eve as everywhere else would be shuttin up early as usual an we couldn't be doin with that kind of nause just at the point when things were beginnin to get interestin, now could we? The day was spent gettin the house an cellars kitted out with various props an party paraphernalia. By the end of the day we stood back with a beer each an admired our accomplishments: three rooms decked out in fine festive style, each with a sound system an a live music room that Horse an Ronnie had sorted out with their equipment.

Yeah man, the place looked like a trip alright an to verify this notion, a complimentary acid excursion was offered to each guest upon their arrival; there were no refusals, in fact the whole cache was gone by the end of the night. I almost felt sad, like it was the end of a special era for me but the thoughts were quickly overshadowed by the craziness of the situation with every man an woman present trippin their Christmas Eve away in style. Funny is too feeble a word to convey the hilarity of the scene those little life-changin mother fuckers evoked that night. It was, in the end, a grand farewell to them an a top Christmas party to boot.

Later that mornin, Christmas Day to be exact, everyone had made their way home to have Christmas dinner with their families, although I suspect a good few of them found the thought of a family dinner a bit too dauntin after the mayhem of the night before an cried off with excuses of hangovers at the last minute.

There was just Horse, X, an myself left in the gaff. The last vestiges of party fever slipped noticeably away with each tick of the clock until the moment when Horse an X left for home an the Christmas dinner that awaited them there. I stood alone in the cold light of day, assessin the carnage that lay knee deep on every inch of floor space throughout the entire gaff. An acute sense of loneliness swamped my mind. I knew I'd been partyin way too hard to not be expectin a few lows at the end of it all but it's that fuckin Christmas Day thing, where the whole world seems to be geared up to ensure it's a happy day an mine never are. What a sad bastard, or is it a sad society where everyone is ordered to be happy as fuck an if you're not, you don't quite reach the mark of approval, an the label of sad bastard is slung in your face to add to your misery an feelin of low self-esteem?

My stomach gave an involuntary growl an I realized I was feelin a bit on the peckish side. I stumbled into the kitchen, riflin through the empty cupboards. Shite! Not a stale crumb was in sight. Now I was really beginnin to feel pissed off. Fuck it, I thought, I'll do what I always do in times of extreme distress an despair – go an sleep it off an get up when things look like they might be improvin.

Something woke me with a start later that day. I sat bolt upright, sleep an confusion fightin for the right to reign in my swimmin head. X was standin at the foot of my bed laughin as I struggled to comprehend exactly what was happenin – I knew the front door was locked, an so came quickly to the conclusion that this was a fuckin stormer of a dream, though it felt just like reality. I could even smell a Christmas dinner in my delirious state, woah, this surely couldn't be happenin. It was, an it was real. The turbulence in my mind settled an I began to get a grip of the situation in front of me. X had been ringin the doorbell an, gettin no answer, he had let himself in through the cellar.

'Come on Bez you daft fucker, get up, me mam's sent you a Christmas dinner round.'

Top one! I was fuckin starvin; my stomach felt like it had been turned inside out, it was so inverted. I set upon it immediately, shovellin the delicious food in without pausin for breath even. With each mouthful, I could feel the old grey matter repairin itself, reconnectin the missin links an restructurin the parts I'd short circuited in my nihilistic quest for partydom supreme. X was buzzin, which I found to be slightly off beat considerin the thrashin he'd given himself the previous night. Why wasn't he feelin just a bit of a come down after the deluge of beer an crap he'd consumed, like me? This man has got a cast-iron constitution, I decided.

It turned out the thing keepin his woes at bay was some very excitin news he'd just received an he could not contain himself any longer. Plans had been finalized for the band to go into the studio right after the New Year to record their first single with Bernard at the controls.

The food had repaired my physical well-bein, but this news was fodder for my soul, an I wasted no time in joinin him in his euphoric celebration of takin that first almighty step into the bewilderin process of puttin music on vinyl. I cast my dull an untidy existence to one side for the time bein an concentrated on the decidedly more interestin aspect of watchin a friend leap out of the hell of life on the dole an mould himself, chameleon like, into the role of lead singer an media magnet.

The Christmas week progressed with the predictable nights out followed by days in recoverin. It was was after one such night out, that had run on into the next day without anyone seemin to notice the temporal shift, that X announced he had plans beyond the next pint.

'Come on Bez, I've got to go down to practise, we're doin the new tune for the single. Yer comin down with us or what?'

'Yeah man, I'm with yer on that one, course I will.'

We gathered a few cans of Special Brew, a weed an our wits an set off down to Little Peter Street where the Boardwalk rehearsal rooms were located. The rooms are below the Boardwalk Club an entry is via a locked door just to the left of the entrance of the main door. We buzzed our way in an went down the painted brick stairwell that led into the communal area where the bands can play pool or get a drink from the machine. It's a sparse place of bare brick with the occasional broken chair propped against a wall an discarded bits of nothinness left to decay in dingy ill-lit corners.

Doors lead off to smaller rooms on all sides an a bewilderin array of noises perpetually emanate from each an every one of them like a mad symphony tunin up for a concert. The Mondays' room was in the bottom right-hand corner, a cell-like affair with hardly enough room to swing a cat an stuffed with an eclectic assortment of acquired equipment. Leads spewed like spaghetti across the floor space connectin one piece to another with no apparent order or recourse to safety. In fact, the whole set-up was a complete health hazard; a real den of iniquity with graffiti litterin the walls, dimps an empty beer cans litterin the floor an all sorts of rottin leftovers from takeaways residin in every crevice. In among this chaos, the band positioned themselves at various openins upon tatty scraps of carpet to thrash out their contribution to the unique sound that was the Mondays. It was, in a strange, comfortably scruffy way, kinda homely. I liked it that way.

The rest of the band were already amassed when we arrived an spyin the refreshments, they immediately embarked on a spliff break, grabbin beers as they went. The break stretched into an hour's worth of idle, stoned chit-chat interspersed with games of pool an slugs of beer until the point arrived at which everyone felt sufficiently oiled enough to drift back in an create some of their special noise.

X pulled a crumpled piece of paper from his pocket; on it were the words he wanted to try out to the new tune. I plotted up in a comfy spot in the middle of the room on a piece of old frayed carpet an sat back against an amp to listen to the tune take on a funky shape. A maraca was casually tossed in my direction an I needed no further encouragement.

After a few twangs an bangs, the band launched into the tune with determination an style, blowin my remainin brain cells in all directions. Their collective playin filled the air with a tangible glutinous funk, the assortment of sounds fusin in an insanely comprehensible non-pattern that stretched my appreciation of music way beyond the point I'd imagined was possible. I began to instinctively nod an sway along with the windin rhythm an somewhere down to my right, my arm, without any prior warnin, began to rattle the maraca in a spontaneous flurry of whirls an beats. X was lost in front of a thousand formless punters, snarlin an intimidatin the imagined crowd an I was out there with him in a massive acid flashback.

I decided that this band was goin to be huge. Don't ask me why, I just knew.

After about an hour of playin the same tune non-stop there was a short break for a couple of joints an then it all started up again. This time round the cohesion began to go a little awry an then decidedly pear-shaped as X kept stoppin it, turnin on Moose in a fit of frustration, 'Moose, you're not playin that bit!'

'What bit?'

'You know, that bit, ping dring stringy bit.'

'You mean this?'

Moose began to ping dring in a Moosey kind of way.

'No you fuckin dickhead, the ping pingy bit you did last time.'

This argument went on for some time, gettin nowhere. Moose looked really confused about which ping pingy bit he was supposed to be playin. The root of the problem lay in the fact that none of the rehearsal had been taped an so no reference could be made to the exact sound he had created previously. The end result was that Moose conceded he could not attain the correct sound without the intervention of another guitarist. X was havin none of it. 'Bollocks, just fuckin do it will yer an stop jibberin about like a fanny.'

Moose, browbeaten an under pressure to perform the impossible, came up with the incredible solution of playin two guitar bits at once an it sounded fuckin *ACE*. What an answer – if you can't play it on one, play it double big on two – brilliantly, complicatedly simple.

The pattern of risin in the afternoon, goin down to rehearsals, goin out on the town an then the same routine the followin day all over again continued until New Year's Eve. This is the anti-climax of every year, when I suffer the same recurrin thoughts year in, year out. I convince myself that this is goin to be my year, one in which everythin goes right an I resist all temptations to follow the wrong path; I'm goin to be a good boy this time round an Him upstairs knows it. This is the pep talk I give myself every fuckin time an before you know it, it is next year an the whole fuckin lot has been a bollocks bag of shite yet again. Life – what a bastard. You've got to give it a go though, haven't you. What else is there to do?

New Year's Eve that year in The Haçienda was actually a top night out, as every New Year I've ever had in there always was, but sadly will be no more what with the recent closure. I think I speak for many when I say that a giant chapter of my life closed along with the final slam of those familiar metal shutters on the corner of Whitworth Street.

New Year's Day found me, predictably, wallowin in my smelly little pit, comin down like a mother fucker an contemplatin my annual January blues. I was cursin like a bastard an buildin myself up for a right royal sulk. I was redeemed from myself by the surprise arrival of Horse an X.

'We're goin down the studio to do the single, do you want to come?'

Fuck, did I! I ripped myself off the mattress an was dressed in two seconds flat, before you could say maraca man at the ready, in fact.

I'd never been inside a recordin studio before an the first thing that struck me was the smell. It was like a smell I'd never encountered before; the smell of lots of electrical equipment in a sealed room. Mmmm, I thought, I like this smell.

Another first for the senses was the taste of fresh bagels stuffed with cream cheese an salmon that Phil had brought in for the lads to munch on as a little introduction to his Jewish culture. Tasty stuff indeed. In fact, they tasted like fuckin heaven seein as nothin of any nutritional value had passed my lips in a good few days.

The atmosphere in the studio was dynamic; everyone was triple excited to be actually makin some vinyl history at last, something positive with a lastin longevity an of saleable value to boot. Bernard was mannin the controls an Tony was buzzin around givin lots of sound advice to the band an arrangin a photo session for the next day. The lads had just received their PDs an had instantly pooled them to purchase a bag of goodies to help keep the creative momentum flowin over the session ahead.

Gaz was the first to get his drum pattern down while the lads sat around limberin up in readiness for their turn. Wow! The first thing that struck me was the amazin quality of the sound; after listenin to them playin on the equipment down the rehearsal room, which had been slung together from various dubious sources, this made them sound like they were in a completely different league altogether; from third division to premier league at the twiddle of a few buttons. It was rousin stuff an everyone's expectations rose ten-fold in anticipation of the industry's reaction on completion. The whole process of strippin the tune bare an bringin in individual sounds in layers was fascinatin to watch an I was spellbound. The day quickly turned into night an then back to day again as the band tirelessly knocked out the tune time after time. The usual temporal markers of night an day are thoroughly distorted in the studio atmosphere as the enclosed space is deliberately designed to cut out any outside influences in order to soundproof an allow the band to fix their focus on the job in hand.

Time was gently glidin by unnoticed, headin closer towards the definin moment when I would officially join the Mondays on a serious an full-time basis. Well, maybe a little less of the serious aspect, but definitely full time.

That mornin Kevin Cummins had arrived to take some photos. It was agreed that he should take some action photos of the band with their instruments in the studio – a bit cliché, but it was a startin point you must remember, an we were all new to the game at the time. Everyone trundled off to take up their instruments an positions, leavin me to survey the unfoldin scene with amusement. Tony stopped mid-bustle, 'What are you doin Bez?'

'How d'yer mean?'

'Go an get in on the photos!'

It was less of an invite an more of an assertion, as if I was deliberately tryin to be coy about my position in terms of bein a band member. I thought he must have read the situation wrongly, an answered as such. X came buttin in before I could pursue this line of evasion any more, 'Come on Bez, yer one of us now.'

I was startled at the proposal. I hadn't genuinely considered myself to be anything more than a friend lendin a bit of support an, I suppose, bein a bit of an honoured voyeur on their path up the success ladder.

'Yeah, Freaky Dancin, it's you!' continued X.

Well, blow me, I thought, now there's a turn up for the books; a fuckin blindin start to the year! I was now a fully integrated member of the Mondays an life would never be the same again. I have to say that I'm still tryin to figure out if that was a good or a bad thing an what the fuck would have gone on in my life if I hadn't turned up at the studio that day. Who knows, who cares? Fate: it's a funny old thing.

'Bez.'

'What?'

'Go an play some maracas!'

'Fuckin 'ell, are you sure? Okay then but I can't play 'em, I just rattle 'em. I'll give it me best go though. I'll make a helicopter noise shall I?'

So there I was sat in the live room, headphones on, maracas in hand, wonderin 'What the fuck!' At the time I didn't know diddly shit about makin music, playin percussion or even when there were four fuckin simple beats in a bar! So this is what they mean by a hands-on learnin experience!

It didn't take Bernard long to suss out that I'd meant it when I said I couldn't play; at least I told the truth. They decided to send X in to help me keep time. Talk about the blind leadin the blind! As it so happens, we got quite into the groove of it, jammin out a half decent sound.

Bez goes down on tape for the first time – top one! The last few days had been packed full of new, mind-blowin experiences an we all felt pretty fuckin good about ourselves, even with an amazin forty-eight hours of no sleep. With the proof of the puddin grasped tightly in our grubby little mits in the form of the finished tapes, we set off, delirious with exhaustion an pride, to burn off the last scrap of nervous energy with a swim at Swinton Baths. Even after that, we couldn't quite manage to get our heads down, so we headed off, Horse, X an myself to X's flat to listen to the tape. Just one more time . . . We sat collectively noddin along, grinnin like bastards, agreein it sounded fuckin *ACE*; our heads noticeably swellin with each successive play. As Horse muttered at the time, 'Wow, that sounds like dough!

With that, we embarked on a mammoth hour-long discussion about what exactly we were goin to spend our millions on, lost in a rose-tinted fog, deep in fantasy land. Yep, can't break the habit to this day; spendin the money well in advance of it ever seein a bank statement. Every time, I tell myself to concentrate on just doin the graft, to see it all through before thinkin about the returns.

Horse eventually wandered off home an left us to get our heads down. Then a strange thing happened. Not bein accustomed to the after effects of bein in the studio for a solid forty-eight-hour session – in fact, not accustomed to bein in a studio at all for that matter – I was disturbed by the fact that every time my head hit the pillow, my ears started to hallucinate. A riot of noise bombarded my thoughts, keepin me wide awake even though I was drained to the point of coma. Everythin I summoned up, I could hear at twenty decibels in full stereo.

'X! My ears are hallucinatin, it's fuckin bedlam in here.'

'Fuckin 'ell, thank fuck for that. Mine are too. I thought I was goin mad for a minute.'

We found it a highly amusin pastime, spendin the next hour or so shoutin up different noises an gettin every one of them back in proper detailed sound. Fuckin amazin. A deep numbifyin coma finally rescued us from certain insanity, removin us from society for a good day an a half of pure medicinal kip.

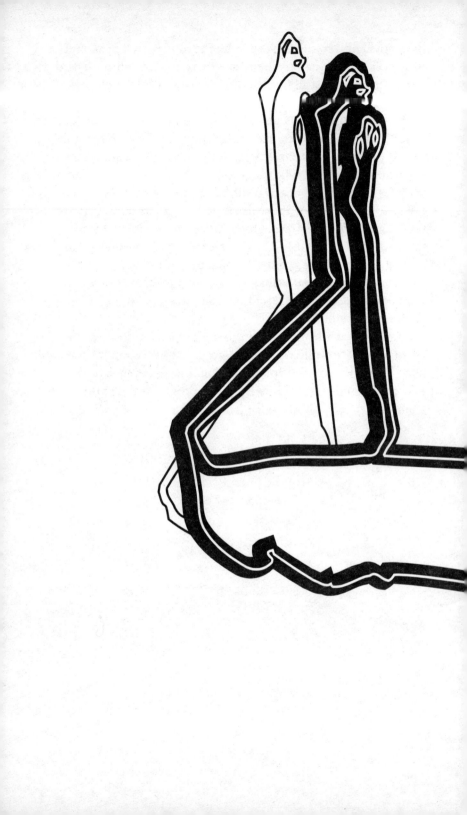

A fuckin bitch of a dilemma was glarin at me full on an there was no respite from the heat I was feelin to do somethin to remedy the situation, fast. I'd been tryin to ignore my cripplin cash shortage followin the Christmas binge, but the landlord was involved now an there were no apparent legitimate means of sortin this mess out properly. I'd left things festerin for too long an other incidents were about to add to the general crappiness of the situation in hand. I was feelin pretty desperate an my life has a nasty habit of goin in a sideways direction at times like this.

It all started with a visit from the landlord, askin for the three months' back payment of rent. I'd managed to stall him for another week, knowin in the back of my mind that the next rent cheque would be arrivin any time now. I was skint as fuck an a plot was brewin in my devious little brain that I wasn't about to admit to myself; I wanted to be a good citizen an do things right but a severe lack of money was pullin me in the wrong direction.

By the time my flatmate had arrived back, my mind was made up; I'd have to tell him I was movin on with the cash an he'd have to find somewhere else to live. That was to be the easy part to face up to in the end, it was the events that followed our little chat that were really goin to fuck with my mind.

He'd arrived back with his bird that night an to tell you the truth I was feelin a bit of a gooseberry an wonderin how I could break the news to him. He'd disappeared into the kitchen straight away to make somethin to eat an this girl had come to sit with me in the front room where I was watchin some crap film on the box. I'd noticed she wasn't exactly dressed for the day-time when she sat down an from the off she started flirtin with me big-style. It was a shock I was ill-prepared for. My mind had been busy rehearsin how I would break the news of my departure an therefore his also an here was his bird comin on all fresh an fruity completely sidetrackin my line of thought.

She had on a very short miniskirt, suspenders an knee-length boots. I was lyin on the floor an couldn't help noticin this fact. I engaged in a bit of general chit chat, tryin my best to ignore the come on vibe an was even feelin a little embarrassed by the sudden attention I was receivin. I shifted my position, tryin to quell the horny thoughts that were swampin my mind. She moved herself, affordin me an even better view of her knickers, liftin her knees up an strokin the inside of her thighs so that the message could not possibly be read in any other context.

I swear, I was tryin desperately to avert my gaze but the bitch was startin to drive me potty. I could hear my mate whistlin to himself in the kitchen, unaware of the damage goin on in the next room. Without warnin, she leaned forward exposin her breasts an started to neck with me in a real passionate way.

Wow, shit! C'mon Bez, I thought to myself, sort yourself out, this is dangerous water you're treadin here mate. I pulled back quickly an shot off into the kitchen to see what my mate was up to before things got totally out of hand. I talked about anythin an everythin to try an get the vision of tits an thighs off my brain.

We sat back in the front room to eat our scran, had a few beers an finished off with a spliff. This kid's bird had settled down a bit by then an I felt comfortable enough to tell him the bad news about the flat. I wanted to scream 'Your bird's a slag too' but that would have been salt in the wound an I'm not generally a malicious person. I sloped off to bed not long after, leavin them to get on with whatever.

Now, I'm a red-blooded male just like the rest, an that little incident in the front room was playin heavily on my mind; I just couldn't shake off the image of those pert tits an exposed thighs. So, like any male with an unrequited horn would, I began to have a bit of a crafty wank.

The bedroom door swung slowly open revealin the silhouette of this kid's bird vampin it in a flimsy little negligeé, like somethin out of a saucy film noir scene. She crossed the room silently makin her way round to the top of the bed an stood facin my frozen features. Slowly she began to caress herself, liftin the negligeé to reveal her naked muff, pantin porn style to really get me at it. I instinctively moved over an she slid under the bed covers.

Christ almighty, I wasn't reckonin on Miss Porn Pants singlin me out tonight, I thought, what the fuck is this little game all about?

My heart was, by this point, in my throat an my breathin wasn't the only thing that was hard. She declared she was goin to sleep with me tonight. There was nothin for it, I couldn't resist any longer an began a rampant mess about, fumblin an tweakin under the covers. I was turned on like you wouldn't believe it an was headin quickly towards the point of no return when, out of the blue, the bedroom door opened again an in walked my mate. Fuck! What the fuckin hell was goin on? A desperate struggle to understand the set-up goin down here was chargin round my heated brain. He simply announced that he was sleepin here tonight as well an dived in the bed on the other side, evidently tryin with all his might to control his jealousy in the face of a humiliatin defeat over his woman.

I was lyin there for about an hour, heart pumpin an loins burnin, wonderin what the fuck to do next. The answer came in the shape of a peachy soft bum wigglin its way into my crotch area an the decision sprang forth in an instant. My body switched on to auto sex drive an I set off slowly takin her from behind, convincin myself that my pal was surely asleep by now. I quickly lost control an forgot all thoughts of keepin the motion gentle, shiftin up a gear or two an finishin in a frenzy of slappin an gruntin.

Shit! Fuckin hell! I leapt out of the bed in a sudden pique of guilt an scooted off to the couch in the front room, leavin her to face up to the certain warp in their relationship that our spent passion would surely cause.

What was it – thou shalt not shag thy neighbour's wife, thou shalt not steal, an the rest! I was a sinner on all counts an surely will burn in hell for eternity for all this, or at least I'm goin to be involved in a fuck-off confrontation come the mornin. I sat wincin at my slack codes of conduct; how could I have made my mate homeless an poked his wife all in the same night, an in the same bed too. I groaned inwardly an tried to physically squeeze the mangled thoughts from my head. I curled up into a defensive foetal position an battled with myself until the sanctuary of sleep took over an freed me from my shame.

I woke expectin the worst, but there was an eerie silence throughout the flat as I went about my business of gettin my breakfast an a bath quickly an quietly to facilitate a swift an trouble-free exit. I had important things to attend to an had resolved to put the previous night's escapades to the back of my mind. After all, it could have been him that instigated an orchestrated the whole set-up. I shuddered an nearly puked in the gutter as I rushed along for the bus. Fuckin sick porno plebs, bet she ends up in the readers' wives section, wearin cheap nylon undies sittin on a Draylon sofa in some seedy hole, being pimped around an . . . I stopped myself, not wantin to think through the consequences of livin a sordid sex-driven life any further. I concluded she was not a classy number to notch up on the bedpost, an directed my attention to findin some change for the bus that had just pulled up.

I was on my way to the council offices to sort out a flat for myself. I'd had my name down on the list for a good four years by my reckonin, an had turned down the offer of a place on Cherry Tree Court two years back in favour of a place with a nicer outlook. I'd done a stint inside an had been abroad in the meantime an realized the time was now ripe to be payin the council a second visit.

It was a fruitful visit; I'd been promised my own place within the next couple of months. A result at last! This in mind, I began to cheer up a bit an set off to see X, who, I knew, would revel in my little tale of debauchery with perverse delight. I was also goin to request a bed while I waited for my tenancy to come through. He listened with attentive glee to my story of sex an shame an agreed instantly to my request of a place to kip. Nice one X.

Now X loves a drama, an was itchin to come with me down to the flat to gather some stuff, anticipatin an interestin scene afoot. He was to be disappointed; all their stuff had been cleared out already in the space of a few hours. Shit! That somehow made it even worse; I was convinced now that he really must have known what was goin on an had taken off in a proper huff.

The chillin thing is, I never did see or hear from him again, but a few years ago I heard down the grapevine that he'd tried to burn down his house with his missis inside. I don't know the full story behind it all, but I do know it can't have done their sanity much good over the years if they'd carried on along the same path that I'd glimpsed that night at the flat. It just goes to show life can play cruel tricks an strike you down in the strangest of ways when you're not lookin straight. I felt sorry for both of them that it had got so out of hand an ended in such an undignified manner, but there you go. Jealousy is human nature an it distorts even the strongest of relationships beyond recognition sometimes.

There wasn't much to pick up from the flat, not much more than the couple of carrier bags of trash that I'd arrived with really. The moonlight flit was over in a trice, my final task bein to quickly sift through the mornin's post that still sat unopened by the front door. There were a couple of glossy mailshots an a plain brown envelope containin my means of survival for the next few months. I said a little prayer of thanks, slipped it in my pocket an remorselessly slammed the door shut with a satisfyin bang for the final time, terminatin a friendship, a tenancy an a way of life. I vowed to stop lookin back at the trail of messy events lyin in my wake, an start concentratin immediately on givin my new found mission in life my upmost all.

I was, by some odd quirk in life, in a band, on a record sleeve an contemplatin a career in the entertainment business, of all places. What the fuck had led to all this then, I wondered, as we ambled down the road to X's flat. I was bein propelled headlong down the path of fate, headin towards a future of indefinite status on countless scary stages across the world. It was an odd feelin. I wasn't to know all these experiences were lyin in wait in the near future, but I could sense that things may never be the same again; even if it only ever led to a greater chance of coppin a better class of bird, it was a start.

The followin day we received our first pristine copies of 'Freaky Dancin'. Finally, I knew it was real. We stood for an eternity, each of us turnin the record in our hands, inspectin every minute detail on the cover an glowin with pride. We were in the Factory offices on Palatine Road, which was actually a spacious flat on the first floor of a large, Victorian-lookin house, set slightly back from the busy road. I cringed to see my emaciated features on the back of the cover, but no one escaped scrutiny, an various less-than-pleasant comments were bandied back an forth about the none too photogenic attributes of the band as a whole.

The artwork on the front of the cover was spot on: Central Station Design, members of Shaun's extended family, had done the job well, creatin a cover that was unique in its stark simplicity but loud in its message. I'm no art critic, but I knew as a record collector that the cover would ensure it grabbed attention on the shelves.

Our attention soon turned to the office itself an, to be more precise, to the contents of the office shelves an walls. Like kids let loose in a sweet shop, we began to rummage an pillage, pilin up all the discs an posters we'd been covetin for the last few years but couldn't afford to go out an buy ourselves. Every piece of shit that could be removed went promptly into our pockets an we left some time later with what must have been the entire Factory back-catalogue.

That wasn't the only gem to come our way that day; we also found out the startlin news that we'd got the support slot on the Colourfield tour. It was a wonder that we ever got out through the doors of the office what with our swellin pockets an heads, especially when we heard that old Tel himself had requested the Mondays to be their support. It was a proud moment that called for some serious celebratin that very night in the local boozer. It's not a cheap do, as I'm sure you can imagine, celebratin bein a pop star an I was thankful for the little windfall that had blessedly fallen my way the previous day; it was my first lesson on how your friends an acquaintances suddenly change their bar tactics, equatin a step up the celebrity ladder as an automatic step up in financial terms too. Heck, who am I tryin to kid, we believed it ourselves at this point in the game; it felt just great to be gettin the rounds in amid animated discussions of the forthcomin tour.

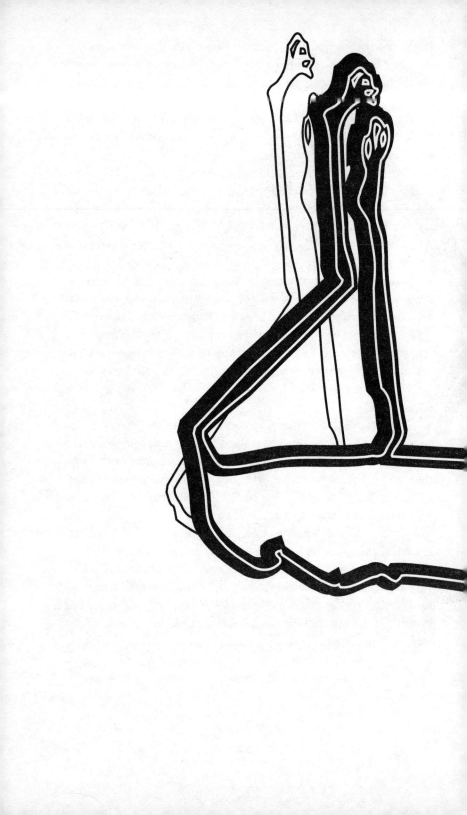

It was around this time, in the early development stage of the band, that the services of a certain Horseman warrant a big mention. In short, Horseman was a star.

Horseman is dad to X an Horse, but to think of him as just that would be a gross insult to his multidirectional input that ensured the band could travel, eat, drink, smoke, play their instruments in a tuned up state an generally exist as an on the road unit with a modicum of cohesion an professionalism. The early days didn't pay large dividends on the gig front; we were lucky if the gig got us a return of fifty quid sometimes. Horseman would often use his own money to enable the show to go on, coverin such costs as petrol, van hire, beers an all the rest. I must admit, they were bobbins; the cheapest, nastiest beers on the market at times, which would cause ridiculous family arguments to erupt out of nowhere as X an Horse ganged up on Horseman, givin him a shitload of stick, presumably for not bein hip an cool enough to get the right kind of beers in. At times like these I'd try an make peace, calmin X an Horse with a few words on how Horseman was really a fuckin cool geezer to be doin all this shit for them an us. He didn't have to, he wanted to, so that his sons could make it somewhere in this dirty fuckin cut-throat business. The arguin was a family thing; bein thrown together on the road for long stretches isn't easy. Most families thrust together on the road would explode at some points along the way. Even so, I am of the opinion that Horseman was the unsung hero who took too much flak an not enough praise. At the end of the day though, I'm sure he knows he was one of the Mondays' most valuable assets.

With the Colourfield tour comin up, Horseman could hardly contain himself an in his excitement, disappeared like Rhubarb, to his shed to knock up a flight case of giant proportions to fit all the gear in so that we could hit the road lookin like a proper outfit, instead of straight out of a somebody's mum's garage. Dedication with a capital D.

The tour kicked off at Hull University an the mornin of the gig found us all huddled in the hired van outside the Boardwalk, talkin fast an furious in an elevated mood of exhilarated anticipation at what lay ahead.

There was no doubt about it: we were the best band ever to walk the planet an our chance had come to prove it to the lot of 'em.

Havin witnessed this same scenario a good few times since, as young bands set out on their first steps to stardom, I've come to realize that every band takin those first falterin steps think they are the best thing since sliced bread. It is a necessary motivation to get a band actually up an runnin an on the road, 'cos without that obsessive, single-minded determination there is no hope. There are too many setbacks along the way that knock your confidence from the word go so you have to have a cast-iron constitution to swallow the criticism an sail through the sea of sceptics with your head above the water. We believed, without a shadow of a doubt, that the world was waitin to hear our music an when it did, everyone would sit up an beg for more; such blind enthusiasm is a vital ingredient for any band startin out in this field of employment. You have to create your own myth. Luckily for us, this entailed the kind of behaviour we were all adept at: gettin pissed, gettin into scrapes, gettin around (in every sense of the meanin) an generally gettin noticed by all the right people mostly for the wrong reasons, but then any news is good news when you have to rely on the press to reach the punters. It wasn't that we lived our lives with the intention of hammin it up for the press, as many punk outfits in the previous years had, it was just that our lives were so raw anyway from livin in such harsh surroundins that the situation was analogous with the rock 'n' roll thing. It was, by pure accident, the real deal. The publicity machine was rollin along quite nicely before we'd even got on the bus.

The real deal on that first night saw us frantically tryin to arrange our equipment in among the Colourfield set without movin a piece of their stage gear. This meant that my allotted space was a clearin right up at the front of the stage next to X, out of the way of everythin, probably to keep my clumsy feet from tramplin some uninsured item an makin a balls up of the set, more than anythin else. It was a very uncomfortable feelin, knowin that I'd have the full attention of the audience trained on my sweatin, amphetamine features, while the rest of the band could hide behind their instruments. It's fuckin hard work hidin behind a maraca an a wooden block, even when you live on a restricted diet of amphetamines, fags an beer. I wandered around the stage lookin for a less exposed spot to slot myself into, but the whole area was awash with leads an amps, which I'd no doubt trip over in my inevitable state of advanced inebriation. That was that then. I was committed to bein the twat at the front, all shake an no sync; there was to be no turnin back.

With the stage gear in place an a quick desultory sound check out of the way we settled back, sinkin beers an psychin ourselves up for the big event. Fuckin hell, it was nerve rackin sittin around, waitin for the night to fall. I couldn't decide if I wanted to laugh or die, shit or piss or simply go home an call the whole nonsense off. I certainly couldn't eat a scrap of food in my excitement an that, in turn, amplified the effects of the intoxicants I was pourin into my body at a steady rate of knots.

When the time finally arrived, I was so off my face an buzzin with adrenalin that I can't honestly remember what occurred, except that there were two crackin girls stood right in the front row, directly below my manic gaze an that they were either givin me the eye or were transfixed with confusion as to what my objective could be in all the shenanigans. It was considered, in our naivety, to be the only way to go about portrayin our pop star status; get wasted, crash on stage, thunder through the set an then slam back into the beers with a silly grin backstage. If this was rock 'n' roll, we liked it, a lot.

Terry an his lot took to the stage a short while later an again we were treated to the sight of the professionals doin their stuff, workin the crowd an gettin the right reactions in return. Terry had been around the circuit long enough to know what the audience wanted an expected from the front man an held them majestically in the palm of his hand with an easy banter between the tunes. Make no mistakes, we were thrilled with the experience, but there was an unspoken consensus that what we ideally should be aimin at was a fuller show with a bit of charm an sparkle to really get the crowd to sit up an take notice. It's all a matter of confidence an X would soon be catchin on to the crowd-baitin vibe, but this was, when all said an done, our first tour. You live an learn fast in front of a live audience that is lookin to break you, rather than make you.

What I do remember most vividly about that first night was a rather timid an quiet Terry Hall joinin us for a beer in the dressin room after the show. Now that was the true highlight of the night for our little gang, well for me anyway. We'd all been fans, to varyin degrees, of The Specials an felt privileged to be chattin on an equal footin to the man who'd bravely stuck his neck out, plucked us from the throngs of wannabes an given us a chance to prove ourselves alongside his own band. We sat for an hour or so, passin idle chit-chat, watchin Terry nervously tear a white plastic cup into strips from the rim to the base. I thought it was ironic that he found it as nerve rackin meetin us as we did meetin him. His wife broke into the conversation with polite but firm orders to extract himself from our company; he was apparently on the wagon an his missis was makin sure he stayed that way. A nano-second after his departure from the room all hands dived on the remnants of the white plastic cup, with the intention of keepin it as a memento of the meetin. X, as I'm sure he will cringe now to remember, came up trumps, an it's a little known fact that that cup remained pinned to the middle of his notice board for years to come. Sorry X, but you should have let me get it, you bastard.

My memory of the whole of that first tour seems to be strangely misty now that I try to recall it. One gig mashed into the next an most of the time was spent uncomfortably cramped in the back of the hire van, nestlin down between boxes of equipment an instruments, under layers of coats to try an keep warm an eatin at motorway services an cafés along the way. We were a long way off the Charlie big spuds treats of air-conditioned tour buses, separate hotel rooms an caterin companies as standard. There was one occasion towards the end of that tour that does stick in my mind as a momentous moment of confusion an mayhem.

We'd done a gig in Scotland an were travellin back through the night with Horseman at the helm. An unnatural lack of sleep, criminally dire food at various motorway stops on a torturous tour schedule, an travellin in a van with little in the way of suspension had left us completely exhausted. We promptly fell into a deep coma not long after the commencement of the long journey home. Horseman, in his role as sound engineer, roadie, tour manager, dad an driver was obviously feelin a little worse for wear himself an decided to pull over into the Granada services to get a kip in himself before he ran the whole fuckin show off the road in his severe state of fatigue. The engine was left runnin to combat the cold an we all slept soundly in the reassurin background hum of the van tickin steadily over.

I drifted in an out of my cosy coma from time to time, lookin out of the window, notin that we'd pulled into a Granada services. My brain was easily tricked into a sense of motion by the purr of the engine an after a few sessions of noddin off an wakin to glance out of the window, I was surprised to see yet another Granada services shinin back at me from across the car park. Fuckin hell, how many Granada services could there be on this strip of motorway, I puzzled, we must have stopped at dozens of them tonight. I calculated that we must surely be nearin our own plot an began to look forward to gettin back home to my familiar little pad with a real bed to collapse into; bein holed up in the van was beginnin to feel like a painful spell in purgatory with the ever pungent stench of sweaty feet an discarded burger wrappers attackin my senses with every breath, the spine-numbin stiffness caused by sleepin in a space between a seat an a flight case an inadvertently usin a spent beer can for a pillow in my dazed an confused state.

Suddenly, the penny dropped. I realized, as I glanced out for about the tenth time that night, that the services were becomin strangely familiar, with the same lorries, the same phone boxes an the same advertisements glarin back at me time an time again. We hadn't fuckin moved for hours. It was a totally disorientatin experience, I could have sworn we'd been busy truckin along all night. I was feelin really pissed off – about everythin. Fuck! I wanted to be home – NOW.

X woke with a start. A barrage of abuse commenced, wakin the rest of the band. We'd all thought the same; it was a seriously agonizin realization to find that home was still a fuckin trek an a half away. The air became fraught with a frenzy of harsh words reboundin round the van as Horseman refused to become the target of our frustration. Not gainin enough ground on the argument for his likin, X aimed an fired the boogie box at the indignant Horseman. SHIT! – it missed spectacularly. A split second later the windscreen was sportin a large gapin hole through which the appliance could be viewed hurtlin across the frosty tarmac.

A tame night then really.

Horseman slammed the van into gear an we set off on the coldest journey ever, freezin our fuckin nuts off all the way home.

We arrived home to the heartenin news that the single wasn't sellin.

BOLLOCKS!

There went the dreams of the first million – an I went to bed.

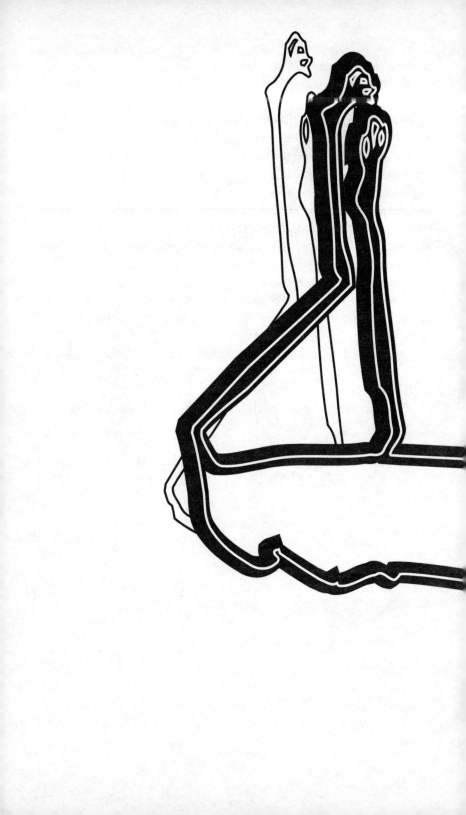

I wouldn't say my life was improvin, I wasn't earnin the mega bucks that I'd dreamed of, but life was definitely changin, takin me off on a decidedly different tangent. By now I felt totally committed to the band an was ready to put my heart an soul into makin it work. Like I said, we were all sharin the same dream an even though it had been slightly soured by that initial lack of response to the first single, we were still focused on gettin it right, somehow. If the truth be known, we had no choice but to make it work. It was the only option available to us that would elevate us out of the present situation we were in. There's the nine to five way of gettin there, which in all truth would never be a route we could get on an survive because of our limited educational achievements an lack of suitable jobs in the area, or there's the method of lookin cool, gettin a name for yourself an goin for jackpot by bein in a band. The latter did seem more appealin to my nature; I'd seen too many an id crushed beyond repair by a cripplin nine to five routine at the lower end of the work spectrum, which is where I would have had to join in the employment sector.

To be honest, I was desperate for this to work out. I'd tried everythin else to get myself noticed in the crowd. In my early years I'd been a fighter, gettin into scraps to prove I was no pushover. Then I moved on to tryin my luck at football, but I was too keen flyin round the pitch employin a lot of gusto, tryin for the ball on all occasions but applyin little in the way of cunnin or skill. So that was out. An then there was the band; my final chance to tell the world that I was worth more than they could see on the surface. I didn't, however, have a master plan. I couldn't play an I couldn't sing, all I could do was perform by expressin how desperate I was to get out of the corner I felt I'd been pushed into by people in authority who thought they knew what would be best for me.

People don't give a fuck, why should they? Teachers, police, social workers, they're all just doin a job an gettin paid; ultimately it's not their responsibility or concern to see that you get to achieve your dreams. They are simply oilin the wheels of a system that churns out a minimally educated workforce who willingly accept a minimal wage because that is a realistic goal. I hate the set-up with all my heart an bein in the band gave me the perfect vehicle to manifest my rage in a resoundin two finger salute to the non-believers, the people who thought it couldn't or shouldn't be done. Yes, I was takin drugs, I liked gettin high, especially with a good weed, I found it exhilaratin as it lifted me up beyond the confines of a 'normal' existence an beyond the reach of the narrow-minded straights who'd written me off from an early age. It was sort of my little war dance to the world, a revolutionary if you like, stompin out a defiant dance of resistance against the machine. Perhaps it was just an acute attack of teenage angst settin in a bit late. Whatever it boiled down to, I saw it as my final shot at doin somethin with my life beyond prowlin the streets an sittin in the boozer talkin about someone else goin for gold.

Though we were disappointed at not havin the instant success we assumed we would, there was no way that we were goin to give in at this early stage. We were hungry for the recognition we thought we richly deserved. We were ACE, it's just that no one knew it just yet. We simply had to figure out a way of makin everyone realize our talents, whatever they were.

The camaraderie was strong within the band, which made the process of gettin the point across to the outside world an easier task than if we were a fractured outfit with little in the way of confidence. In fact, we were teemin over with the stuff an eager to get out there to prove our point.

Me an X would often spend hours locked in deep conversation discussin the various merits of the band; our strong points an our even stronger points. We were confused by the apparent lack of interest; adamant that we shouldn't be wadin around the shitty small-time circuits in search of a chart success. We spent hours geein each other up, completely focused on the glitterin future that sat just beyond our grasp, wonderin how we could stretch out just that little bit further to attain our goal. There was no doubt in our minds that our time would come, it was merely the how an when of the equation that baffled us.

There was an encouragingly positive vibe goin down in small pockets of the North, in such places as Leeds an Blackburn, where a growin army of supporters gathered, addin to the existin fan base that we had secured on our own patch in Manchester. The fans were lads like ourselves, the kind of people who heard their own lives echoed in the slightly left of centre an definitely inside out aspect of the music. They were young, unemployed, angry at the futility of their own existence an subsequently out for laughs, takin drugs an absorbin the music as an antidote to the depression they faced in tryin to eke a future out of half a prospect in the job market.

We knew that there was a whole fuckin army of kids up an down the country in the same predicament as us who would recognize the truth in the music; the embodiment of the struggle we all faced. They smoked the dope, they took the drugs an they heeded the same clarion call of anguish as us, an we reckoned it wouldn't take much to win them over to our style. It was takin just a little bit longer than we had anticipated.

It slowly dawned on us that we would have to slog it out like the rest of 'em to prove our worth. It was goin to be a great shock settin out on our own, havin been spoilt rotten by the big openin we'd achieved supportin New Order an Colourfield. To come down to earth with such a bang, earnin fifty quid a gig an gettin minimum audiences in backstreet dives was painful, to say the least. It's fuckin hard keepin the momentum of a performance goin when the band an entourage nearly outnumber the punters, as happened on occasions in some of the very early shows.

The money earnin side of the venture was still a long way off in the future, we were still signin on the dole an havin to pull roguish scams to finance our existence. It would have been nice even to say we lived a hand-to-mouth existence, but at the time it was more like a rolled up note to nose affair as a constant input of amphetamines kept us rollin along an had the added benefit of keepin hunger at bay – food on the road is stupidly expensive.

Much of the time was spent down the rehearsal room below the Boardwalk goin over an over the tunes in an attempt to rise above the consortium of small-time outfits all drivin at the same objective; to be seen an heard an recognized as the best.

The nights were spent prowlin the Manchester club scene, preachin the word to all who would listen, gettin our faces seen, croppin up in as many places as possible to make sure no one missed the point we were tryin to make. It was durin one of these night-time forays into the city that I stumbled upon the girl who was to become my long-time girlfriend an, ultimately, the mother of my children. We'd noticed that her an her mate had been cornered in a bar by some fat blokes an realizin that they were none too plussed by the chat-up techniques they were bein plyed with, offered them the choice of our company instead. It came in handy bein in a band, givin rise to the opportunity of gettin girls into nightclubs with a certain amount of flair an, of course, not havin to pay for them. We invited them to join us on our night out in The Haçienda, showin off our powers of influence with the doormen. It was a handy trick to pull, never failin to impress the girls. I couldn't figure out if she was impressed or not. Bein from Sheffield an new to the Manchester scene, she hadn't heard of the band an I'm not sure if she even believed me. It didn't get me a shag this time, but I didn't give up hope.

The gigs were startin to attract a slightly bigger audience an the atmosphere generated by the throngs of lads that were startin to turn up created a palpable charge that rippled through the small crowds as they tested our authenticity; were we really one of their kind or were we imposters takin the piss, was the general feelin we sensed at the time. The question was resolved at one rowdy gatherin in Blackburn that quickly evolved into a full blown riot. It was one of our finest moments of the day. The gig had set off at a frantic pace an we were givin it our all when, to my utter astonishment, some fuckin stupid dickhead took it upon himself to jump up on the stage, grab a mike, an rant *zeig heil* at the top of his voice. I couldn't believe the audacity of this kid, not only had he taken it upon himself to invade our space in the middle of a set but he also had the gall to shout a load of fuckin Nazi nonsense through our PA. I wasn't havin it. The blood rushed to my head, turnin my face a strange purple colour, an I felt a sudden stab of intense anger in my gut. In a flash, I was over the other side of the stage, givin him a top smack under the chin with my maraca.

Never has my percussion been so offensive. He dropped to the ground with a satisfyin thud. With that, a few more kids jumped up an a full-on rampage commenced, the whole place runnin amok as the battle cry went out. Each time a punter clambered up to try his luck I lashed out with force, tryin with all my might to defend the stage an equipment from the onslaught.

It wasn't really a battle aimed at us, we were just the spark that lit the fuse as the crowd were just as happy to be kickin each other. It was the result of a shitload of testosterone-filled young lads full of beer an bravado lettin out a torrent of pent-up frustration an enjoyin every fuckin glorious minute of it. It was match fever without an opposin team to scream abuse at.

It wasn't long before the police turned up an seein me, appearin to be orchestratin the whole crusade from the helm, they made a B-line straight for the stage an began to drag me out by the scruff of the neck.

'But I'm in the fuckin band. It was some Nazi cunt messin with the mike!'

I pleaded in vain an they proceeded to oust me from the buildin.

'Stop. I'm goin to be sick!'

The officer wasn't about to listen to my wind ups, only this was no wind up. I spewed up all over him; a putrid brown slime clung to his crisply ironed pants an freshly polished boots, an an insipid odour of regurgitated burgers an beer hung thickly in the air.

He wasn't impressed an swiftly threw me in the back of the van. The promoter, havin seen the mistake, came hurtlin out to my rescue implorin with them to let me go as I genuinely was with the band. They finally released me an I went back to join the others. We continued the set, managin to do a couple more numbers before it came on top again an the whole thing was called off. That night was one of the most memorable of our early gigs, not least because it made the front headlines of the local Blackburn paper the next day. St George's Hall was trashed to bits an we went down in folklore as the band that incited a riot. Top laugh or what for the lads. At least we were grabbin the attention of people, an you know what they say, any news is good news when you're startin out.

A similar incident occurred in Leeds after we'd just finished a gig in front of about forty people an were relaxin in the bar, chattin away with the punters. Some kid approached X an stood in front of him in a challengin manner, ready to test his character. It was obvious that he was tryin to incite X to fight him an was on the verge of takin the confrontation one step further when I stepped in to ask him what his problem was. He turned an snarled in my face an I snapped, givin him a flyin headbutt before he could do any damage to either of us. In retrospect, my intolerance of such behaviour was probably a throwback to my prison days when you made sure you got the first dig in so that it would be clear from the start that you were no pushover. The fight commenced as he stood his ground tryin to retrieve the upper hand in the face of a humiliatin blow to his ego. A couple of other people made a move to join in but were stopped by the majority who proclaimed the lad to be a dickhead for tryin it on in the first place. It's a shame but it always happens when a band begin to get a bit of recognition, there's always some nutter who takes up the challenge of knockin you down, as if you have no right to be puttin yourself on a stage in the name of entertainment. I suppose it's inevitable that the minute you take to any rostrum, you leave yourself wide open as a visible target for them to vent their anger on an this is what had happened.

It was a triumph for the band among the Leeds crowd at the time because from that moment on we were respected an viewed as equals; there was no pretence to our music an the lads knew it. They began to follow us everywhere, offerin unconditional support in everythin we did.

Our very first London show, at The Clarendon pub in Hammersmith, was the breakin point we needed, openin the floodgates to a very desirable rapport with the national music press that lasted throughout the years an afforded us the chance to reach a much wider an varied audience.

We were very lucky in that we'd been offered the services of a boss sound engineer called Oz, who'd expressed a wish to do this particular show for us an was even willin to forego his fee completely to ensure we gave the very best performance in the light of such an important gig. What a man! We got down there to find that instead of a throngin mass of public, beggin to hear the tunes, there was a cynical bunch of journalists ready to rip us to shreds with their pencils sharpened an note-pads at the ready. They'd been invited along by Dave Harper, our then 'press' officer, an we surveyed the gatherin with some trepidation, knowin the response could make or break our future. As it goes, we launched into a powerful set, aided by the services of Oz, who, to his credit, made damn well sure that the sound was top fuckin notch for us. We put our heart an soul into the show; it was our most motivated an polished to date an the gamble paid off. From that day, the press gave us continually favourable reports which, in turn, swelled the formerly regional fan base of a few hundred staunch supporters to one of thousands on a national level.

I was really beginnin to enjoy myself, havin a proper purpose in life for once, an one that didn't readily cause me to brush up against the law in any seriously freedom-threatenin way, as all my past endeavours to earn a crust had. Time was flyin by quickly an before I knew it we were makin plans to get the first album underway. It was to be called *Twenty Four Hour Party People Plastic Face Can't Smile White Out*, derived from a chance remark on an afternoon session down the boozer. We'd been on a mammoth whizz session for days, an were sat nursin pints in the throes of a massive comedown. In walked a friend of ours an seein the vacant expression of our faces he announced, 'What the fuck is up with you lot. Fuckin 'ell plastic face can't smile white out!'

The remark made us all perk up as we realized what a bunch of sad bastards we looked, especially as it was all self-inflicted abuse. We stopped wallowin in our depression an got another pint in to mark the occasion. The observation was a classic an it was agreed that the comment summed up the order of the day an must therefore be included in the title of the album.

John Cale was drafted in to do the album with us. Fuck me, the Velvet Underground were a legend in our record collections, an absolute must for accompanyin the smokin sessions at the time. We were all a bit nervous an excited about just gettin to meet, never mind work with, one of our heroes. In the cold light of day, we found him to be a bit on the strange side, never talkin much an constantly stuffin his face with oranges an extra strong mints throughout the entire recordin session. It was his recipe for stayin on the straight an narrow, not somethin we were really sure about, particularly as we were busy headin, fast an furious, in the opposite direction to achieve our creative consciousness.

He did manage to refine our sound to some extent, by addressin the abnormal speed at which the songs progressed: always slow at first, gettin faster in the middle an gettin double fast an manic towards the end. He assured us that it would be a better composition to get them all runnin at the same pace throughout, to get a more complete an aesthetic feel to the tracks.

The whole album was accomplished in six days without hardly a word passin between the producer an the band, an incredible feat of musical engineerin in itself, if ever there was one. It was durin this time that X was developin his jacked up, smacked up love affair with drugs, especially the heroin. I tried it myself a few times, but that inward-lookin, mongin on the couch business was not for me. I liked to be up an about, doin things, meetin people, seein places an generally livin. I'd been alone with myself plenty enough in my time inside so while everyone around jacked up an goofed out, disappearin into their own secluded sphere of oblivion, I'd be neckin acid an trippin the light fantastic in some club or other. Life ain't for sittin in a dingy doss hole, with your head too far up your own arse to even see the people around you.

Smackheads – the ultimate selfish bastards.

The first time I tried it, I have to admit, I pumped it into my veins with unreserved glee, willin to give anythin a shot, literally. I was young an stupid but not so stupid that I didn't heed the numerous warnins from older users who'd passed the point of no return themselves an had lost the strength to crawl their way back to normality. Don't get me wrong, I tried without any success to become that bleedin heart artist, once takin it for a whole five days to try an really get into the buzz of things, but I just couldn't do it with the panache that X did an I had to accept that it wasn't my idea of utopia. It bored me stupid. I was lucky really that my temperament wasn't suited to heroin, someone else might not have the aversion so bad an then it's yet another young life gone to the dogs.

I stood back from that moment an viewed the ruins of countless lives that lay in splinters around me, people who were content to wallow in their own shit waitin for nothin but the next fix. It's a sad existence an I'm glad I had the impatience to rush ahead in search of somethin more. I wanted to be up an about an smack just gets you down an keeps you there, whingin about what could have been.

X liked it, he does the bleedin heart artist thing very well. He *was* David Essex in *Stardust*. The drama of it all suited his countenance down to the ground as he followed the rock superstar manual to the letter. It's his shut off mechanism for dealin with the world, or not dealin with the world as the case may be.

X had found himself a girlfriend about this time an was busy fallin in love. I was the proverbial gooseberry an decided it was time to leave the flat we shared – his flat – an get one of my own. I managed to secure myself a council flat in Little Hulton on Owlwood Close. It wasn't a palace by a long stretch of the imagination but it was all I needed an it served its purpose well on the occasions that I chose to sleep there. Okay, it was a squalid dump, full of cheesy old milk bottles, an ashtray for a floor an nothin but a smelly old mattress to eat, read an sleep on, but it was home.

One mornin, not long after movin in, I woke to find myself covered all over from head to toe in what appeared to be a nasty heat rash of some sorts. It itched like mad an I felt like shit. Amazinly, for all the abuse I poured on my body, it usually held up pretty well so I was gettin particularly concerned about my condition as the mornin progressed. We were due to do a gig in Scotland with New Order that night an so feelin a soft cunt, I hauled myself out of my pit an made my way down to X's so that

I wouldn't miss the off. I arrived at his flat an began moanin about the worryin rash that was drivin me round the bend with the itchiness of it all. We emptied his bathroom cabinet an poured all sorts of possible remedies over me but none worked. In a fit of panic, I went round to the chemist's, lifted my top at the counter an showed him my spotty torso. He gave me a box of pills which I downed without hesitation; I was completely focused on gettin to the gig, no matter what it took to get me right again. Hey presto, within half an hour I felt like a new pin. The gig was back on.

The show was a blinder an I felt on top of the world, knockin back a bottle of tequila afterwards with my usual fervour. The anaesthetic qualities of the alcohol ensured that the journey back was a painless one an I made it back to my pit in a happily drunken state, indifferent to the damage I had inflicted on my already poisoned body.

The followin mornin, I woke feelin worse than ever an it wasn't just the average tequila hangover that was goin down; I could feel a real illness comin on thick an fast. To make matters worse, I was expectin an American girl to stay an she was arrivin that day. I'd met the girl in the recent past. She was a bit of a Factory groupie at the time an we had got as far as exchangin bodily fluids, just the once, on a one-night fling. On her return to America, she'd kept in touch, sendin me letters – as is the way with young girls sometimes. She'd written to say she was comin over an had asked if she could crash at mine for the duration of her stay. I wasn't too keen but, like a fool, had agreed to the arrangement in a moment of madness.

I was in no fit state to be receivin guests, an I was in no mood to be civil an polite to one, especially one with a gratin American accent. The poor girl lasted all of ten minutes in my company. I barked at her to shut up, snarled at her for fussin about an in the end told her in no uncertain terms to fuck off out an find somewhere else to stay.

Needless to say, she left. About fifteen minutes later she came back, great sobbin tears rollin down her cheeks. Not that old blackmail trick, I thought, please don't start playin that game on me now, it's all I need.

What had actually happened was, in my mind anyway, quite funny at the time, but it had completely freaked the daft cow out. She had been standin at the nearby bus stop to return to town when a bus had appeared at the top of the road. As the bus came nearer, she noticed that it was bein pushed by a large gang of young kids an another of about twelve was steerin the thing, laughin manically an headin straight in her direction. As the bus got closer, it began to career out of control, slidin round the corner an just missin her in the process by a few metres. She was petrified an in shock.

I still told her to piss off. Like I said, I was beyond showin grace to visitors. I was ill.

I desperately wanted to get out an pretend that things were actually quite normal an decided a mooch down to see X might clear my head. I wanted to talk over the previous night's gig, as was usual the day after an event. I made it over there but couldn't concentrate on what was bein said. The pains rackin my limbs an the strange fuzzy feelin in my head made it impossible to join in any of the banter an I soon made my excuses an left to go back home. I needed my bed badly. It took me an age to slog the distance back to my flat as I repeatedly slumped in the street with the effort to move my limbs in a co-ordinated manner. I crawled back into my bed, never havin felt so exhausted an ill in all my life. A friend called the doctor out for me but in the dim an dingy conditions of the flat, he failed to make any positive diagnosis. He issued me with another set of pills an told me to call back in a week if it hadn't cleared up by then.

I tossed an turned an sweated an writhed for a further few days but the illness was gettin the better of me an I knew I needed some care an attention to help me through. I thought I was dyin an no one seemed to be doin anythin about it. In one last desperate attempt to get some help, I hauled myself the considerable distance to see a relatively sensible friend of mine. He was slightly older, was one of the few people I knew who had a real job an, consequently, led a far cleaner an healthier existence than myself. He cooked good food an kept his place clean an nice an generally knew how to look after himself properly; I hoped he would take me in an look after me.

I collapsed on his doorstep from the effort of gettin up there an he found me lyin with my head against the door, barely conscious. He immediately put me to bed an called the doctor out a second time. Once again, the dim light of the room made a definite diagnosis difficult an I was given yet more medication, told to rest, an to call back if the condition worsened. Why won't they accept that I'm really fuckin ill, I thought, but I was too weak to protest an so stayed in bed eatin the soup an sandwiches that my mate brought to me at regular intervals. By this time, my whole body ached with a deep an dull pain. I could hardly move to turn over in bed an my head felt like a dead weight on my bony shoulders. I went on like this for another week or so, bein tended by my friend who looked unnervingly worried every time he entered the room to survey my physical state.

I realized I would have to go into the doctor's an demand a proper diagnosis, this simply couldn't go on any longer. The minute I staggered into the surgery, the doctor took one look at me an proclaimed, 'My God, hasn't anyone told you that you're yellow?'

Of course they hadn't, I'd been holed up in dimly lit rooms, skulkin about under bedclothes for the last two weeks.

I was promptly bundled into an ambulance an rushed off to Monsall Hospital in Manchester. It was an isolation hospital an I didn't like the sound of it one bit. That's it, I moaned to myself, I'm goin to die in a fuckin dreary ward in a spooky old hospital an nobody will know. I had advanced yellow jaundice an pleurisy, caused by a nasty bout of hepatitis which in turn had been caused by usin needles to inject drugs. Not somethin you can drop into the dinner conversation too often. It could be treated an cleared completely, they assured me, but it didn't alleviate the immediate feelins of doom an despondency as I lay there in the isolation ward, hurtin like fuck an wantin to go home.

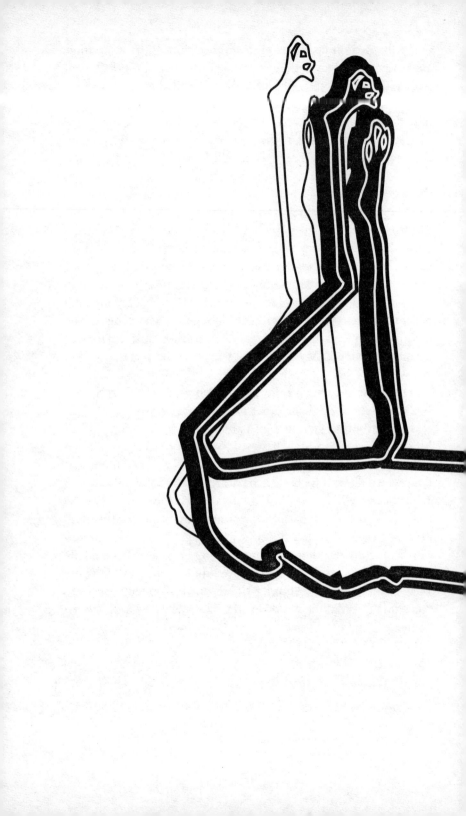

The band were goin on their first trip to America in just under two weeks' time to play at the New York music seminar. It was an important showcase of new sounds an we were goin with Factory Records to show off to the big wigs in the Big Apple. I lay there, in isolation, in my hospital bed, willin myself better. There was no way I was compromisin my chance of goin to the States over some nasty infection. It could be my first an last chance, I had to get there. I stuck the hospital thing out for about a week an then discharged myself in a panic about gettin my shit sorted out in time for the flight. The doctors thought I was fuckin barmy but I was feelin better an decided to risk it.

I went round to a house where some of my stuff had been left, to pick up my passport. Fuckin nightmare of nightmares, it had been lost. I scrambled about an managed to get it together to go to Liverpool for a replacement. Time was tickin by at an alarmin rate an I still had to sort out my visa through the American Embassy before I could go anywhere. On the day of the flight, I rushed down to London, burnin straight round to the embassy an pushed my way to the front of the queue; I had no time for decorum. I got my visa sorted with just an hour to make it over to the airport in time for the check in.

YEEESSS! I'd done it. What a result! I was on my way to New York with the band. Big fuck off cheesy grins all round.

We landed at Kennedy Airport buzzin our socks off, makin a B-line for downtown Manhattan. It felt like a scene lifted straight from a film; it had just been rainin an steam was comin up from the sewers along the sidewalks. I quickly got a crick in my neck from lookin upwards in amazement at all the towerin buildins. I'd never seen anythin like it, the scale of everythin took my breath away as we scurried around, tryin to absorb everythin at once: the sounds, the colours, the smells, the people, the whole fuckin lot just bombarded our senses stupid. It was like I'd eaten the strongest trip in the universe an had been transported straight into a 70s celluloid world of yellow taxi cabs an delis, half expectin Starsky an Hutch to come boundin across the enormous stretch of tarmac that seemed impossible to cross without seriously puttin your neck on the line.

We were stayin at the infamous Chelsea Hotel where, in a macabre set-up some years earlier, Sid Vicious had killed Nancy an then OD'd himself, or some such nonsense, I forget all the gory details. Fuckin rock 'n' roll legends; fucked up bunch of selfish bastards. None the less, we couldn't help but be intrigued by the incident.

We dumped the bags in the rooms, had a quick check round the hotel to find The Room, were disappointed at the distinct lack of evidence of anythin untoward havin ever happened, an then raced out to soak up some more of the Big Apple. First things first, we darted into the nearest shop an bought a bottle of champagne to celebrate our arrival in style. Wastin no time, I popped the top an threw the brown paper bag in the bin, engagin the first passin black man in conversation as I did so. I thought it's what you did when you travelled to another country – get a drink in an talk to the locals.

Rule number one – don't throw away the bag that the booze came in an definitely don't drink it on the street in New York.

Havin literally just got off the plane, I had no idea there were any such rules an that I was casually breakin the law. I soon did. A big fat bully of a cop came boundin over from nowhere, snatched the bottle from my lips an put it in the bin. I was gobsmacked. 'What the fuck! Ey, what yer doin yer fuckin prick, I just bought that champagne in the shop.'

I was utterly confused by the incident. I couldn't work out if he thought I'd stolen it or if his problem was that I was stoppin the locals an talkin to them, or if he was simply bein an arrogant fucker who wanted me to know it was his city. I continued to argue the toss with him an went to recover the bottle from the bin. He pinned me up against the wall with one hand, took it off me a second time an put it back in the bin again. He issued the warnin that if I attempted to go back for it this time, he'd blast me. Fuckin hell, he got out of the wrong side of bed this mornin,

I thought. I was not gainin any ground on the matter, that was clear. What could I do, he was a big motherfucker with a gun an I was a skinny young lad with nothin but a sore case of indignation at his rude an unfriendly manner.

Someone pulled me aside an quickly explained the laws about keepin alcohol in a bag an the no drinkin in the streets thing. Why didn't he just say so in the first place? I could have saved myself a full bottle of champagne. You live an learn.

We slouched off, mutterin to ourselves an cursin the New York Police Department for bein top pricks, but not too loudly, just in case. Once round the corner we seized the opportunity an vented our anger on a passin stretch limo full of fur coats an gold chains that had moments earlier come out from the opera opposite. We gave it a top bootin an immediately looked around, laughin nervously at the ludicrous nature of the little scene that was quickly developin on our first jaunt out an about in the big city.

We were terrified, but it felt fuckin ACE. At least you know you're well an truly alive an living every minute on the streets of New York. The senses are keenly sharpened by the frenzy of activity goin on constantly in all directions.

Horseman had us all in hysterics, strollin nonchalantly round the streets with his Tesco carrier bag, lookin the token eccentric English nutter abroad, but he wouldn't ditch it for nobody, insistin it contained all his little essentials. Funny as fuck an not gettin mugged.

We went off to meet the American girl who had naused me up in my ill state the few weeks previously an I cringed, rememberin the cruel treatment I'd given her. It hadn't dampened her keenness, it seemed, an I soon put the memory to the back of my mind. She'd secured herself a job with the New York branch of Factory Records an was willinly playin the ambassador, busy organizin a meal out for the band. Fuck that, we want to score some drugs, we told her, pressin the issue until she finally gave in an agreed to take us to an area where we'd find somethin to smoke. All the way there she was tryin to tell us that the New York drug culture wasn't to be confused with the set-up in Manchester, things had to be done differently round here. What does she know, we laughed, we're the lads, we've got oodles of street cred, we know how to speak to these dudes. Drug lingo has to be the same in any culture, we shrugged.

She dropped me an X in an uptown area just by a little park an got off straight away, not wantin to take any active part in the goins on. We scored straight away, we couldn't believe our luck. We looked at each other an laughed about the rest of the band sittin in a borin restaurant while we fearlessly scouted about on the night-time streets, soakin up the real life dramas that were goin down all around. The kid came back with a few small vials of crack. Whey hey, we were off, back to the hotel to get into some serious crack session. It took fuckin ages to get back as we'd spent everythin we had on us on this one deal an couldn't even afford the cab fare. We walked for what seemed like miles as we kept gettin lost an doublin back on ourselves in the haste to test out our goodies.

We finally arrived, buzzin with the little kit an ready to do the lot. The first vial was ceremoniously cracked open, 'scuse the pun, to find a mass of tightly packed polystyrene balls that came spillin out, bouncin everywhere. Our faces blanched at the sudden realization that we'd suffered a humiliatin major rip-off on our very first venture into the underbelly of the city. What a pair of naïve bastard pricks!

We began to fume, firstly at our own stupidity an then at the twats who'd pulled the scam on us. 'Bastards! That means we'll have to go back out again. Now, quick, what's the name of that fuckin restaurant again?'

We weren't about to let it lie. Scurryin round to where the rest of them were sat, just about to tuck into their dinners, we burst in an began demandin to be taken back down to the area where we'd just scored the pure-quality polystyrene. We wanted to go immediately; we were ragin over the incident, which had been made ten times worse by havin to go an admit it to the others in order to get a lift back up there. The poor girl asked if it could wait till she'd finished her food,

'No! It can't wait!' we barked at her in unison, faces purple from the desperate need to get back out there an DO SOME-THIN! She relented under the pressure an took us back to the area we'd recently vacated but a little further down this time, where it was slightly busier.

This time we struck it lucky, meetin some fuckin right on funky dude who invited us down into his den to smoke his pipe. We followed him warily along a short, dark passageway an down into the dank an musty cellar of a big brownstone buildin. Think *New Jack City* an you get the picture. This really was the bowels of the city an all my senses were busy screamin this fact at me, but the buzz of gettin that hit together kept me glued, unflinchingly, on my upturned crate in that dimly lit basement, waitin patiently for my prize.

The dude pulled out four vials of crack an a little glass pipe an invited us to stay with him to do the session. He filled the pipe with crack as me an X sat watchin intently, notin the method of sortin it all out. He placed a small ball of opium in the middle of the crack an passed it over. WOW! FUCK ME, the instant dreamy whoosh of the high was too nice. The crack shot you to the moon an the opium floated you back down on a liquid silver cloud. I was burnin for more straight away an so was X, but the dude turned all crazy on us all of a sudden: 'I'm feelin spooky man!'

We got the message loud an clear an fucked off into the night. Walkin out of the den we couldn't help actin like we were ten men; we'd just had our first proper hit of crack with opium an were feelin fuckin massively mighty. There wasn't a problem in the world that we couldn't deal with.

The Puerto Rican gang that saw our exit from the crack den an instantly surrounded us wasn't a problem. I could deal with it. Even when the geezer at the front began to accuse me of spittin at him, it wasn't too big a problem. I was tryin to explain that the problem was actually theirs, 'Fuckin hell, we come down here tryin to be friendly an all you lot want to do is cause trouble! What's your fuckin problem?'

'You just spat at me!'

Maybe I was a little excited an overly animated at the time but then that's my nature on drugs, I can't help it if a little spittle escapes my mouth when I talk too fast.

The kid pulled out his gun an shoved it at my throat. It

suddenly dawned on me that I might possibly have a problem on my hands. Yes, I concluded, this was definitely goin to be a bit of a problem, possibly a big fuck-off problem to my health.

God must have looked down an thought, Fuck that, I've got no time to be dealin with these nutters just now, 'cos a few seconds later, the dude who'd served up the crack appeared at the end of the passageway an quickly diffused the situation, draggin me away forcibly as I still tried to argue the toss. He fished in his pocket an gave us a dime bag of weed to be goin on our way with, tellin us to fuck off out of there before we got done in for real. At those words, I became fully aware of the seriousness of the set-up in those parts an we didn't need tellin twice. We knew we'd had a lucky escape an burnt it all the way back to the hotel to finish the session in the safety of our room.

It slowly dawned on us that we'd actually done all our PDs for the week in just one drugs mission. Not only that, but the word had got back to Factory about our little foray into the uptown night-time scene an they were shittin themselves that we might try it again an not be so lucky the second time round. We really didn't give a fuck at the time, we were as high as kites an were simply glad to be just buzzin about, doin our thing in New York.

We woke to the prospect of havin no more money for the rest of the week. Then X hit on the idea of workin the same scam that we'd done a few times back home in times of dire emergency. The Factory offices were full of brand new saleable records that the company were happy to give away as perks to visitin bands, if you were on the label. We ran in, raided the shelves an took the records straight round to the nearest music shop. They took the lot off us an we ended up with $150 each, linin our pockets nicely. Sorry Tony, you know what it's like when you're peppered, or perhaps you don't.

Later that afternoon, we went down to the Limelight Club, the venue for the gig that evenin. We wanted to check out what kind of gaff it was an to make sure the equipment that we'd ordered had arrived. Had it bollocks, the whole organization was in chaos. The organ that we'd stipulated turned out to be a piano. The Mondays with a piano, can you believe it? Fuckin ridiculous. We turned our attentions to the actual buildin, rompin around, lookin in all the nooks an crannies for anythin interestin. We stumbled upon somethin very interestin in no time at all. It was the manager of the Limelight, who invited us into her office for a little chat. The little chat turned out to be two fat lines of charlie; this little cookie was definitely completely off her nut. Fuckin fantastic. Now this is just what I thought New York was all about.

She must have liked us as in the next breath she was inviting us back to her pad to spend the rest of the afternoon gettin blasted on coke. Not wantin to offend, naturally we agreed.

It was soon clear that her intentions were to get seriously sexy as she emerged from the bedroom clad solely in a dainty pair of knickers an proceeded to chop out the lines as if it was the most normal thing in the world to sit in front of complete strangers with your tits out. I sat there with X, frozen on the couch, nudgin an gigglin like two naughty schoolboys, eyes wide with wonder an astonishment at the sight before us. She presently began to give us a bit of a lap dance routine, only we weren't payin, just snortin, absently watchin her gyrations an pussy rubbin techniques. She was completely an utterly, dangerously, off her fuckin face, frantic for a shag with all the coke. It didn't end there either. Her flatmate came back halfway through the session an immediately joined in the porn show, strippin off an gettin high an dirty like her mate.

We took the coke, drank the drinks an casually declined the shag, but none the less enjoyed the show. We weren't so callous, the coke was ours after all. We'd bought an eight ball with the money from the scam we'd pulled off earlier.

We'd stayed longer than anticipated, arrivin at the club wired to fuck, an hour an a half late, just before the point we were due to go on. Everyone was growlin an pullin faces, goin berserk, but we'd known it was goin to be a shit performance since the chaos of the afternoon. We were coked to the ras an didn't give a flyin fuck at this late hour.

The set was one of the worst we'd ever played, an absolute shambles. Tony Wilson said at the time that he'd never been so embarrassed in all his life. He'd been biggin the band up to all his American contemporaries an promisin them a real treat. The only treat in store that night was a near fight flarin up between me an X as we snarled at each other from opposite ends of the stage, a result of doin far too much coke, in various forms, over the previous two days with no proper sleep. We were off our fuckin heads an pissed as farts, way off mark for doin a gig. I ended up smashin a bottle down on the stage an it bounced off into the audience, missin someone's head by just inches. At the time all I could think of was fuckin hell, we'd better get out of here fast. We came off stage to be met by, of all people, a bunch of kids from Blackburn who'd come all this way to offer their support. They didn't seem to mind that the set had declined into a farcical version of the sets they were used to seein – like us they were havin a ball just hangin out in New York. They crashed their charlie on the table an the party wore on.

The followin mornin found us skint again an plunderin the stores at Factory a second time. No one questioned our actions an we shot out to find another record shop, cashed in our goods like the cheeky bastards we were an set off to meet up with the rest of the lads to go for a jaunt on the Staten Island ferry. One of the best photos of the band, in my opinion, was taken durin that ride on the ferry, with the New York skyline providin an atmospheric background. It's a bit clichéd, I admit, but I like the atmosphere it conjures up, an all the memories of the madcap an mayhem that were part of the set-up back then. We knew we were on the verge of somethin special, an it coloured everythin we did with a deliciously rosy hint of the glory yet to come.

Later that night we went cruisin the streets of Manhattan in an open-topped Spider sports car, all eight of us. A proper sight to be seen, it was fuckin brilliant. I'd never felt so good in my young life. The air was warm an still an the neon signs lit up the night like a never-endin circus with freaky people paradin on every sidewalk. New York on a first visit is mindblowin, to say the least. A cop saw us comin an grabbed hold of his bollocks in the middle of the street shoutin, 'Fuck you, fuckin mother-fuckers!'

I couldn't believe my eyes an ears. No way would you get the stiff English dibble bein so loud an abrasive while on traffic directin duties in front of hundreds of watchin people. We were pulled over an ordered out of the car for bein overloaded. Me an X volunteered to walk the rest of the way back to the hotel. We didn't mind, it's an addictive thing in itself just strollin in the heat an the bustle of the city, watchin the world zippin by an all the odd little scenes of life bein played out on every street corner.

Before too long, we had managed to acquire a hanger on, who sold us our last lot of coke for the visit. A few seconds later, he reached into his coat an pulled out a big fuck-off knife. Oh no, not again, we can't be that naïve, surely. I couldn't figure out his motive at first when it became instantly obvious that the blade was not for us. We'd been approached by a couple of girls who were tryin to rub us up, fondlin our bollocks in an over familiar way. The kid flashed the knife an the girls backed off. 'See that guy down there, he's gettin ready to mug you man!'

He pointed across to a dark doorway just a little way up the street. A figure moved furtively in the shadows, dartin off at the sight of the flashin blade. I had no reason to disbelieve his claim, an thanked God that he was with us. Yes, we were still that naïve an yes, it really is that dangerous a place.

New York certainly lived up to its reputation as the twenty-four-hour city that never sleeps. It hits you hard an it's unre-pentin.

We saw the scandal, did the vice, I loved it.

New York had been the biggest eye opener yet. We came home floatin on a cloud of euphoria, big ideas formin about the shape our future would take once the music took off. Even the long flight home didn't dampen the exhilaration the trip had infused us with. We went straight from the airport to The Haçienda, burnin to tell of the adventures we'd just had. Mike Pickering was in the DJ box. He was our first victim of the night as the tales came effusin from our mouths in an incessant stream from every corner of the small room. His ears got a proper batterin – an there was no escape because he couldn't move from his DJ station all night.

Even though the set in New York had been a wipe out, it didn't lessen the feelins in the band that somethin big was brewin on the horizon. We all thought at the time that the new single, taken from the first album, would be the trigger that would set the ball rollin in our favour. In retrospect, we all harboured the same notion every time a single was released, each of us thinkin it would be a dead cert number one every time. It never was, of course. The climb up the ladder of success was long an slow an any milestones passed along the way, although each added a dimension to the band's development, at the time seemed remarkable in their ordinariness.

'Tart Tart' was the single that was goin to make us massive. It was a personal favourite of mine an I was confounded as to why it didn't do better than it did. It was met with pretty decent reviews, but maybe the public needed a little longer to acquire the taste for X's growlin, cryptic lyrics an the rawness of the musical accompaniment. I had a special affinity for the tune because of the references to one of the very first people we had met in the early Haçienda days. Her name was Tart Tart.

She was a strange type of woman, an old groupie from the 60s, somethin she wasn't adverse to admittin. The drug culture of the hippie era hadn't treated her too well an she was lookin pretty rough an haggard by the time she met me an X, but we liked her friendly disposition an slightly kooky ways. She looked upon herself as an abstract artist but I think her main way of carvin a livin was by wheelin an dealin on the darker side of life. The first time we came across each other, me an X were sportin freshly barbered skinheads an were bobbin an weavin about the club in our usual fashion, up to no good. She told us a spooky little tale of how a few months earlier she'd painted a picture of two young skinheads in The Haçienda, an hadn't known why the image had taken over her canvas at the time. It transpired that our meetin crystallized the meanin of the paintin for her: she took it as fate that she was destined to take us an the rest of the band into her life. She did so willinly an often laid drugs on the lads in times when money was short.

One weekend we'd called by as usual to pick up a bag of goodies, promisin to pay up on the followin Monday. She was happy with the set-up an we went away thinkin no more of it, but the chillin reality of the situation was that we were never goin to get to pay her the debt.

On returnin with the dough a few days later, there was no reply at the door. We went back a few times over the next couple of days but again there was no response. Eventually, another friend of ours went round an forced the door. Everyone was startin to get a little anxious by now as she hadn't contacted anyone for some time. He found her dead at the bottom of the stairs. She'd died of a brain tumour an was black an blue from throwin herself around, smashin her head on the walls an ultimately down the stairs in a desperate attempt to stop the pain an agony. The police assumed they had a murder case on their hands because of the extent of her bodily injuries an even dragged the lad who'd found her off for an interview as prime suspect. Obviously, the post mortem put the record straight.

Her sudden an lonely death was a shock for the band as we'd all come to look upon her as a special an unusual friend. Her death gave rise to the immortal lines in the song:

T T, she laid it on,
an a few days later she's gone,
back to the womb,
to get drowned drowned drowned drowned drowned.

The poignant reality of the words touched me, they meant so much, like I found most of the lyrics in those days did. They were all taken from our collective life experiences, with X effortlessly shapin the form of the language to fit the tunes. To me they were classic words that spoke volumes about the times we were livin in.

WHERE DO WE DRAW THE LINE?

There is no escapin the blatant fact that drugs were a drivin force behind the work of the Mondays. We turned what the Government termed as a no good, low-life existence into a fuckin huge, mega money-spinnin, fantastic adventure. I believe the attraction of the band lay in the fact that the music an our publicized lifestyles mirrored those of a vast multitude of disillusioned kids an young adults. X articulated the everyday goins on in life in a way that other people only wished they could, but they instantly recognized an appreciated the observations in the lyrics fused to the mish mash of nearly, but not quite, familiar sounds. We made no bones about the fact that drugs played a major part in our daily lives, an also in the quest for producin a certain amount of the *je ne sais quoi* sound of the Mondays.

The hypocrisy of the Government drawin the definin line of which poison is legal an which is not riled our young an fevered brains as we watched the destruction that alcohol an tobacco alone wreaked on the communities around us. Now I don't want to be puttin around the word that takin drugs is good for you, but I do want it to be known that I find it hard to stomach the anti-drug campaigns of the last decade or so that have constantly victimized the illegal substance user when more deaths are recorded per year as a direct result of usin legal drugs such as tobacco an alcohol. Here is a small example of how legal drugs seriously marred the life of a member of the Mondays in just one evenin.

PD had been out drinkin in the boozer with Ronnie one night. They'd had a few too many to drink an got on the wrong side of another gang of lads. A violent, alcohol fuelled attack commenced in which PD suffered substantial injuries, havin chairs thrown over his head an bein launched by a kid wieldin a baseball bat. Ronnie got a hammerin too, but it was PD who took the biggest beatin. He was completely done over in the attack, coppin for some nasty gashes on his head an a split lip from his mouth to the base of his nose. The important fact to consider though, is that he'd suffered physical injuries that quickly healed but the attack left him in a state of psychosis for some time. He recovered after a while, of course, or so we think – it's hard to tell sometimes with PD – but the point I'm makin is that his life suffered a major setback as a direct result of takin legal drugs on licensed premises.

Ironically it gave rise to one of his more amusin quotes. When questioned by the doctor about how he felt when walkin down the street after the event, he replied, 'Great – when there's nobody there!' The off the cuff remarks became more an more bizarre after the attack, an he was either a genius comic or completely fuckin solidly off his rocker. Like I said, it's hard to tell.

Booze an fags – fuckin scandalous.

I say this with some conviction, as recently I made the decision to give up smokin weed. Nothin in particular prompted the act, well nothin I can pinpoint anyway. Perhaps I'm realizin the momentum gatherin pace, racin towards the premature demise of my own life, who knows, but the important thing is that I've stopped smokin weed for whatever reason. Those who really know me will realize what a momentous statement that is for me to make, an if you've read the rest of this book, you might too. But anyway, what I'm gettin round to is that, no fuckin way on this earth can I say the same about smokin cigarettes an havin the odd pint or brandy, it's just fuckin impossible. Now I never, in all my young days, thought I'd be sittin here sayin that I can't give up smokin puny fuckin cigarettes but it's true, an the Government don't give a fuckin shit about it. They wouldn't bat an eyelid if I died of cancer or whatever, but give me a dodgy E death an watch the authorities report that with glee as concrete proof of the evilness of illegal drugs an their effect on the health of the nation. I mean no offence to the people who have suffered a bereavement due to any kind of drug, but I find the whole set-up a stinkin mass of cover ups an propaganda lies by a Government that can't afford to lose the tax returns on these so-called safe, legal drugs.

Who's to say that what I choose to alter my state of mind

with is worse than what the next person chooses. Each to their own, but with knowledge an maturity, not youth an ignorance. It's hard to prevent but education an discussion has to be the key now that drugs are so widespread in any community.

Over the next year things jogged along quite nicely, with the fan base increasin with each passin month. It wasn't long before the venues began to increase in size too. Slowly but surely, our reputation for puttin on a full an rowdy show filtered out to the masses via the press who were willinly chartin our rise to success in every weekly publication. It became a common occurrence to see my mug in some music paper or other, gurnin for all my worth on this stage an that, goggle-eyed at the wild frenzy of the growin crowds. I was havin a fuckin ball at this point in my life; I was permanently shacked up in a proper home with my new girlfriend, who'd just returned from America, travellin here, there an everywhere, an gettin loads of lovely attention from adorin female fans – heaven. We weren't gettin rich though, far from it, as any money that came back from any of the early ventures went straight back into makin the band a more professional outfit. As you get more attention, so does the quality of the sound, which means you very soon need better equipment, better recordin facilities, better crew, better drugs, of course, an better management, all of which cost mega money.

It was around this time that the original manager decided to quit the team. There were a few reasons for this, any one of which could have been the real decidin factor so I'm only surmisin here. Firstly, Phil wasn't puttin in the time needed to get the band to the top, what with his other work commitments. Secondly, X was gettin agitated at the slow pace at which the band as a business was tickin over, an thirdly, I reckon that Phil's strong Jewish background was a natural barrier to him goin any further with the likes of us lot. I got the distinct feelin that his family did not approve of the ragamuffin bunch of hooligans he was promotin with their errant an ungodly ways. I could be wrong, but there you go, that's my opinion anyway.

This is where Nathan McGough comes prancin into the picture to take over as manager on a majority vote, but I've got to say here that he never got my vote. Personally, I knew he was a prick from the moment we met, an as if to prove the point I was shoutin to all who would care to listen, he went an lost the band's dough on the very first show we did with him as official manager. We were playin a gig away somewhere, I can't remember where, but we were stayin in some hotel anyway. Nathan was already enjoyin the perks of life on the road as a band manager, takin an extra-special interest in the many young an naïve groupies that often hung around. Maybe this night though, the young girl he chose to entertain wasn't quite so gullible as he thought. Come the mornin, all the money for the band was missin, either lost or, as I suspect, pocketed by the girl who'd whiled the night away with Nathan. But then that was Nathan, always preoccupied with what was goin on in his pants rather than what was happenin or not happenin in the band. Nathan thought he was the chief shag an silent celebrity of the gang, we thought he was our manager; maybe we both had the wrong idea about his job title.

Whatever, it was an embarrassin scene that mornin, an one that should have served as an omen of things to come. In fact, from that moment on, I found myself bein constantly embarrassed by my unavoidable association with him. Maybe he felt likewise, but then, in a set-up with more than a few people to organize, there's bound to be a certain amount of friction in certain areas, an managers do tend to bear the brunt of frustration in any business. But then, ironin out the wrinkles is what they get paid for, only Nathan left a few too many creases, an not just in the beddin.

The band's potential was, in spite of the choice of manager, increasin with every gig, to the point where we were takin the main act of the night out of the picture. I refer to a gig in Manchester in some place or other where the Bodines were headlinin an we were the 'support'. It was pissin us off that the Bodines were given a precedence over us, especially as on the night the place was rammed with our crowd. Needless to say, the Mondays stormed the gaff an took the whole audience for ourselves. The Bodines were never to be seen. It seems they didn't want to play their set to a soiled an saturated audience, an went home instead. One-nil.

Later that very night, I found myself alone at X's flat in fear of a premature death through misadventure – take heed! In my boredom I'd fashioned myself a pipe out of an old talc bottle. In my greedy haste to smoke my weed, I'd forgotten to wash the chosen vessel out properly an must have inhaled a good few lungs full of Marks & Spencer's finest Lily of the Valley talc. I felt fuckin ill within minutes of the mistake an the little dangly bit at the back of my throat swelled to about twice the normal size, stickin to the back of my tongue an almost chokin me with every breath.

I sat up all night, pushin my fingers to the back of my tongue to allow myself to breathe. I was fuckin exhausted come daybreak an close to tears, kickin myself for inflictin such stupid an unnecessary torture on my own body.

I'd been lyin awake all night thinkin about the borin predictability of the outcome of takin drugs in a never-endin quest to get a buzz, but never quite gettin beyond an anticlimax followed by a huge comedown followed by an attempt to get back up there again, each time failin to reach that pinnacle of excitement by a growin margin. I had to admit it to myself, drugs weren't fun any more; I was lookin for somethin more to put me somewhere else, but definitely not down.

THE LITTLE
FELLAS STEAL
THE SCENE

Little did I know, the little fella that was goin to change the face of clubbin around the world was just around the corner. I'm talkin, of course, about Ecstasy. The E explosion was also to have a massive bearin on the future success of the band, in that the lads element of the audience who were previously preoccupied with the football terraces, gettin drunk an havin a good fight, were suddenly transformed into serious clubbers who weren't afraid to be seen dancin at gigs. It was no longer seen as a puffy pastime to get down on the dance floor an shake your funky stuff till it hurt. I believe it is this major change in the way the young kids began to behave that propelled the band an many like us into the spotlight.

My introduction to the little white fuckers came about in The Haçienda one night on the run up to Christmas. I think it was 1987. I bumped into a friend who'd just come back from a mission to the Dam an was lookin for all the world like he'd just copped a million. His eyes were shinin, he looked like he was goin to explode with excitement an I'd never seen him so full of enthusiasm for the club scene. He was buzzin his socks off, completely convinced that all the girls fancied the pants off him. Immediately he began to engage me in tales of the life-enhancin properties of the small white pill he had popped with a pint in the boozer earlier. I couldn't believe it, this usually shy an retirin kid, not particularly known for his attractive qualities was bumpin an grindin on the dance floor, shimmyin up an down the stairs an rubbin up to all the girls like he was some big sexy mother fucker. He asked me if I wanted to get one down my neck, but at a score a go I was a bit reluctant to part with my readies for such a small speck in my palm. It was all I had on me at the time, the big bucks were still evadin my pockets.

Over the next few weeks I kept my eye on his small group of friends. I was splittin my sides at some of the antics they were gettin up to an was taken completely aback by the outward show of affection towards everyone, even sworn enemies were bein let off the hook. Every time a top tune came on, they were up there, leadin the corner in a helluva funky stomp, dancin all over the gaff. The mad fuckers just couldn't get enough of it. It was like *Saturday Night Fever* all over again. I wanted in, but costin a score a go I needed to get some serious dough together to get my lot on the buzz; you can't go doin these things on your own, it's just not club etiquette. I could see all this nonsense goin on an couldn't get into the set-up 'cos I didn't have enough money. I was gutted.

A week or so later I got a rise an carefully put it aside, waitin for the right moment. It didn't take long for the right night to come along an I was ripe for the off. I found the kid an made the purchase, necked the pill, an waited. Phew! Fuck me, I was not ready for the initial rush at all, it took me completely by surprise. I felt so fuckin good man, like never before in my entire lifetime of samplin this an that. The name said it all.

I flew all round the place, dancin like a bastard for all my worth an lookin around in wonderment at all the beautiful women who had mysteriously climbed out from all corners, especially to dance with just me, the sexiest thing on two legs. It's true, I was a fuck-off love magnet an all the girls adored me, well I adored them so it must have been mutual – wasn't it? I poured with sweat, strippin off as the heat became furnace hot. I put it down to all the energy I was expendin at the time. The feelin was so heady, it made me sick if I stood still for too long but once I began to move again, I was off on a wave of funky explosion, all arms, angles an hands, grinnin till my cheeks ached.

That night the handful of secret E explorers congregated after the club an went off to a warehouse party. It was different from all the other late night parties we'd been used to which were usually the blues clubs or private parties in some house or other. This was a completely new vibe goin down. The music an atmosphere were beginnin to veer off in a completely new direction, but no one knew at this point just how massive it was goin to get in the very near future. It felt bigger an better than anythin before, even though there were only a few people around at the time. The music sounded fuckin amazin. Suddenly, my ears were receptive to the most minute details of sounds on the tracks the DJ played. It was fuckin strong stuff, an I couldn't get over the rush of that euphoric tide that was sweepin me along with the flow of the music.

It was a massive fuckin eye-opener. Soon, no one would be content to be paddlin around in the small ponds any more, they would be lookin towards swimmin with the big fish, samplin all that the world had to offer. A lot of people suddenly had the opportunity to make a lot of money very quickly, an in true entrepreneur fashion, they seized it with both hands.

About three hours after neckin my first ever pill, I'd turned into the most confident an cocky bastard in town, but completely lovable with it. In short, I was flyin off my fuckin face, drippin with sweat, double enthusiastic to any suggestion that sounded good an generally up for it in a big way, whatever 'it' happened to be. I wanted horny sex, I wanted to gorge myself stupid on the funkiest grooves, an most of all I wanted to live, right here, right now.

Fuckin hell, what a night out that was. I knew, the following day, that I had to get nearer the source of these little white wonders to get the price brought down to a sensible level. I wanted to know just what the dibble have been tryin to suss out ever since; just who was bringin in this new fandangle drug goin by the name of ecstasy? No way was I prepared, or even able, to pay £20 a time, but, fuck me, I was knocked sideways by that first night on this new E buzz. It was the fuckin mustard.

I'd arrived home that night absolutely smitten with my new find. I couldn't wait to tell my girlfriend about my night's adventures an to get back out there, to spread the gospel far an wide.

I started early the very next day, goin straight down to tell X about my discovery. He half listened, huffin an puffin, his mind wanderin off to the next blast of brown that he was contemplatin. He wasn't into goin out much at this point in time, he preferred to gouch on his couch, stayin in, all cosy an safe with his girlfriend. My revelation had fallen on deaf ears. I was givin it my best shot at gettin him out with me that night to give it a go.

I applied as much peer pressure as I could muster but he was too content with his tootin to be takin any heed of my new interest. I didn't hang around too long, I wanted to get down The Hac nice an early to spot this kid an get right back on this life-changin venture.

I took up my usual position in the corner, bobbin up an down, waitin for this kid to turn up so that he could score me one from wherever they came. It was doin my head in, I couldn't see him anywhere. About halfway through the night I was beginnin to give up hope that he would show. I was fuckin gutted, pacin up an down from the bar, slowly gettin pissed to pass the time.

I'd resigned myself to the fact that every night can't be a party night when a tap on my shoulder made me turn round. This young kid stood there, grinnin like he was my long-lost cousin or somethin.

'You don't remember me do you?'

Fuck! I hate it when that happens. I grappled desperately in the depths of my mind for a flicker of recognition but it was takin too long an I finally had to admit my ignorance. 'I was out with you last night.'

'Fuckin hell, yeah, top one. It's all comin back to me now!'

I immediately brightened at the prospect of bein able to reflect on the previous night's escapades with someone who knew exactly what I was talkin about. My spirits lifted even further when I realized that this kid might know where I could get sorted with another E. Of course he did. I should have known by the look in his eyes; he knew where to score alright. He led me over to the stage, in among a small crowd of people who looked like they'd all cracked the secret of life the way they were all smilin an dancin. I was introduced right there an then to one of the main players who'd had the amazin foresight to see that these little pills were goin to be the smash of the year. I'd no idea of the extent of his involvement in the matter at this early hour in the game.

That night, I was unofficially initiated into what can only be described as an elite club that was slowly takin over the dark-ened area at the back of the stage, growin like a sea of algae in the sweatin recess of the club, ready to float outwards over the dance floor an take over the writhin masses. I looked out across the crowds, an little did they suspect what would be comin to them in the very near future. I knew somethin massive was about to happen, what exactly I didn't know, an I could never have imagined the extent to which the scene would grow into one of the biggest youth culture movements in our time.

For the second time in my life, I slipped one of these tiny, innocuous-lookin pills into my mouth an twenty minutes later took off with a big fuck-off smile. I was brought back into the fold by the distinct whiff of skunk weed teasin my nostrils. I enquired where the skunk was comin from an the same kid pulled out a huge stinkin bag of the green sticky stuff, slippin a bud the size of a thistle into my hand with a smile. Fuckin marvellous, I've died an gone to heaven I thought, an settled into a non-stop groove as a blinder of a night began to unfold. Another great night out goes down in the history of The Haçienda, an little did I know it then but I'd managed to find the source of my new leisure aid, savin myself a pile of readies in the process. Fuckin *ACE*.

I went out again the next week to sample some of the same. Here was the acid test; it was a Tuesday night, nothin ever happened on a Tuesday night, it was renowned for bein the one night that everyone stayed in, ate properly an sat watchin the TV with their slippers on till bedtime. Now, if these little fuckers can brighten up a Tuesday night, I thought to myself, then they really are the fuckin business.

I ran into this kid again an he joined us for the duration of the evenin. I was out with my girlfriend an her mate who had come over from Sheffield for the night, so I was pretty glad of his company to tell the truth. He took it upon himself to treat the night as a bit of a blind date set-up an to get his intended in the mood, he slung half an E round to each of us. It was enough, plenty enough.

I had, at the time, the misfortune to be drivin a handpainted white Maxi around town, which is a serious confession for anybody in any financial situation to be admittin, especially an aspirin pop star, but there you go, I was. I did at least have the decency to wait until dark before turnin out in it though but, no kiddin, it really was a sight to be seen. It wasn't mine, you understand, it was on an extended loan from someone who lived in the house where my girlfriend's flat was an it seemed better than gettin taxis everywhere, well marginally. It was, it has to be said, the worst car ever. It had bald tyres, big fuck-off gunners in the paint work that had literally been applied with somethin like a yard brush, an to top it all the back seat – covered in a really tasteful maroon leatherette – wasn't even tethered to the chassis in any sense. This meant that whenever I put my foot on the accelerator, anyone who had the bad luck to be sittin in the back would tip neatly backwards into the boot, as though some massive G force had mysteriously taken hold of the car's contents. We found this out quite by accident on the very first spin in the car. I was talkin to my girlfriend who had chosen to sit in the back as it was slightly less embarrassin than bein up front with me. She supposed it would look like she was in a taxi, completely unconnected to me, the driver, in any way. She was completely unaware of what was to come; it was divine retribution for abandonin me at the helm.

I set off confidently down the road an instantly became aware that I'd misjudged the speed of a car comin up behind me, so to correct my manoeuvre I slammed on the accelerator to gain some speed. There was a fuck-off shriek from the back of the car an I looked in my rear-view mirror to be met with the sight of a pair of spindly legs stickin upwards from the direction of the boot. George an Mildred eat your heart out.

The point I'm gettin at here is that we just so happened to be out in the crapmobile that very night, an actually ended up cruisin conspicuously round the streets of Moss Side in the wee small hours lookin for a party. We found one, in some scruffy, dark, blues club. We stormed it, massively confident even though we were in a minority an made the joint ours, rockin in the corner amid bewildered stares. They just couldn't make out what kind of buzz was goin down in our little gang an luckily they left us well alone. The rapid explosion of the E scene saw the very same gaff rammed to the roof only a few months later an playin a completely different set of tunes as everyone became desperate to party on after the clubs an the organizer realized that these people were willin to pay more than his regulars.

The young kid with all the E's turned out to be quite a grafter, in the sense that he travelled around a lot, takin opportunities up whenever an wherever they arose, mostly out of this country. I hadn't realized just how much money it was possible to make leadin that kind of nomadic existence until he offered me a lift home in his car one night after the club. I followed him to the underground car park beneath the G-Mex an was amazed when he stopped dead beside a brand new, gleamin BMW 325I with leather trim. For one awful moment, I thought he was about to try an have the car over right there an then in the middle of the brightly lit car park. Then it dawned on me that he was the actual owner of this fine specimen of wheels. He was only about nineteen years old at the time, wearin nothing but top-quality labels an drivin a car that lads his age usually only get to wank about in their dreams. As we got in, he began to explain how he an his partner had 'done' Ibiza the previous year, off-loadin huge amounts of this E drug at the big clubs an parties over there. There were massive returns to be had in this E business an he intended to take this corner of the market by storm. He did, an after makin his fortune in the initial scramble to secure contacts an buy the new drugs, he bowed out gracefully, leavin the locals to fight out possession of the inner-city black markets, retirin along with his partner to a sunnier climate with fat wallets an massive grins.

They'd well an truly smashed it.

The following week was spent goin down to the rehearsal rooms gettin ready for the forthcomin tour. I'd hardly stepped through the door before I began to spout about my previous week's adventures. I couldn't help it, I wanted them to understand the potency of the little pills an how they'd be totally surprised by the new kind of buzz you got off them: how they'd be feelin double sexy with it. That wound them up alright – as soon as I mentioned the pure sexy vibe they were all ears an wide eyed with interest. Apart from that, everyone was ripe for tryin somethin new after all the years of amphetamine sulphate nonsense. My overspillin enthusiasm for my new drug affair must have been convincin, as one by one they soon came round to the idea of neckin one.

The issue did become slightly sidetracked as we were all buzzin quite naturally at this point, what with the thought of gettin off on tour round Europe; this was what we'd all been waitin for, the chance to get out of our immediate, dismal routine of doin the rounds of the houses, boozers, rehearsals, back to the boozer an so on. We were ready to set out on a real bender, spreadin our music an our style of livin far an wide around the globe. Rock 'n' roll, on the road. We'd finally cracked it an it felt good. I felt fuckin fantastic an was chompin at the bit, ready to go, havin discovered the weapon with which to launch an atomic dance attack on the unsuspectin audience.

The tour was all set for off, an with a newly appointed, unofficial, tour manager, this time in the shape of Muzzer. He was a big bastard with a commendable streetwise head on him for his tender years. He was an asset the Mondays could scarcely do without as he had the amazin ability to locate stray band members, round them all up an get them movin all in the same direction at the crucial moment. He was the only person who could possibly have pulled it off without the situation digressin into some fuckin huge showdown; it's not easy dealin with six egos, especially as at least four of them would be in the throes of a confusin comedown, a bitter testimony to the previous night's frolics.

X had come across Muzzer quite by accident durin a tricky moment in some boozer in town where he was sufferin a bit of hassle with a group of kids hell bent on causin him an injury. Muzzer had seen the band about eighteen months before at some small gig in Middleton Civic Centre, where we'd played to a crowd of about fifty, most of them bein his pals an associates. They had found our antics on stage a bit strange but funny with it, an consequently had developed a soft spot for the band. Seein X gettin some stick, vergin on the seriously violent side, he decided to step in an diffuse the situation before he got a proper batterin. It was a somethin an nothin argument that had flared up in an instant over some girl from the previous night. Muzzer told the other party to fuck off, which they promptly did, much to X's relief. Obviously, X was very grateful for his intervention an they have been in a firm allied partnership ever since.

The tour was about to begin.

Thinkin in terms of travellin an scorin drugs on tour in this country, we set off across Europe smilin, full of a false confidence that it would be as easy as orderin up cheese pasties to get whatever we needed en route. What a top pause of a decision that turned out to be. The small amount of draw we had on us at the start of the journey lasted all of one an a half days. In our excitement, an bein slightly anxious about playin to foreign audiences, we smoked like bastards on the first leg of the journey. The small van we'd hired for the trip was continuously enshrouded in a haze of ganga smoke. I say small van but, compared to the previous hired vehicles we'd suffered, it was actually a pretty swanky affair. In fact, it was to be our first taste of travellin in somethin approachin comfortable from which we could never look back.

So on our first ever venture across Europe, we had the good fortune to be ridin in a twelve-seater luxury minibus with reclinin coach seats, a TV an video, an adequate little sound system an even a fridge to keep the beers cool. Smart as fuck; we felt like gods for once, instead of a bunch of skinny-arsed no good fuckers, bein rattled to death, goin from one town to another in an orange tranny van with bench seats. Those days were, thankfully, fadin fast into the past.

This was the life, or at least it was until the draw ran out. We didn't even have a single line of whizz between the lot of us. Worse still, I'd forgotten to get hold of a handful of the new little pills that I'd been busy ravin on about for the last week. In my excitement to get off on this momentous journey, I'd barely remembered to pack my toothbrush an clean grumps. It was a large scale disaster, an soon, after we'd got the first gig under our belts, the shit began to hit the fan.

The first night in Germany went surprisinly well. Everyone still had enough draw to quell their nerves, helped along by a fervent samplin of the local beers. The show went down better than we had anticipated an we were pleasantly surprised when three of the lads from back home turned up to lend their support. They'd been in Germany doin a bit of graft an had seen the gig advertised locally. They were as taken aback to find us there as we were with them turnin up out of the blue.

The next day we piled back into the van, which was now full to the brim, what with the addition of the three kids from the night before an Gunter, the tour promoter. With Nathan, Muzzer, the sound engineer (big natty dred – Si Machin) an the driver on board as well, we were packed in like sardines. A heady mixture of tiredness, hangovers, hangers on an no draw began to stir the occupants of the van into a dangerous cocktail that threatened to bubble over an explode as the tension rose in relation to the need for SOMETHIN! to calm us all down. We asked Gunter, who seemed like an alright geezer, if he thought we could score somethin in the next town. AH! YAH! OF COURSE, he replied in his German accent. We had no reason to suspect that he was bein anythin but straight with us so for a while the tension eased as we sat back to contemplate the gig to come.

The next town came an went but still no sign of Gunter makin a move on our behalf. It slowly became apparent, as Gunter began to show his true colours, that he was intent only on doin his job, an that was to deliver us intact, smellin sweeter than a rose an as sober as a judge, to each venue. He thought he could apply army-type rules to this bunch of straggly musicians, tryin to shape us up an get the outfit gleamin as if we were a bunch of young squaddies on their first manoeuvre. We were a British band on tour, for God's sakes. We lived to take drugs, get out of our minds an dance about on stage, an didn't take too kindly to bein told when an where an even how to jump in fuckin bastard Nazi overtones – ALRIGHT!

At first, we took it on the chin, hangin in there with the promise of that draw turnin up sometime soonish. As it didn't materialize an it became obvious that it might never do, the small reserve of patience we had left became dangerously depleted. We started drinkin as soon as we arrived at the next venue, an things started to turn nasty. The lads were pissed off, pissed an a long way from home, an therefore a long way off from a guaranteed shitload of whatever we wanted.

It kicked off royal.

After gettin no joy from Gunter, we decided to turn to the punters in the club for a little help on the drugs front. They looked at us as if we were aliens as we tried, as pleasantly as we could, to get the request understood. Either our confusin north Manc accents had stumped them, or they were incredulous that the band were out in the crowd openly askin for drugs. Whatever the reason for their dumb countenance, it soon became apparent that the only outcome for a night like this would be a spill out on to the street for a drunken brawl. An that's exactly what happened. I think the final score was ten Germans on the deck an all British representatives still standin. It had nothin to do with the war, before you go drawin conclusions for our behaviour towards them, it's just that we simply weren't on a level with these blond-haired, blue-eyed, humourless sour Krauts.

The three Salford lads had such a ball that night, bouncin the locals across tables an chairs, that they decided to stick it out with the band for the whole duration of the tour. They'd stay behind in each town, do their graft an then catch us up at the next venue in time for the gig. They smashed it in every town an could afford to do as they pleased, stayin in all the same hotels as us. But then again, we weren't exactly overdoin it on the hotel front in those days, just your normal everyday Teasmade an trouser press in the corner kind of places – If we were lucky!

In every hotel they initialled the register with the letters SCW, standin, of course, for Salford Crime Wave. Perfect nonsense. The terrible trio swept through the country like the bubonic plague, leavin a trail of infestation of the criminal kind in their wake.

The mood of the tour was set. The big show was, however, yet to come, in some paltry two-bit town in France. Our reputations, by this time, preceded our arrival. This resulted in the unfortunate predicament of bein thrown out of the hotel we'd booked *before* we'd even stepped foot in the place. Undeterred by this minor setback, we took off down to the club to have a mooch about an set up the equipment. We were met with the same stony reception there too. We shrugged it off, an downed a few beers while waitin for the call to take to the stage.

It became glarinly obvious that they were tryin to do damage by just two songs into the set, when a couple of security men grabbed hold of Muzz for no apparent reason. He, in turn, grabbed hold of the microphone on the desk at the back to shout for help an the whole band an entourage downed tools in readiness for the battle to commence. The major part of the action took place in the changin rooms between the band an the security firm. Weapons of all descriptions appeared from nowhere addin weight to the already charged situation. The funniest was seein X swingin a big piece of scaffoldin around like a knight with his trusty sword, hittin people on the back of the neck as they came past. It was like a scene from a proper old time Charlie Chaplin film with full on slapstick effects, only this was for real an the digs hurt like fuck. I wouldn't have missed it for all the world though, it was a classic.

By the time it had spilled out into the street, the French police had arrived an there was a whole mass of people tryin to scatter themselves to avoid bein arrested. One of our lads from Salford was nabbed by the dibble. He hadn't seen then comin up behind even though we'd been screamin, 'DIBBLE! BEHIND YOU!'

It was too pantomime to be true an in the total confusion of the moment, he realized too late an couldn't make a run for it. He got frogmarched off to the dibble shop, literally. There was lunatic chaos goin off everywhere.

Our next port of call was the hospital to get a few stitches put in Muzzer's head. While hangin around the casualty department we came across one of the security men from the club, his arm hangin limply by his side. In the furore, one of our lot had completely wrenched it from the socket. He didn't look happy.

In truth, we didn't really have a lot to smile about ourselves. We had no hotel to go to an no money on us. We ended up kippin outside the police station, like a bunch of scruffy bastards, awaitin the release of our mate in the mornin. We woke early at the sound of the town comin to life. My mouth tasted like shit an we all had huge hangovers an bruised stiff limbs. To top it all, the kid we'd loyally been waitin for couldn't even go with us on the next leg of the journey.

We were off to Austria that day but it turned out he an one of the other grafters couldn't get in the country because of previous convictions. They decided to sit it out in the Dam, where they intended to get supplies together to meet us with back in Paris. Sounded a good scheme to me! Better late than never.

Things started to run a little smoother the minute we got out of reach of the Germans an the French. On hittin Austria, we scored a trip, so things must have been lookin up.

Now I'm no slacker when it comes to neckin trips but even I was taken by surprise by the mightiness of this weird little fucker. It sent me flyin sideways into a state of total disorientation. I couldn't decide the simplest of things – did I want my shoes on or off bein the main topic of debate in my head for the entire first gig there. I was in a complete quandary over the issue; I took my shoes off to bust a few moves, then decided, nah, that's not right! I sat down to put them back on again an tried to break some more moves, but that didn't feel right either. I spent the whole set tryin to work it out, utterly obsessed with the whole shoes on/shoes off thing, to the extent that I kept forgettin where I was an what I was supposed to be doin. Every time I remembered, I tried to do somethin about it, but this just seemed to exacerbate the problem further. The strange thing was, I was alright once I'd stepped off the stage, an proceeded to have a stormer of a night with the rest of the lads. Needless to say, it was one of the best, most memorable gigs of the tour – I think!

By some miracle, we made it back to Paris in one piece. An there we found the most beautiful of sights awaitin us at the hotel. The Salford lads had turned up trumps for us; everythin we needed an everythin we didn't need even was laid out like some baroque banquet, sparklin before our eyes. After the two weeks of burnin round Europe, clean as a nun's habit with not a drug in sight, we couldn't believe that we'd only just managed to get it together for the final gig. It wouldn't be happenin that way again, that *was* a cert.

Myself, I couldn't wait to get back home to the little scene I'd left brewin in the corner of The Hac. I was feelin gutted because I was sure I'd missed out on crucial new developments on the club scene, even though it had only been a few weeks since I'd discovered the plot. I had a gut feelin that this new thing was about to take off in a massive way, an that, once it started, it would happen fast an I didn't want to miss a single beat when it did. I needn't have worried. Everyone was still there, same as always, gettin pissed, whizzin their tits off an talkin a load of shite in corners.

I was out the night I returned home, anxious to see my new acquaintances an get back into the groove of things. I was fuckin flabbergasted by the reaction I got when I walked into The Haçienda. It was nothin to do with the band or anythin of the sorts, it was all about people literally runnin up to ask if I knew where they could get hold of these new E things. It seemed they'd heard of my ravins about them an had been waitin for me to get them back on track an to get things sorted for them. What a predicament; the only bastard in the crowd that knew how to get hold of the things wholesale. Here I was with thirty or so people houndin me to 'sort it out'. Of course, I put the order in for them, purely on a non-profit basis, an they received their E's just like they'd asked. The kid who'd got them together had never had an order so big. It was a fuckin riotous turnin point in the history of the club. It was a crazy sight, seein thirty or so people goin for it big style, centre stage, no messin. It was as if the clouds of an eternally dismal day had finally parted to let in the most brilliant rays of sunlight, the kind that warm the body right through. It was like lyin on a Caribbean beach in the middle of Manchester, no worries to plague the mind, no more fidgettin about in corners, paranoid about the way you look or dance, just goin for it an feelin on top of the fuckin world.

What a top release.

The switch had been flicked, the illuminations had been turned on an they were blazin. Nothin could dim that kind of brilliance, not even the law.

The followin week, an order for sixty was put in to the same kid. He couldn't believe it. It was at this point that he came clean an admitted that he an his partner were the drivin force behind the set-up. He thought I was makin a mint out of it but I explained that my money had gone into the kitty just like any-one else's, so he ended up with the exact amount he'd quoted every time. I wasn't interested in makin money out of friends. I was in a fuckin bang-off band, out every night surrounded by all my mates, havin a fuckin riotous ball. What more could I want?

Everyone was happy, ecstatically happy in fact.

On comin home from the tour, my girlfriend an I decided to move to another flat across town in Fallowfield. Edgerton Road in Fallowfield was where Mat an Karen an sometimes Pat lived. They were, an still are, Central Station Design, the team who designed all the album covers an posters for the Mondays an, in later years, the Grape. Mat an Pat also have the unfortunate bur-den to shoulder of bein X's cousins. We moved into the bottom flat in the huge old Victorian terrace where they occupied the top flat. The house had three levels an it wasn't long before another friend of ours took over the tenancy of the middle floor flat. It was a cosy set-up that lent itself conveniently to a party atmos-phere.

One exceptional night, we had decided to stay in an give our legs a rest when, around midnight, there came a knock on the door. I opened it to find X in a proper state in the doorway. He'd found out that while we'd been away on tour, his missis had been shaggin some other geezer an had actually left him for this other wanker. He was devastated, they'd been together for a few years by this time an he'd had no idea of what was comin up. To add insult to injury, he knew the other bloke really well an con-sidered him to be a prize prick. He was furious on top of bein deeply hurt; she'd humiliated him an it had driven him insane with anger an jealousy. Tanked up with Valium an beer, he'd completely smashed the flat where they'd lived together. In his blind rage he'd slashed his hands an arms badly an was bleedin all over the place. He had massive bumps on his head where he'd been buttin everythin in sight too. He stood there, drippin with blood, hurt an anguish twistin his face, askin for help. He was my mate an I didn't like to see him like this. I took him straight in an tried to chill him out.

'X, you're goin to be a top fuckin pop star, why are yer doin this over your bird goin astray on yer. There are plenty more fish in the sea, it's fuckin teemin with 'em, all waitin to get a little bit of Shaun Ryder for themselves. Come out with me tomorrow an see what you've been missin, see how things can change when you least expect it, overnight.'

I was of course talkin about comin down The Hac to do an E in with me an the growin army of party people that were startin to gather down there. I was sure that if he could get out of fillin himself with downers all the time, he'd soon perk up an get it together again. It has to be said that there were a lot of smackheads around at that time who managed to give up because they'd tried the E scene an liked it. People who'd never been out of their front rooms in years were known to transform in a matter of days into funky, struttin sex machines, dancin on stages an huggin relative strangers all night, every night. It was as though a generation had suddenly woken from a zombie-like existence an were goin double hard at livin to try an make up for the time they'd missed. I wanted X to get out there an see all this as it was happenin. I knew that once he'd got in there, there'd be no stoppin him.

I was right. He went from bein a ragin smackhead to a ragin E head in an instant.

Like I said, the whole house had been taken over with our friends by now an it was an unspoken agreement that the bottom an middle flats were used for pure partyin, every night, after the clubs threw out. The clubs all shut at two on the dot in those days so it was crucial that the party gaff was sorted out prior to goin out for the night. At first, it was just a small crowd of people crammin into the middle flat with a ghetto blaster, a bottle of brandy an a crate of beers. Later, the party spread to include the whole of the bottom two floors, with a top sound system installed permanently in the downstairs flat. There were girls off their fuckin nuts strippin for the lads an dancin all horny to the music, shaggin on the stairs, bongs in the kitchen; it was a full-on fuckin orgy of pleasure seekers an anythin went. It occasionally verged on the dangerously subversive at times as things got out of hand in the loved up environment. There were a few casualties who went a little too overboard in that department an lost the plot a bit, never to return. For the most part, though, everyone behaved themselves an kept a grip on reality. Most of the people involved had long waved goodbye to bein teenagers an therefore they weren't about to make a complete arse of themselves by losin it in public. What went on in private, of course, is a different matter altogether!

The parties raged nearly every night for about two months an the address became known to the locals as 'the hostel'. Unbelievably, hardly anyone complained about the noise comin from the house at all times of the day an night. Except perhaps the man next door who, after a particularly heavy session that had lasted three days or so, knocked to say that he was sufferin from exhaustion from lack of sleep an could we please keep the noise down. Exhausted from just bein next door to it! He should have been thankful he didn't live in the middle of it. I was fuckin completely knackered an in the thick of it with no escape mate.

There was an unassumin Asian family that lived nearly opposite the house who, one night, sent one of their clan over to see
what was goin on. He looked like their grandad an he had
donned his coolest hippie hat to come an investigate the apparent non-stop celebrations. He fitted in quite nicely, lookin for all
the world like a bona fide, top ganja smoker. You had the feelin,
on lookin into his wise old eyes, that he could tell this motley
crew a thing or two about weed. After all, he was from the right
corner of the world to know such things. I was spot on with my
judgement; while his family an his wife waited for the intrepid
explorer to return with an explanation for the constant din, he
was happily ensconced in a heavy smokin session, his eyes
sparklin as he lit yet another bong. He became a regular at the
gatherins, always takin up a quiet position, such as on the stairs,
away from the crowd, smokin to his heart's content. He looked
as if he'd found his nirvana in this cruel country at long last. No
problem there then!

Poor Pat an Karen tried desperately to keep their corner of
the house in order, but it was pretty tough for them at times with
all the mayhem goin on just down their stairs. The thing is, it was
all escalatin way out of anyone's grasp. The only way to tackle
it seemed to be to ride out the storm of parties an sit in hope that
it would all eventually burn itself out – or move on.

The Mondays were goin from strength to strength but still
not makin any money so it was decided that the band should go
on an Enterprise Allowance Scheme to keep off the dole an keep
the dole off our backs. This meant that we could now officially
operate as a bona fide band without the pressure of worryin
about annoyin trips to the dole office to sign on every other
week; it gets a bit tricky when you're tryin to sort out gigs
abroad.

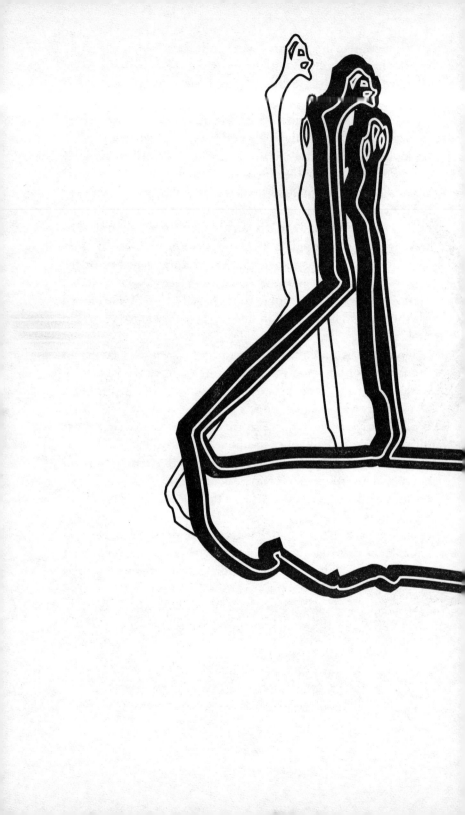

Just like anything that is good, too much of it for too long an you start to get bored with it. The parties in Edgerton Road were, at long last, comin to a natural end. People started to get on to the fact that there was a market for party gaffs in the post-two a.m. bracket an they started to open up all over the place. Advantage was also bein taken of the longer, warmer nights of approachin summer to arrange the odd outdoor event. The party scene had never been so good. All the time, though, I kept thinkin about the stories I'd been told about Ibiza: the clubs, the girls, the sun – the lot. I decided it was time to go check this place out for myself.

By the beginnin of the Ibiza summer season there were twelve of us on a four-hour flight, our meagre stashes stashed, an clubbin gear packed, ready for the party. I say meagre stash because the twenty or so percys I'd got together for the trip had been in my pocket the previous night in The Haçienda, an inevitably they had all vanished within an hour of me bein out. So there we were, on our way to party land with no proper resources, no traveller's cheques, not even an apartment to go to, just a plane ticket an a couple of stray T-shirts that I found stuck to the linin of my pocket. Two out of twenty ain't too bad, I suppose.

I didn't really give a fuck about such minor problems, to be honest. I'd travelled around with far less in my pockets in the past, an I knew that the future held somethin a bit special after the reaction we'd had at the last gig.

By this time everyone had heard of or had taken an E. There was an incredible explosion of fans that coincided with the onset of the tidal wave of interest in the drug. No coincidence I say. Just how our fan base was changin became apparent at the gig in The Haçienda, just before the summer kicked in properly. It's not that I don't think our music was good enough in its own right to have attracted such a followin, but it was fuckin lucky for it to be happenin when it did, put it that way. I knew, after that night, that any future gigs would be divided into roughly two halves. On the one side there would be the punters buzzin their nuts off, almost slobberin in anticipation of the event. On the other side, there would be the punters that were a bit astounded by it all, but, by the end, would be wantin to get in on the buzz they could see all around – badly. All the rest could fuck off home an sip their cocoa for all I cared. They obviously didn't know a good thing when they saw it.

I was busy thinkin about all this as I sat on the plane to Ibiza, mullin over the changes that were goin on all around an smilin quietly to myself. It had been a top fuckin night at the gig. I'd felt completely at home with where I was at, partly because I was occupyin the very spot on the stage that I had made my home in the last couple of months, an partly because I could see the audience respondin to the music in a way that they never had before. For the first time, I'd seen the recognition in their faces that they knew the chaotic scene in front of them made perfect sense for the times that they were livin through. The rest of the band were beginnin to feel that there was no turnin back now that we had come this far. It was beginnin to dawn on us that this was for real an that the record buyin public genuinely liked us.

We were a bunch of fuckin hooligans with a big bunch of fuckin hooligan fans, an we were on our way to the top. That's what the press was sayin anyway, an we all know they don't lie!

I was sufficiently pleased with the direction that things were goin in anyway an I was lookin forward to soakin up some serious sun an fun on this two week break. What I was breakin from at the time I don't know, life wasn't exactly tedious back then. Really, I was just flittin from one party scene to another. A change is as good as a rest! Thinkin about it, I had no mortgage, no kids, no car, no bills – no worries. I didn't need to think twice – just off mans, like a shot with no lookin back.

I'd heard that Bernard was goin to be out in Ibiza at the same time as us, recordin an album with New Order. I resolved to look him up when we arrived. I think he'd resolved to have nothin to do with our lot, havin heard on the grapevine that we were on our way. Ibiza, it turned out, was too small to be able to hide for long.

As soon as we hit the ground, we set off for some apartments that one of the girls in our lot had stayed in a few years previously. She was convinced that the owner would remember her from back then so we gave it a shot. I didn't ask why he would remember her.

My mind raced ahead to thinkin about who I could go an visit to boost supplies. I'd been given a verbal list of vague addresses of people that I sort of knew from back home who were on the island. Things weren't lookin good. Thankfully, it turned out that some of the other girls with us were a little more organized than the rest. One of the girls had brought a *small* bag of whizz with her. Another had made sure there was enough weed on board for a good few days to allow us to settle into things nicely. We managed to blag the apartments, got out the kit an began to relax in the knowledge that things were turnin out alright. Every now an then a few sharp digs came my way about givin all our stash out at home but what can I say – I just can't keep a good thing to myself.

The first afternoon passed without a hitch, sittin round the pool, drinkin beers an generally feelin fuckin ACE to be away again. As the night began to fall, everyone got their act together to go an hire cars. Bein stuck round the peninsula from where all the action was goin off an realizin the clubs that were really worth a visit were all situated either inland or down the other end of the island in Ibiza Town, it was essential to get the transport front sorted out quickly. Pissed up, lager fuelled San Antonio was alright for daytime activities, but a fuckin pain in the arse to get a real party goin at night.

I was gutted. I didn't have a licence to my name. I was even more gutted when they all started to turn up on mopeds; I wouldn't even be able to cadge a lift anywhere. I was ready to go into a top sulk when I remembered Bernard across the island in his plush recordin studio surroundins with a sparklinly clean drivin licence. I knew he'd lend it me to hire a car if I could get up there to see him. He'd understand.

I got Leah, a friend of ours, to drive me up to the studios. I had to talk Bernard round to the idea for all of twenty minutes; it was like takin sweets off a baby! I even got a handwritten pass to all the best clubs from the owner of the studios. Result! The only condition of the deal was that I was to call round with the car to take B out every night. It sounded like a fair deal to me! Thankin him heartily for his kind trust I sped off down the road to get a car sorted. There was just the one hitch with the plan, which nearly tripped me up at the last hurdle. The bloke in the hire shop looked intently at the drivin licence an then back at me. He commented on how amazinly young I looked for thirty-three! The bullshit poured out of my mouth in hot an gushin streams. Phew! What a charmer. He fell for it an I was off.

That first night was the most disastrous night of the holiday, everythin went fuckin sideways within a few hours of us all gettin transported up.

First of all, one of the kids came buzzin back from the shops with his newly hired scooter, rippin up an down the road like he was on some top Kawasaki. He'd literally only gone up the road when, on the way back, he got the speed wobbles, started skiddin like Torvill an Dean all over the road an ended up smackin head first into a stone wall. It was birdies tweetin round the head time. An ambulance arrived an he was whisked off to hospital to be stitched up an kept in under observation. One down, eleven to go.

While in the hospital, his girlfriend looked into his holiday insurance to see if he was covered for accidents of this nature. There was zero cover for moped accidents written in minuscule writin at the very bottom of the policy. It was goin to cost over £700 to get him out.

Meanwhile, he'd been stitched an cleaned up but was bein kept in an doped as they waited for him to pay for the treatment. We decided there was nothin fundamentally wrong with him an after a few hours' deliberation, it was agreed that there was nothin for it but to break him out of the hospital an do a runner. Little did we realize how it would come on top later, we were just up for it at the time. It was a funny stunt though.

I was on the crack team that was dispatched to get him out. He had wires attached to his wrists that were unceremoniously ripped out an tossed aside. It was all just part of the conspiracy to make him look ill an keep him in longer anyway. He didn't need painkillers, he needed his friends! We draped him by the arms, doped up an in his pyjamas, round our necks an dragged him off to the waitin car, tryin to look as inconspicuous as possible. It was a fuckin blinder of a break, a resoundin success.

By the time we'd managed to get him out an away from the hospital, it was teemin it down with rain. Fuckin hell, I thought, what else could go wrong? It had all seemed so idyllic a mere few hours ago.

No one was goin out that first night. I couldn't sit still, even with the pourin rain bouncin off the sunloungers, I had to go out. Besides, I'd promised Bernard that I'd go an pick him up. By the time I'd talked one of the other lads into accompanyin me to help with directions, it was gettin quite late. Undeterred, we set off with the intention of bringin B back down to our gaff for a drink with everyone else.

The studio was situated well inland up a thousand tiny back lanes an it was pitch black. To cap it all, the rain wasn't easin up. In short, the drivin conditions were fuckin horrendous an this, coupled with my renowned shit sense of direction, was turnin the journey into a bit of a crusade.

As we neared the studio, by reducin the concentric circles around the area for a good hour or so, the full Mediterranean storm peaked, an cranin my neck to see the sign ahead through the drivin rain I ran the car up a high kerb an off the road, bucklin the suspension right back underneath the wheel arch.

I think the road sign I'd been tryin to read had been a warnin that the road narrowed just ahead. Not much cop on a pitch-black night in the middle of a torrential downpour.

We were fucked.

No way would the car go forward. The wheel was catchin an jammin fast; we were goin nowhere. I looked at The Chef, the kid I'd brought with me, an he looked at me. Obviously, I'd have to stay with the car an he'd have to run up to the studio to get some help. It wasn't that far an if he ran really quickly, he wouldn't get that wet. I sat in the dry, warm car an waited. I found out that the car did actually go in reverse, but only in reverse. Tryin to spin the car round so that I could maybe reverse some of the way up, I realized that it would only go in a straight line also. The wheel would not turn at all. It was a long shot an the car wasn't havin it. I sat with the stoop of a defeated man, starin absently out into the bleak night an waited. Bastard!

It felt like a fuckin lifetime had passed before they got back. The Chef came back with B. He was soaked to the skin. Neither of them looked happy. There was nothin we could do to put things right.

Come the mornin, I went round to see the bloke in the hire shop. I told them I needed a new car because the other had had a blow out resultin in a crash. They gave me a new one just like that an in return for their gesture of goodwill, I told them where to find the old one. Sorted. I don't know what all the panic was about.

Eventually, we managed to get it together for a night out an Ibiza opened up before us like the magical adult playground it is, showin us its true colours. There's nothin quite like sittin in an open-air club in the mornin after the night before, watchin the sky turn all shades of the rainbow with the sun comin up an the brandy still goin down. It was the whole picture that I'd been waitin to see an more. In the pastel shades of mornin, with the sun's rays spillin across the whitewashed walls of the club, it seemed like paradise. The buzz of the club wound down to a contented hum as the clubbers sat decidin where to go for breakfast. I was beginnin to really enjoy myself an at last it began to feel like a real holiday.

As we'd arrived right at the beginnin of the season, the main club we'd gone to see wasn't open yet an so we spent our time in KU an Pacha. In the latter, it took me a whole week's worth of visits to work out that I'd been usin the girls' khazies, liberally slappin on all the perfumes an lotions without payin, much to the delight of the attendant who I later realized was a screamin transvestite. I thought at the time that they were bein very generous puttin out all this after-sun stuff for the poor, ravaged, baked an peelin clubbers like myself. I hadn't realized also that the podiums were there solely for the paid dancers. Every night

I was flingin myself up there, grinnin away like a madman an they never once tried to throw me off. Don't know why.

Bernard was busy doin his own bit to keep the rock 'n' roll myth goin, I seem to recall, by resortin to the classic attention-seekin blackout in the middle of a club. I know for a fact that he thinks to this day that I spiked him, but that's just not my style. I'm sorry B, you just have to admit it, you keeled over from your own doin. Pernod an E is a lethal combination when all's said an done. It was a bit strange though: one minute he was bobbin about with the rest of us an the next he was out cold on a stone seat. To make matters worse, it was rainin again an bein an open-air club, there was little escape from gettin wet. The rain streamed down B's cheeks an dripped off the end of his nose. He just carried on snorin like a baby, mouth gapin wide open.

It was decided that we should bundle him into our car an drive the short distance back to our apartment before he caught pneumonia. Halfway home, he came round an demanded that I drive at two miles an hour so that he could keep the car door open while he threw up. Alright, I was a bit pissed myself an was findin it difficult to keep the car in a straight line in the drivin rain when I realized that the best policy was to follow the white line in the middle of the road. To see the white line in the middle of the road, I had to drive with my head stickin out of the window, as you do. It was a sight to be seen. The two girls sat silently in the back, jaws clenched, prayin for a safe delivery home. We made it an everyone crashed with the exhaustion of it all.

B came round the next day to find he'd missed his flight home. Shame. We'd have to do it all again to pass some time till the next flight.

The ten day break was over quickly. There were only a few days left before we were due to fly home an we'd hardly seen the sun. I got away from the others with my girlfriend to Formenterra, a small, very quiet island that lies a few miles away. We hardly had any dough left after all the clubbin an couldn't afford to stay in the hub of things any longer. Apart from that, we were knackered. It was only a short ferry ride over, which is probably a good job the state we were in. After seein the unspoilt beaches an undeveloped landscape, we decided it would be perfect for a few days' rest in the sun, away from all the insanity.

Vastly restored an topped up to the brim with vitamin D we ventured back over to Ibiza for the last night of frivolities. We were glowin all over – an I really do mean all over – from two days' solid sunbathin on an empty beach. We hit the town with renewed fervour, buzzin to fuck over our newly acquired suntans.

The Amnesia Club was open on the last night of our stay an we had a fuckin ball, havin secured a top source for sortin everybody out. It was another open-air club, packed out with all the top grafters, beautiful girls an yet another gaggle of trannies struttin their stuff. It was an exclusive kind of place which, as is usually the way, translates as expensive. It didn't matter as it was the last night anyway. No one had the slightest intention of goin home with change in their pockets.

Dehydrated with birdcage breath an eyes barely open, we hit the airport with our hastily repacked bags an very little in the way of taxi fare for the other end. I seem to have spent a lifetime nursin hangovers in airports, an it never gets any easier. This time, however, I had good reason to count my lucky stars as all I had to do was board the right plane an go back to sleep till we hit Manchester Airport. Pity then my poor friend, Eric, who after havin made a miraculous recovery from his scooter crash, had spent the remainder of the holiday on the run, movin from apartment to apartment, leggin it from the hospital mafiosi. They wanted his dough an they were serious. So serious, in fact, that they set up a welcomin party just for him at the airport, takin him off to his own private cell until he promised to pay up. Why is it that the worst nightmares always appear to begin just at the moment that you are in chronic need of a good kip to rebalance the jigglin brain cells?

Utterin sincere words of sympathy an encouragement, we watched as he disappeared into the interrogation room – an then we left. Well the plane was waitin, what else could we do? Actually, his girlfriend did stay behind to help sort the pickle out, so our consciences were salved a little. They followed on a few days later after havin the money wired over to cover the costs.

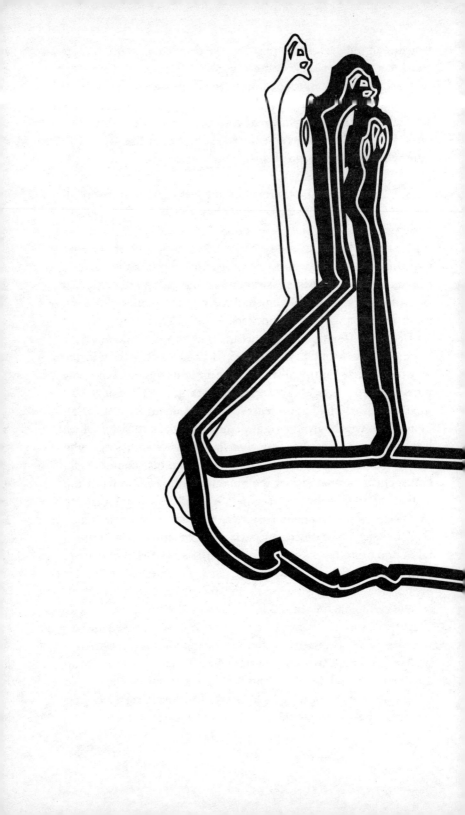

Back at the flat in Fallowfield, X's feet had become a real bone of contention. No amount of air freshener could remove the rank odour. It hadn't been too bad prior to us goin away, he'd been polite enough to keep his shoes on, except for bedtime. While we'd been away though, he'd made himself more comfortable, paddin about everywhere in his diseased socks, infestin the carpets with stinkiness. Radical action was needed. I moved out.

My girlfriend, sick of all the goins on, had in fact already moved out. She'd decamped to her friend's house on the other side of Manchester before we'd set out on the holiday but so much had been happenin at that time that I'd barely noticed. I'd not taken the move too seriously anyway, assumin she'd be back at some point. She wasn't. On returnin from the holiday, she went straight back to Blackely an stayed there. She'd said I was too insensitive. Can't think why.

So there I was, homeless, single, young an on the verge of becomin the most unlikely pop star in the business. Maybe it was my increased intake of this new wonder drug, I don't know, but I was findin it all a bit fuckin confusin to say the least. Luckily, I had my new team of mates around me, who spared no expense in gettin me set up an back on my feet. These lads were rakin it in by this time; the transition period in the main clubs from a uniform diet of whizz an booze to everyone gettin turned on to the E scene had been amazinly rapid. Hundreds of people had approached me to find where to buy the tabs. I didn't want to be personally caught up in the business an merely steered the inquisitive in the right direction. The suppliers were more than happy with my unwittin promotion of their bumbles an consequently took me under their wing, offerin unlimited use of the luxury apartments, top of the range motorbikes an all-expenses-paid trips to London to see first hand how massively the scene had taken off down there. How could I refuse? I was constantly out at places like Schoom an Heaven, soakin in the electric atmosphere an meetin the organizers an DJs who were pullin the whole thing together, playin the new sounds freshly imported from the clubs in Ibiza.

I was buzzin like a kid let loose in a sweet shop, wearin the best clothes, pamperin myself with saunas, eatin in the best restaurants an, to round it all off, stayin in the luxury of five star hotels. For someone who was out every night of the week, I was bearin up pretty well. Paradoxically, it was the biggest drugs binge I'd ever embarked on an yet I was treatin my body to the best food an the healthiest skincare regime that my face had ever known. All that dancin an sweatin an eatin an pamperin was raisin my stamina levels, tonin me up an fillin me out, all in one go.

I felt fuckin fantastic – party on.

The shows with the Mondays were gainin in strength as we began to feel the growin swell of the audience behind us all the way. The band were on top form, neckin E's like Smarties an turnin in blindin performances as a consequence of their new found confidence on stage. The buzz had given the whole package a new dimension an the stage was becomin more an more animated, givin a much more visually arrestin experience for the audience.

X began to swagger about, more at ease with his stage persona than ever before, smirkin at the crowds an preenin himself, playin them up with barely discernible one-liners, more to amuse himself than anyone else. The more he took the piss out of them, the more they loved it. I can honestly say that at that point in time, bein in the band an doin gigs was fuckin good fun. It still felt like a top blag an the band remained genuinely amazed at how seriously everyone else took the whole thing.

The way things were goin we needed another album out soon, to strike while the iron was hot. We put our business heads on to get a strategy together of how we wanted to go about this next album. The only strategy we kept comin up with was Martin Hannett. This went against everyone else's wishes, but we were adamant that this was the man for us. We'd heard various stories over the years about Martin an the *unusual* way he went about his business. For us, it was a simple decision, nothin to do with Factory protocol. We liked the stuff he'd worked on in the past an couldn't give a fuck about his personal wrangles with the other Factory heads. X dug his heels in: he wanted Martin Hannett, The Legend, to work on our next album an that was that.

We just knew that he'd be right up our street, on our wavelength. The man was off his fuckin rocker in a musically genius kind of way. It was the magic ingredient we thought we required, to slightly adjust our sound an take it one step beyond the already shiftin boundaries of mainstream music.

Before they were willin to take what they considered to be a risk, in takin Martin on as our producer, Factory wanted us to do a track at Yellow T to prove that together we could cut the mustard. They were still unsure of the unlikely combination of a bunch of roughneck lads, completely off their heads, mixin with an old timer who was similarly off his head, comin up with anythin remotely feasible in the way of a saleable record. We went off with Martin to record 'Wrote for Luck'. Admittedly, it was nothin like the tune that hit the charts, in fact Martin had been so nervous about doin it that it came out soundin a complete mumbled, jumbled mess where you couldn't really tell what was supposed to be goin on.

Even so, the potential for the track to be developed was there; we were all confident that it could be salvaged an reworked into somethin mega. Besides, X was still adamant that Martin was the man for us. The way he had to get completely off his trolley to get into the work appealed to X, who could relate to it immensely. We were sure that if we could get Martin to chew on a few E's, we'd have it cracked an a whole Pandora's Box of ideas would come floodin into the studio.

In the end, the track was taken to two prominent London DJs, Paul Oakenfold an Steve Osborne, to be remixed. They'd played at the clubs over in Ibiza, had seen first hand the rapid turn-about in the essence of club culture as a result of the ecstasy influence an, therefore, knew exactly the sound that would work in the clubs back here. No amount of E's poured down Martin's neck could budge him from his 80s trip. He didn't understand the essence of what we were about or wanted to become. That's not to say that the work he was doin wasn't of any use, it's just that he hadn't looked around an caught on to the vibe that was evolvin out on the street an in the clubs. Still, he did take our music to a different level, givin us the key to open the door to the future, even though he didn't actually fling the door open himself.

We were shortly sent off to record the album, which was eventually to be known as *Bummed*, in a two-bit town in North Yorkshire, of all places. It seems the plan was to place us in the most backwater studio in Britain so that we wouldn't be too tempted to indulge in class A pastimes.

We took our own an set about shaping the small town of Driffield to fit around our needs.

Driffield, a town that time forgot, so borin that the British Army put a base there: a place where people are sent to learn how to behave – or not.

I could foresee that the squaddie business was goin to be a bit of a nause in the one an only club in the town. It was a problem we were goin to have to tackle head on if we were to get any fun of a night without gettin our heads kicked in every time. The inevitable rumpus began to develop as soon as we sauntered in an began downin pints in what they saw as their territory. They really began to take exception to us when the local women started to veer in our direction. We were E'd-up an dancin all over the gaff an they didn't like it one bit.

One big motherfucker of a squaddie started flickin beer mats in my direction. It couldn't be ignored. I had to front it out there an then.

'What's your fuckin problem?'

'You, ya fackin off ya heed!'

This Scottish geezer started goin on with himself, risin up to his full height, ready to take the confrontation full on into a fight. He was itchin to get to grips with all of us. I wasn't about to be his punchbag for releasin his pent-up frustration on. It wasn't my fault he'd joined the army, the straight bastard. He turned out to be a sergeant major with the vocal cords to go with his rank. He stood inches away from my face screamin with all the authority he could muster. 'Don't I scare ya!'

'Nah.'

The whole thing was strangely amusin from where I stood, deep in the throes of an ecstasy trip. All I could think was that he'd bust a blood vessel if he didn't chill out. There was nothin for it but to give them all a nibble on a tab each.

Problem solved. Within half an hour they were jumpin about with us instead of on us; it was a worthwhile investment. Of course, every time we saw them they wanted more, but at least it kept the peace. We gave them bits of draw from time to time, too, for good measure to enhance the harmony. Peace never comes cheap.

Repercussions from a slight mishap I'd had in the recent past in Manchester meant that I had to dismiss myself from the Driffield proceedins to take a few trips back to the city to appear in court. It was not a pleasant experience. I was hoppin about on pins, scared shitless that I might go down, shatterin the promise I'd made to myself when I'd walked out of borstal an back into society. I felt a fuckin idiot for lettin myself down at a time when I should have had no worries at all. My future up to this point had been lookin sparklin, we were ridin high in the press, were busy cuttin a new album, an the girls were flockin round in droves. The court case was becomin a bit of a top nause. I was doin a lot of drugs too an the ups an downs weren't helpin matters.

It was a pretty serious charge I was facin an I couldn't believe how I'd managed to tangle myself up in a mess which, fundamentally, had very little to do with me. I'd been tryin to do a favour for one of the lads an it had seriously backfired on me, like you wouldn't believe.

About a month previously, one of the lads had asked me if I'd give him a hand in takin a bike up to Altringham to sell. He had a hire car that I could follow him up in, so that I could give him a lift back when he'd offloaded the bike. Sounded kosher to me. We set off, my mate rippin ahead on this bike, drivin as if he were on a getaway, dodgin in an out of the traffic like a top idiot. I tried to keep up without lookin conspicuous with the speed we were doin. I managed to get in front of him in an attempt to slow his progress down to a relatively legal speed. It only served to encourage him all the more as he took the manoeuvre to be a challenge. Daft bastard. I clocked an unmarked police car up ahead just at the very moment that my mate seized the opportunity to overtake, givin it full throttle an really playin the road for all to see. I tried to flag him down on his way past my car but his focus was set dead ahead. The police pulled him within seconds.

Now, you have to remember that I was doin a lot of E about this time, which does very little for the human brain in terms of thinkin on your feet an applyin the best logic to stressful situations. That day, I was bein particularly slack. In a panic, thinkin that the lad in front knew nothin about the bike, I decided to pull in behind them to give him a hand. As I did so, I realized that I knew diddly shit about the bike myself an not only that, I wasn't in a legal position to be drivin the car I was in either. Fuckin shambles or what?

They nicked us both an trawled us straight down to the police station. The strange thing is that because I was E'd up, I felt indignant that I really was innocent of committin any serious crime. Then they came back from searching the car I'd been drivin. It was rammed with bits of draw that had been left languishin in side pockets, on the floor, in the glovebox, you name it. These lads had more money than sense. There was also a small selection of spirit bottles, just in case a party shout went out, an to top it all, the essential bag of E's. I was done for. To add insult to injury, they let the other lad out after he'd given them a false ID an here was I, pleadin total innocence, givin my own name an address, thinkin everythin was sweet.

I sat in the stinkin police cell, waitin. How the fuck did I end up here in this fuckin hole with the stench of dibble all around? It was a smell I thought I'd never have to encounter again, but here I was frettin once more like a dumb twat about sloppin out an countin days.

Eventually, they let me out on bail. I was bein charged with takin a car without the owner's consent (TWOC), an possession of cannabis. They weren't quite sure what to make of the little bag of pills; I think I was probably one of the very first people in the city to be nicked with a stash of ecstasy in tow. It was a lucky break: in just under one year from that time, to be caught in possession of anythin more than two of the little pills was taken very seriously, an could earn you a short stretch inside. It was a panic reaction by the authorities in the face of an avalanche of the new drugs floodin the black market. There was no legislation for ecstasy at the time that I was taken in because they simply hadn't encountered the drug before.

The way I saw it, it was irrelevant anyway, as I was pleadin not guilty all the way down the line. The only charge they could get to stick was the TWOC business an then they would have to concede that if the car wasn't mine, the drugs weren't mine either. They would be right of course.

It took a good few train journeys backwards an forwards from the studio in Driffield to Manchester to settle the case. Tony Wilson played an absolute blinder in court for me, givin a sterling character reference an outlinin the bejewelled path to stardom that I was about to be travellin. They were convinced an I was charged with just the TWOC, which carried a hefty fine of £700. Given the circumstances, I couldn't grumble.

My problems were seriously dwarfed a few weeks later by an encounter while on a mission up to Blackpool for a night out. We'd stopped off at a house along the way to pick up some money an to take a welcome spliff break before hittin the town. I'd met the lads we were visitin in Ibiza a few months earlier an the conversation flowed easily. Everyone was in good humour, sippin beers while decidin where to go that evenin. The relaxed mood was shattered by the sudden arrival of a lad I didn't know too well. He burst into the room an began shoutin his fuckin head off about his family at the television.

I thought he'd gone fuckin mad for a minute, he really had lost it. It was a few moments before I could register what he was so upset about. There was a news item on the TV, it was the first broadcast of the Lockerbie disaster. The plane had crashed, only hours earlier, right on top of this kid's family home.

'That's my shed, that's my gatepost. That's my house.'

The kid was screamin, hysterical. His family was dead. He looked around the room, his eyes frantically dartin from one person to the next as he cried out for someone to lend him a car. He was trapped in a cripplin moment of realization. The shock was visibly ripplin through his body in waves. I'd never seen anyone in such an acute state of pain an confusion. No one knew what to say or do. We sat there like dumb, mute bastards while this poor kid's heart was bein torn to shreds in front of us. The raw human emotion, stripped bare an bleedin, was surreal. I almost didn't believe what was happenin. I glanced at the others. They sat motionless, eyes unblinkin, hardly darin to breathe, stunned into silence. No one offered their car. No one put their hands in their pockets even. Fuck! I'd never felt so inadequate in all my life.

As suddenly as he'd arrived, he was gone again, wild with desperation to get up to Scotland, to see the destruction an know that it was real. He stole a car an drove himself. We should have given him the help he needed. Someone should have taken him to Scotland. The police arrested him for stealin the car. The tragedy worsened. He became permanently, mentally scarred. The large sum of money he received in the wake of the tragedy was useless: it couldn't begin to fill the gapin void it had left in his life.

I saw him out in The Haçienda some time after the accident, trying to spend all his money, his inheritance, on everyone around him. Pullin him to one side, I asked him to put his money away an think about what he was doin. I tried to reason with him to see sense, to see the importance of makin the money last.

Not long after, he went to Thailand. People assumed he'd gone to sort his head out away from all the crap at home. Word came back that he'd died, alone, in some hotel room. I was gutted for him. I was gutted about the way we'd all handled the situation so badly. I felt as if we'd failed the test of humanity, even though I knew deep down that there wasn't really much we could have done to lessen the blow.

That whole fateful life an death thing is just too fuckin strange to dwell on sometimes.

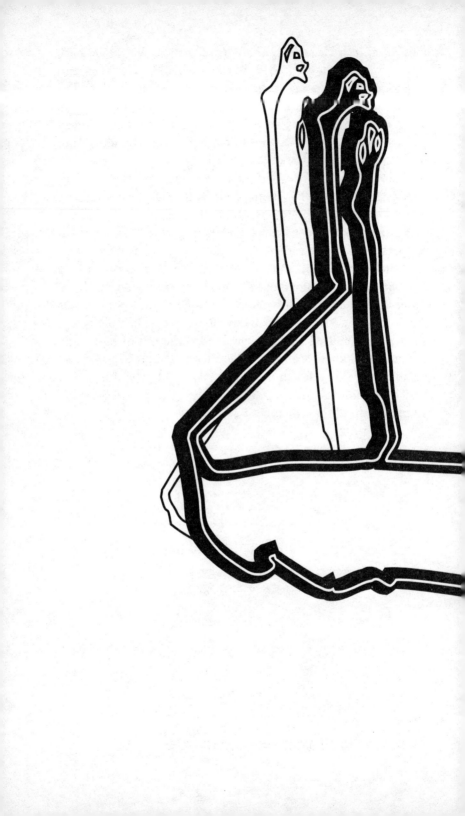

Anyway, back on the music side of things, *Bummed* was released to a baffled reception from the critics. They thought they liked it, but weren't quite sure. Maybe it was an acquired taste.

Some time later we were gettin ready to do the legendary gig at the Free Trade Hall. It was the night before the gig, an the band were supposed to be givin it one final practice before the big event, but you could tell that X was in no mood for it an was lookin round about for any excuse to get out of doin it. The perfect opportunity reared itself in the shape of Horse. He sauntered over, oblivious to the sudden about turn in X's mood. 'Yer big nose cunt!'

Startled by the completely unprovoked, aggressive verbal assault from his brother, Horse instantly rose to the bait, givin X the perfect chance to repeat the insult. 'You what!'

'You 'eard, yer big nose cunt!'

The shit hit the fan, right on target, an sprayed the furore out into the street. I decided to take a step back, I couldn't be arsed gettin involved because it was always a handbags affair with the two of them anyway. Apart from that, it usually provided some damn fine entertainment.

Horse quickly got the upper hand in the skirmish, bloodyin X's nose. Lookin very happy with himself over the small victory, he turned to jump in his car to make a quick exit while he was still on top. He wasn't quick enough. X had jumped over the bushes into a garden an scanned about for a brick to smash the car with. Just as Horse was about to start up an go, the brick came flyin into the street, smashin straight through the car window. I'm chucklin away to myself on the sidelines by now, this was quality entertainment from the Ryder brothers.

The curtains up an down the road began to twitch with all the commotion an a few brave neighbours actually came out into the street, threatenin to call the police into the proceedins. It didn't make the slightest difference to the warrin brothers as they carried on regardless, blind rage stamped all over their kippers.

Horse emerged back out of the car as X came leapin back out of the garden, ready for the second round. He lunged at Horse, sinkin his teeth into his nose an snarlin like a rabid pitbull. Horse began to panic. This was fast approachin a hospital situation an he began to plead with me to help. By this time, I'd seen enough an was beginnin to get a little nervous about it becomin a stretch in the police cells the night before an important gig. I stepped in to try an prise them apart. It was ferocious stuff an in the scuffle, one of them bit me on the thumb. Bastard! I resolved never to get involved with splittin them up again, not unless I had a large stick an a tranquillizer gun to hand.

The followin night it was pure pandemonium at the Free Trade Hall where the guest list threatened to outnumber the people with tickets. There were, in fact, a couple of hundred on the list but many more considered it their God-given right to be on it also. I'd never been in such demand an couldn't decide if it was a good feelin or a major pain in the arse.

There were trade disputes goin on out in the street in the front of the venue as rival merchandising set-ups argued the toss over who should be on the patch. It was kickin off all over. Suddenly, everyone wanted a piece of the cake. I just wanted to get as completely out of it as possible. I didn't think I could make it on to the stage in front of all the madness otherwise.

The pre-gig problems reached crisis point when the doormen, in their infinite wisdom, tore up the guest list an refused to allow anyone else in. I suppose they thought it would be a simple solution to the perplexin task of matchin heads in a heavin crowd to names on bits of paper. The reaction was to steam in in force, rushin the door in a show of strength. There was little the security could do in the face of such an angry mob chargin at the entrance. It was later reckoned that about 700 stormed in to swell the already packed crowd to the maximum possible for the size of the venue. It was heavin out in the front of the house.

Reports filtered back to the band sittin nervously consumin large amounts of alcohol an any other substance to hand to get them through the next couple of hours. The adrenalin was pumpin in my veins an no matter how many drugs of various descriptions I threw down my neck, I just couldn't get stoned enough to cope. I came to the conclusion that an acid would maybe do the trick. It didn't, so I necked another. Fuckin hell, it's a good job that we had to get on an do the show soon after or I could have been stuck there all night tryin out different combinations to put myself into a coma, literally.

Obviously, it soon became apparent that the trips were a major mistake. The sight of all those gurnin an sweatin faces, packed in like sardines, completely took my already short breath away. It was absolutely rammed full. Even the third tier was open an full to the brim an that hadn't been opened for years because it was considered too unsafe. The whole fuckin gaff looked mightily unsafe from where I was standin. I was utterly gobsmacked by the turnout an the way the audience responded when we first walked on stage. Alright, so a good few of them were our mates out there, but it was still a scary scene to deal with on acid. I knew as soon as the music started up that I'd taken far too many drugs, even for me, an that's sayin somethin. The rush I was gettin up there was enormous, like a tidal wave of shock washin right over my head an makin me feel unpleasantly sick an totally fuckin fantastic all at the same time. I didn't know whether I wanted to sit down an throw up or stomp around an laugh my bollocks off. Woah, the first couple of tunes were spent doin my best to just keep my head from blowin off an stomach contents down. By the third or so tune, I'd completely lost my body, somethin bigger than me had taken over control of the old arms an legs. I took a back seat somewhere in the top of my head as my body moved around the stage of its own free will – all I had to do was fly along with it an smile. The gig seemed to be over in no time at all.

On the way back down off the stage I spotted my girl, Debs, an grabbed hold of her to steady myself. Woo hoo, that felt good; somethin normal goin on to ground myself with. There was pure sweat pumpin out of me, as though I'd just stepped straight out of a sauna. My heart was leapin about like a super ball in a lift shaft, I thought I'd never regain my senses an slow down. Fuck, I needed a gallon or two of water, I was dehydrating to the point of meltdown an I needed to lie down somewhere nice an cool an quiet to get my shit together. It took me over an hour an a good few fat spliffs to come back down to earth an feel somethin close to normal again.

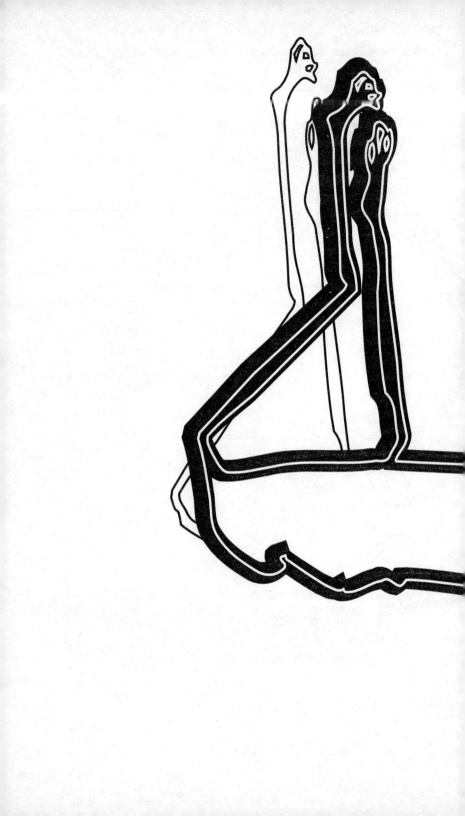

We'd arrived.

The next month or so was spent on the road, burnin about the country from town to town, tryin to convert everyone to our madness. A small mob of Mancs came along on the tour to offer their support at every stop, an to help put the people in the know.

There was a top feelin of togetherness an love even among the band: six fuck-ups comin together to make one massive right. Singularly, we were nothin, but united, we were stormin it. It was the first time that we'd all felt good enough about the abilities of the band to relax an accept that we really were goin somewhere at last.

There was still no dough rollin in though, a major drawback of signin to Factory, but they were givin us a free rein to take the band in whichever direction we wanted an so the sacrifice didn't seem too bad for the moment. The wages we were receivin were actually pitiful – a mere £150 a week, topped up by a £40 Enterprise Allowance that we were still claimin.

With the continuin success of the gigs an the constant generous support of the music press, we thought that it would surely only be a matter of time an patience before we could begin to reap the rewards. I didn't like Nathan though, an occasionally secret doubts crept into my head an I delighted in givin him as hard a time as possible, just in case he wasn't up to the mark an would let us down. He could never understand what he'd done to deserve it an the truth is, it was about what he might do in the future rather than what had been. I didn't think he was strong enough to hold the outfit together in the face of giant success an I felt it was my duty to constantly test his armour for that telltale chink.

A message filtered through from one of my mates who'd been workin on the continent doin bootleggin an ticket toutin at the big gigs. His little firm was off on another jaunt soon to do the Pink Floyd an Simple Minds shows in Denmark an Sweden. It was a graft by day an party all night set-up an it sounded pretty fuckin good to me. There was one condition in me joinin them out there: I had to get him a kit bag together on tick till we got back an he would sort me a top drink out as part of the deal. I had the kit packed an was ready for the off before you could say press conference comin up.

I did check that nothin was on the horizon in the immediate future an took great pleasure in seein the colour drain from Nathan's face as I told him of my plans. To be fair, I did promise to call back home a couple of times to see if anythin was about to happen. Things were buzzin with the band an there was a big chance that I might just be needed to do some press or somethin at a moment's notice, but I was no puppet about to sit around waitin for a record company or manager to organize my life when I still needed to earn myself a crust to survive. Pay me an I'll stay was the message. You have to feed your soldiers or they can't fight the battle. I took off the mantle of pop star an set off to join my mates, £300 to cover my ex's burnin in my pocket.

I was buzzin my socks off, glad to be doin somethin else after bein on the road for a few months, seein the same faces day in an day out. Although there were always good times on tour with the band, bein out of the country with the grafters had a different feel to it. There was no pressure to perform for people an so I could sit back an enjoy the mayhem an take in the laughs which came thick an fast, one a minute.

It was clear from the beginnin that it wasn't about to be any old ordinary trip. My pal an me arrived at the port, all set to board an get off. Then we noticed the price of the crossin an remembered what the other lads had been sayin about the jib over. They did it every time, sneakin the boat an gettin free food an accommodation all the way. I looked at the paltry £300 in my mits an thought, Fuck it! I'll do like the rest of 'em. If it came on top, the worst that could happen would be a deportation home again. Nothing to lose then. It was amazingly easy to do: everythin I'd been told was true. The only hairy moment came when we woke up in the mornin in some cabin on the boat. There were two girls starin at us, waitin for some sort of explanation. We smiled impishly an offered them to join us for breakfast after the good mornin splitt had been passed around a few times. It did the trick. They thought we were *ACE* in fact. I was astounded by how accommodatin an pleasant they were about the whole situation. It could have turned really nasty if they'd been a couple of middle-aged straights. Just our luck, though, to have sneaked into the women's only section of the ship. It just goes to show, you're not safe anywhere these days.

As I suspected it would be, with the lads out in full force, the whole mission was a resoundin success. We made an absolute killin. It seemed slightly ironic at the time that here I was, bein hailed as part of the next big thing to hit the music scene an I had to go toutin to make enough money to take myself for a holiday. Somethin wasn't addin up somewhere along the line. It's sink or swim, even near the top of the pile.

Six days had flown past by the time I remembered to phone home to check up on things. I phoned Nathan an found, to my horror, that I was needed in Barcelona the very next day. Fuck! I'd only just got back to the hotel from a shit-hot party that had lasted till dawn. There was no way I could make it back to England in time to travel out with the rest of them. There was a small stash of money lyin on the table opposite. Shit, I'd just have to spend it on a flight down there an try to get it back off the organizers. Shit shit shit an double shit – I was tired out an in no fit state to be arrangin movin my body to a different country via a plane. I was still flyin from the previous night for fuck's sake.

I arrived at the airport an tried to focus on the information boards flashin from all corners. Where the fuck was the desk I needed then? After an hour or so of shufflin up an down the concourse, I located the correct desk an started to explain my needs. It was impossible: I'd been out for far too many nights by now an the communication thing wasn't in operation. The more I tried to explain myself, the more twisted the whole scenario became.

I went off in a total huff to phone Nathan. I was there. I was ready to go. I had the money. I just couldn't make the bastards understand what I was sayin. Talk about frustratin. Nathan would have to sort it out from his end, I decided, an relinquished all responsibility for my passage to Spain from here on in.

The daft twat ended up gettin me booked on a flight that cost me £700: club class, the only one available. I was only goin from fuckin Sweden to Barcelona, not Bangkok. I reluctantly handed over the cash an boarded the flight. I was fumin like fuck by now. Not only was the money thing doin my head in, I was flyin into Heathrow to change for another flight on to Barcelona, an it was becomin a logistical nightmare. What a farce. What a fuckin hangover. What's all this about anyway, I wondered, as I settled back with a hair of the dog to calm my battered an frayed nerves.

Heathrow – the customs are doin my head right in. I'm wrecked in every sense of the word an I've lost the transit route to the next flight, findin myself headin straight towards customs. At the last minute I noticed the error an tried to double back upon myself. The bastards had clocked me. I was in no fit state to be conversin with the likes of customs officials by this time, especially in the bedraggled mess I was in after what had amounted to a six-day, non-stop piss-up. I began to explain my dilemma to the nice man at customs who was by now rifflin through the contents of my bag as if he had a proper hard on, as if it was a sure-fire dead cert that he would come up trumps with the contraband he was lookin for. I might have been off my face but I sure as hell wasn't that dumb. A top bit of jugglin ensured that the rest of the adventure wouldn't be a wash out. I couldn't get out of goin officially into England an back through customs again to board the next flight. I was convinced that it was a con-spiracy to make me miss my connection. This meant I had to go through the whole thing yet again, sweatin like a bastard this time as I was gettin more an more disorientated by the minute. Terminal stress: it was killin me.

Eventually, I caught up with everyone about five hours late, but at least I made it with the contents of my pocket intact, ensurin a top night out for the lads on my arrival. Well, you can't return not bearin presents now can you? Their faces were a sight for sore eyes; everyone was in top spirits about the way things were developin. What a difference a week makes. We went out that night in Barcelona with the promoters who promised to get the refund for my nightmare flight sorted out as soon as possible. Nathan was nowhere to be seen. Too busy bein a token pop star himself, no doubt. I began to have even deeper reservations about his ability to keep the show together in the face of a real dilemma. Fuckin hell, wasn't I supposed to be the one takin all the drugs an shaggin everythin in sight without a care in the world?

Okay, so his job was pretty impossible in the light of tryin to get us altogether in the same place at one time, but I still didn't trust him.

A CLOSE CALL

From then on in, we were goin to be workin our bollocks off. We were constantly tourin all over the place an the audiences were growin in size an enthusiasm all the way along.

Details of the individual gigs become very confused at this point as the pace of things quickened considerably. The year was over before I even knew it.

There had been time to squeeze in the odd do along the way, though, one of the most memorable bein a warehouse bash thrown by two brothers, notorious for their quality parties. They had organized a few large outdoor events over the summer that I'd unfortunately missed. Everyone was still talkin about them when I got back an it made me determined not to miss out on this one.

The place was rockin, with all the usual party antics well underway, when the call went out that the police had arrived to close the party down. They were politely shown into the caged goods lift an promptly sent up to the top floor before the power supply was turned off. There was no other way out from the top floor except down the lift shaft. They were left up there for hours, an as all the large metal doors had been securely bolted shut, no one could get either in or out of the gaff. This suited all those inside just fine. The police, on the other hand, were less than impressed, especially as their shouts couldn't be heard over the sound of the PA which was cranked up to max in a bid to ignore the problem.

The real reason why I remember it so vividly, however, has nothin to do with the raid at all. What I found really funny about that night was that a well-known personality from Manchester, who shall remain anonymous, was captured on film gettin up to all kinds of nonsense. It was career ruinin stuff an the person who'd filmed it knew exactly which buttons to press to get what they wanted. A blackmail situation developed an by all accounts went on for some time.

There had been a few nasty events in the past year too, most notably the scary incident in The Haçienda that had seen me in real danger of bein chopped to pieces by a gang of around twenty.

The club atmosphere had been on a steady decline since the initial year of mayhem. The clampdown on drugs in The Haçienda, forced by a threat to its licence followin a drug-related death an the increase in gangland violence, had soured the dance environment for many. I'd returned to Manchester durin a short break from tourin an had gone down to the club with some friends. Oblivious to the new rules in force since our absence, we skinned up an relaxed in the usual way only to be approached by an aggressive trio who instantly tried to evict us. Not bein used to such repressiveness on their nights out, my mates took offence to the attitude of the doormen an a small battle exploded in a flash. One of the doormen copped a gash in his head from a bottle launched by one of our lot. Other members of the security got involved, one of whom was in the process of puttin in a bid to buy our flat. I'd always got on well with him an thought it would be a good idea to step in an try to negotiate a truce before the trouble went any further.

The group of lads I was with cut out at the rumour that another firm had been shouted up to come down an wipe them out. I went back to the corner an carried on with the night, thinkin that everythin was sweet now that the offendin bunch had left the buildin. A short while later, a mob of about fifteen to twenty, all tooled up to the eyeballs, came wanderin over to the corner an the doorman that had copped the injury pointed me out as one of the troublemakers. I was gobsmacked.

I was surrounded in seconds an they literally picked me up with the intention of draggin me outside to do me in. They formed a circle, flankin me on all sides, pullin out knives an machetes to stop anyone from gettin in to help me. All I could think of was that under no circumstances was I goin outside. I started to wriggle like fuck in an attempt to save my life. They weren't expectin my reaction an tried in vain to hold on to my arms an legs but I was flippin like a greased eel out of water. I managed to cause them to lose their balance an there were so many of them that they came down like dominoes on top of me, swipin at each other in the confusion. By this time, the incident had got so out of hand that the doormen couldn't ignore it an were forced to come over in the light of such a public floggin goin down in their work environment.

I seized the opportunity to wriggle some more to get out from under the writhin mass of murderers an legged it at great speed up the stairs an on to the balcony. I was lucky. The only injury I'd sustained in the incident was a top cauliflower ear from a savage boot to my head just as I was gettin away. It turned pure purple an wobbled like fuck for weeks to come.

I'd used up every ounce of energy in the escape an stood pantin like an out-of-breath dog that had faced the whole pack of hard bastard neighbourhood strays, lookin down on the carnage below with half a smile, wonderin how the fuck I'd managed to get out of that one alive. I was so relieved that I spent the rest of the night boppin away as though nothin had happened.

The next night, I wanted to go out as usual but no one would have it that the whole incident had been well an truly sorted on the actual night. I was adamant that there would be no come back. I was right. I arrived at The Haçienda to find a well-known kid from a notorious inner city area waitin for me. He'd heard all about the nonsense that had gone down the night before an wanted to step in on my behalf to make sure that I wouldn't be the victim of yet more gangster politics.

I'd taken him an his mate to various parties down in London in the recent past where he'd had his first E an, as a consequence, the time of his life. He reckoned he owed me one. I wasn't about to get all modest an argue the toss with him.

A couple of months later, in a totally unrelated incident, he was gunned down in the street with his mate. His mate took a fatal shot to the head an he took a few bullets but survived by the skin of his teeth.

I looked back at the close shave I'd had an realized just how fuckin lucky I'd been. The gangland mentality was seepin into every club in the city an turnin an already dyin scene into a dead one.

Time to move on.

The video for 'Wrote for Luck' had been recorded in Manchester at Legends nightclub at some point in the previous year. All the band an the vast rent-a-crowd brought in to bulk out the crowd scene were completely off their nuts. Half of Manchester had heard about the shoot an they all turned up in full party spirit, even though it was the middle of the afternoon, rarin to show the world an its grandma what was goin down on our plot. The scene was goin fuckin bonkers by now. A couple of A&R men from America had turned up in the city to attend a few of the do's that had become a nightly occurrence. They couldn't believe what was developin right before their eyes an the scale to which the E-fuelled frenzy had ascended.

They loved the urgency of it all an desperately wanted to capture the essence of the music an the party vibe, wholesale, to import to the American audiences. Unfortunately, the package lost some of its flavour in transit an the Americans weren't quite ready to embrace the lifestyle or the soundtrack that we lived by. I don't know why, perhaps they just weren't clued up for it at the time.

Electra wanted us badly after witnessin the effect our music was havin on the scene an, before too long, me an Shaun found ourselves gettin off to America to do some interviews over a deal signed with Electra. We were made up to fuck over this new development because it meant we were now on the same label as The Doors an Love, the very legends that had inspired us an many other bands of our time. They were the classic bands of the 60s that everyone wanted to emulate in some way. Maybe not so much in the sounds they'd produced but definitely in the way that they had broken new ground an opened up a new era in the music business.

We arrived in the States full of optimism an were greeted at the airport with stretch limos an given the full monty pop star treatment. It was a first for us an we were enjoyin every fuckin celebrity perk they could throw at us, happy to take their generosity to the limit. The interviews were peppered with breaks to indulge in the new pastime of smokin the ridiculously intoxicatin crack that was bein tossed in our direction by some kid who'd latched himself on to us from the word go. He was up for goin to the extremes to satisfy our wants an so we took it to the extreme, thinkin that it was the norm in the whole rock 'n' roll set-up over there. If they were willin to supply the goods we were more than willin to oblige their idea of hospitality. Well, it would be ignorant not to, wouldn't it?

By the end of the week, I was threatenin to kill the poor kid. I must have lost the plot with the constant drip of the pressure to appease an the steady fix of intoxicants that were enterin my bloodstream an addlin my mind to the point of no return. In spite of the non-stop top ups, we worked relentlessly to promote the band the entire time we were there, doin eight hour days of pure interviews, one after the other, until the point that we didn't have a clue what day it was an who we were talkin to.

A few weeks later, we were back again, tourin with the Pixies, another of Electra's new signins who were doin alright on the American circuit. The tour was goin okay, nothin sparklin, but without incident – until we decided to go out an score a weed one night in Cleveland. There were three of us, me, Muzz an X in the taxi, which was like a little minibus affair with a door that slid open on the side. When the driver heard our plans an where we wanted to go, he refused to take the job. We offered him an incentive an eventually he agreed, but was none too happy about the situation. It was a no-go area even for the police, but we only wanted to score a weed an get out. We thought it would be sweet.

Pullin up outside what looked like a crumblin an condemned apartment block from a Sarajevo war zone, we spotted the dude an he approached the car. We sensed that all was not as it should be. The deserted streets an obvious lack of law an order should have been a major clue. Still, we tried to plod on with the deal, frontin it with as much attitude as we could muster. The dude insisted that we get out of the car to do the business but it didn't seem to be a good idea. He stood back, pleadin honour an respectability – he was just a simple drug dealer tryin to make a livin, not a low down street robber on the rip. It was a ridiculous thing for such an obvious vagabond to be sayin but, like the daft twats we were, we took him at his word when he showed us he wasn't desperate for our money by lettin us see his own wad. We wanted a draw an weren't goin home without one now we'd come this far.

As soon as we stepped out of the door, the rest of the team turned out in full force, swingin bats an goin straight for the kill. We shit ourselves an tried to jump back in the taxi but he was already movin off, tryin to save his own arse. The gang started to smash his car up which gave us just enough time to leap in an tell the driver to get the fuck out of there. Muzzer copped a brick straight in the kipper an was bleedin badly. All of us had suffered some injury or another in the storm of blows from the baseball bats. We were in a pretty bad way an could have done with a hospital visit, especially as bits of Muzzer's face were flappin in the wind. The taxi driver, on the other hand, wanted us to go with him to the police station. He was holdin us accountable for the damage to his car. We talked him into goin via our hotel where we deftly jumped out an legged it to the safety of our rooms, lockin the doors behind us.

A new rule was brought into bein: no more missions into the ghetto, purely bona fide deliveries only, an from known sources, from now on.

The street gangs weren't the only source of danger in Cleveland as X found out later that night in some bar down town. He'd taken a shine to a lap dancer an after droppin a shitload of acid together, they vanished into the night for a mess about. This bitch was no class act though. She must have weighed all of five stone, with shoulder blades an hip bones that would make Jodie Kidd look obese. She also had a healthy dose of some sort or another, which she obligingly handed over in an act of free love.

X was beside himself with grief the followin mornin as the full implications of his endeavours were realized. No one could console him as he scribbled suicide notes from the twelfth floor to his girlfriend back home. He was convinced that he had contracted Aids an the shame was killin him before the disease had even shown any signs of kickin in. It was all a false alarm, of course, brought on by the nasty confusion of an acid comedown of mighty proportions.

I just want to reiterate, before I go any further, an referrin to any past discrepancies in the chronological order of the stories also, that my memories of tourin an the various gigs an events along the way are a bit fuzzy when I try to remember the sequence with any accuracy. It gets to the point when doin a gig is equatable to goin to the boozer every night. Obviously, you tend to have a crackin time in the boozer or you wouldn't keep goin, but you don't remember every visit with absolute clarity, only the exceptional times an then perhaps not in the right order. Tourin is exactly the same in that not all the gigs are spectacular enough to warrant a mention an there are the odd few that should but you can't recall until prompted.

I'm not sayin that tourin with a band is borin, it's a fuckin fantastic way to live your life when it all comes together, but the constant whirl of buses an hotels does leave you disorientated an wonderin at which point you did last change your underpants or phone home. Tour buses are a real threat to the health of the occupants, in every sense.

I'm not complainin though. I really enjoy the set-up when it's all going well, there's nothin to beat flyin around the world with the sure knowledge that you're improvin musically with every set, providin the punters with the best entertainment that you're capable of an seein them appreciate the price of their ticket along the way. For job satisfaction, there's nothin comes close to it.

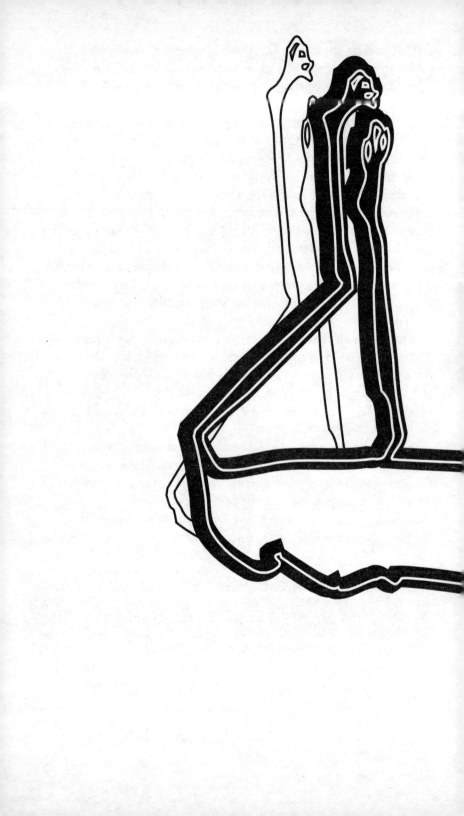

'Wrote for Luck', as I've mentioned, had been passed out to a few choice people to do remixes on an Paul Oakenfold, with his partner Steve Osborne, came back with the best of the bunch. It was a classic mix that proved pivotal in the future direction of the band's sound. It had the production we needed to facilitate the dance cross-over that we'd been lookin for to enable the clubs to pick up on an translate our music to the masses. It was a collaboration made in heaven.

We were about to take on the final production prowess of Martin at the Manor Studios in Oxfordshire, owned by Richard Branson. Martin sadly passed away some time after the session due to an over exuberant session of his own, doin what he liked doin best – takin his indulgences to the extreme. The constant barrage of abuse on his body in the quest for creational inspiration was too much for his system to take any more. He passed away in the night, with a heart attack. A sad reminder to us all of the downside of livin life on a constant edge.

I went down to the studios along with everyone else, but I fucked up badly an never got to see the project finished. I'd been out practically every night for the last two years without givin my body an soul one break from the madness. The strain of keepin it all together was beginnin to take its toll an the bubble finally burst within the confines of the studio. I was like a spring that had been wound too tight an it just needed one last turn for the whole fuckin thing to snap an fly off in all directions.

We were all sat in the studio, listenin to Mark Day do his bit, an I happened to mention that I didn't think his guitar sounded quite right an X turned on me, snarlin, sayin what the fuck did I know about anythin being right or wrong. I pounced on him, takin the challenge to be a personal slur an within seconds the whole thing had turned heated an was gettin totally out of hand. My girlfriend happened to come in just as I was in the throes of issuin a threat to kick his fuckin head in an she wrongly got caught up in the messy business. I couldn't stop myself an set about on a twelve hour rampage, takin the worst of it out on my girlfriend an smashin about the place like a lunatic. I was a human whirlwind of destruction, smashin in doors an threatenin to do anyone in that tried to come near me. In the end, I was packed off home before I went so far that the police would have to be called in. I managed to upset everybody there, to the point that they couldn't cope with havin me around them any longer. My girlfriend got herself off to London an I was sent back to Manchester to cool off, out of harm's way.

My head was in bits. X had managed to turn the situation around sayin that I was bein a right wrong un, an maybe I was, but I was fuckin gutted the minute I got back home an realized what I'd done. Suddenly, it looked like I'd lost my girlfriend, my place in the band an my chance of a future, all in one twelve hour bout of insanity.

It had been the first time that I'd really wanted to kill X, or at least do him some real harm. I've felt that way a good couple of times since, but the outbursts usually only lasted a matter of ten minutes or so before it all blew over. He's pretty harmless under all that front anyway. I've learnt that if you get past all that shoutin an stand your ground with X, givin as good as you get, he soon crumbles an goes off in a top sulk. He reminds me of one of those little fuckin horrible terrier dogs that run at you snarlin like fuck till you give 'em a good kick an they soon fuck off yelpin to sit in the corner for a good whimper. That's X man. A fuckin terrier in a bulldog's clothin. He shouts well though, I'll give him that much. Dog eat dog.

The project was a four track compilation to be entitled 'Madchester', in the wake of the success of the 'WFL' release. We were fumin over the title of the EP as we didn't want to be associated with all the other crap bands that were ridin on the success of the city's reputation at the time, gettin inflated deals on the strength of the surge in interest in all things Manc. Our view of the music an happenins was on a worldwide scale an small-town mentality appeared nowhere on our agenda, especially as the whole thing had been blown out of proportion by a media that was hungry for a sensational new slant after the complacent yawn that was the 80s.

Oakenfold did a remix of the 'Hallelujah' track an played it to the London crowd. It was an instant hit in the clubs an we knew then an there that his little outfit would be doin the business for us in the future. They had an amazin knack of pressin the right buttons to transform the sounds we were tryin to create into the sounds we needed, to transmit our musical message to the people out there in the clubs an venues.

Our popularity was growin beyond our wildest expectations at a rate of knots. The response to the vibe we were tryin so hard to put out just the year before had accelerated to the point that we found ourselves in the unlikely position of considerin a gig at the G-Mex. We were fuckin astounded at the stupidity of suggestin such a massive leap in such a short space of time. We were convinced that it would make us look like the biggest bunch of nob-heads this century. It seemed like the perfect set-up to knock us down to size an it was with a nervous intake of breath that we waited for the response to the announcement. To our complete an utter amazement, the gig sold out within a day of the tickets goin on release.

What was even more mind blowin was that the whole set-up had been the idea of two of the young up-an-comin promoters, Jimmy 'muffin' an John 'the phone', who had previously only ever dealt with the merchandise side of the operation. They were confident enough of our pull to put their necks on the line, but still we were diggin our heels in an screamin bollocks to the notion of playin one of the biggest venues in town.

The phenomenal response prompted them to go for a second night. Surely they're off their fuckin trolleys, we ranted, they must be really trippin if they think we can fill it two nights in a row. We were spectacularly wrong. Both shows sold out. Credit to the lads who believed in us an managed, in the face of a possible calamity of mega proportions, to pull off the stunt an send us flyin into the league of stadium fillers overnight.

For the first time in my entire life, I began to let the fact seep slowly into my consciousness that we might just be on to a winner here. It still wasn't time to go house huntin just yet though.

The feedin frenzy moved up a notch as all the people involved with the band clambered to get their piece of the cake. The band were left virtually potless in the mad scramble, an reelin from the speed at which it was all careerin along. A lot of cash was disappearin on the extras, as we upgraded our surroundins to befit our new status. Good hotels an luxury tour buses don't come cheap.

In true rock 'n' roll style, we invited all the people who had supported us over the last few years back to the Midland Hotel in Manchester for an after show party on the second night. It had begun in the vast bar in the foyer an was later moved into a private room at the back of the hotel in a bid to keep all the nonsense away from the other guests. In a massive gesture of generosity, I ordered up the beers on my own room bill an was hit with a £4,000 bill the followin mornin. Intent on takin the party into the daylight hours, the party people dispersed to various rooms throughout the hotel, causing havoc along the way as fire alarms went off all over the place. The police were called in to catch the maraudin troublemakers who had taken the celebrations to the extremes, lettin off fire extinguishers in the corridors an generally makin a fuckin nause of themselves as they refused to leave. A giant concrete urn was hurled at the front glass entrance as a couple of idiots wouldn't accept that it was time to go home an had been physically evicted from the buildin. We were swiftly banned from the hotel for an indefinite period an any other hotel within the same chain throughout the entire UK. Oh well, it had been a good do. No regrets, except that we had to bring in a policy of honin down the guest list to a manageable throng in the future. At least it was cheaper, if not as much fun.

Havin said that, we managed to bag the headline at Glastonbury that year an everyone wanted to come along for the ride. The possibility of damage was lessened by the fact that it was set in a field an we could relinquish responsibility for any mishaps. We asked the organizers for an impossible amount for our guest list but they were havin none of it. The entrepreneurs on the firm set about makin up their own laminates on site an distributin them around the Manc contingent to make up for the shortfall. No one, it seems, was disappointed at the gates.

The journey down there was an adventure in itself, gettin lost an only findin our way back on to the trail by smashin into the wooden signpost for Glastonbury in our big luxury tour bus up a small, narrow lane. We arrived in style with a big crack in the windscreen which, before too long, was joined by a pair of lacy black undies, hangin mysteriously off the wing mirror. It proved to be a very useful distinguishing feature for locatin the correct bus on returnin at dawn after a full night of it in the fields.

There were camps containin battalions of Mancunians all over the place. One lot had got their own cosy plot set up in a prime position on the hill, away from the threat of the ubiquitous mud, complete with quads to facilitate ease of movement with minimum messiness. They were bombin about the gaff all day long, sellin their imported cargo of lighters an Rizlas at vastly inflated prices to any passer-by willin to part with their cash. They even had a stockpile of booze on board: a proper mobile offy.

The passes were workin a treat as they zoomed in an out of the backstage enclosure on their quads, deliverin supplies an givin lifts to girls too proud to get their feet wet, but not so proud that they wouldn't get their tits out as they screamed past the crowds. It was playtime on a grand scale an we were intent on havin it large. I wandered out into the crowd an instantly got caught up in the lunacy, as trips an pills came flyin at me from all directions. The lights an sounds soon merged into one big carry on as I ventured deeper an deeper into the makeshift, mad max land.

No matter which way I attacked the path system, I always managed to end up in the travellers' field, stoppin off for mushroom tea at every turn an gettin caught up in their genius, tripped-out sounds comin at me from every tent flap.

The atmosphere down in the centre of the festival was gettin a bit frantic as men stood around in balaclavas, sellin E an crack. E was makin its big debut at the festival that year an the city dealers had infiltrated the site, bringin a menacin presence to the party. There were reports of a rape an of stallholders bein taxed, along with a noticeable increase in tent robberies an mindless violence. I must admit, I didn't really notice much of it as I bobbed along quite content in a happy acid haze, but I was aware of the possible dangers facin my girlfriend an her mates as we lost each other in the confusion of the night.

The gig, it has to be said, was a bit of a blur for me. I remember gettin up on the pyramid stage an lookin out over the field of revellers just as the night was creepin in an the sky was changin colour. It really was a purple haze as the many fires an burnin torches cast an eerie smokey blanket over the valley. It looked like some mad pagan ritual goin off with all the giant candles an fires lightin up hundreds of little pathways through the sea of tents in the distance. I was totally entranced by the magical sight in front of me as the crowd appeared to ignite in a sudden burst of activity as the tunes kicked in. I'd been swallowin trips from the moment I'd arrived on site an was completely lost in the surge of energy risin off the crowd. I've been told that the set wasn't the best musically that the band could have given, but to me it was irrelevant. I could see for myself the potency of the reaction from the crowd.

I was in a perfect state of bliss that carried me from set to party without ever consciously leavin the stage, but I must have done because later that night, I caught up with Debs in a field near the stone circle an created another little life to compound the sheer happiness I felt at that moment. It was Midsummer's Eve an life was fuckin ACE all round. I knew that somethin special had happened at Glastonbury but hadn't yet realized that we were goin to have a baby on board as a consequence of it.

Just before the Glastonbury thing, we'd been asked by Electra to contribute to a historical compilation album that they were puttin out to celebrate their fiftieth anniversary. Every band on Electra was to do a track from their back catalogue. They sent over a few samples of tracks that we could do a cover of, an one of them was 'Step On' by Johnny Congos. We recruited the backin vocals of the mighty Rowetta to add a bit of depth.

Rowetta was ace, an the track turned out so fuckin good that we wanted to keep it for ourselves an ended up givin them a cover version of 'Tokoloshe Man' instead. It was still good, but it wasn't as good as 'Step On'.

*

I remember a package arrivin at my flat one mornin an openin it to find a really nice Omega watch starin back at me. I'd completely forgotten that one had been promised to every band member for contributin to the album. It was a fuckin belter of a surprise when it turned up out of the blue. Unfortunately, I'd just bought myself a really nice watch on my travels in America an so it was a bit superfluous to my needs. I gave it to my grandad, which was probably a pretty shrewd move as all the others either lost or sold theirs an later regretted it. At least I can say that mine is still in the family.

After makin such an impressive debut on 'Step On', Rowetta quickly became a permanent feature in the band, addin a new dimension to the shows with her kinky dressin an her whips. She was really a top girl to be around on the road, guaranteed to be good fun, although she did break down in tears a few times with the sheer exasperation of bein holed up constantly with six lads on her case. She sometimes got a little frustrated by our ignorance of the fact that she wasn't one of the lads an felt that she couldn't cope with all the goins on. For all her talk of not bein up to it, though, she didn't do too badly on the party front. She's funny as fuck with it too an I loved her to bits, as I still do to this day. I'll always have time for Rowetta. Not enough credence was given to the massive boost she gave the Mondays with her vocals an her character. Well, I say – Rowetta, you're *ACE*.

The tight work schedule saw us gettin straight off to Ibiza to do a gig at one of my old favourites, the Ku Club. I was made up; I hadn't expected to be goin over there at all this year with everythin else goin off. Rowetta wasn't booked to be comin over with us but turned up out of the blue havin won the holiday in some competition in Manchester. Now if that ain't destiny, I don't know what is. The date had been squeezed in at the last minute an it was regarded as a welcome five day break. Break my arse. It was fuckin harder work than workin with all the distractions on the island. I only made it back to the hotel on a few occasions an that was only to get dressed. The band had been given their own car; amazin since it was common knowledge about my many past four-wheel fuck ups. Somehow, this time, for once I managed to keep myself an the car in one piece. Well nearly. I almost missed the flight home 'cos I was havin such a ball an shot up to the airport just in time, leavin the car with some kid, with the instructions to do what he liked with it. I was feelin mighty generous after the easy time I'd had of it. It wasn't my car anyway, so fuck it, I thought.

I collapsed into my seat on the plane an fell instantly into a coma. I'd hardly slept the whole visit an my body decided a total shutdown was in order. Halfway through the flight, the air hostess woke me to hand me my dinner. I lifted my head, eyes rollin an mouth dribblin an tried to form the words to say thank you. Nothin but a weird grunty sort of chutterin noise escaped before I neatly nose-dived into the dinner before me an fell straight back into the coma, all snug in the warmness of the food. The air hostess was gettin really flustered tryin unsuccessfully on a few occasions to wake me, thinkin somethin was really amiss an that I might possibly die or somethin messy like that on her shift. There was a young school age girl sittin in the seat next to me an apparently her parents were lookin none too plussed about the whole situation. What can you do if you need the kip? There's no law against sleepin violently that I know of. Not accordin to the cabin crew though. They called ahead for me to be met off the plane on landin at Manchester. I woke up just as the plane was comin in to land, completely oblivious to the commotion I'd caused by bein tired enough to sleep. I found myself in the strange position of apologizin to people for causin offence, not fully aware what offence I'd actually been guilty of. The threat of the police escort was removed an I went home to finish the kip off in the safety of my own bed. After Glastonbury an Ibiza, almost back to back, it felt really good to see a familiar pillow in a sleep-friendly environment again.

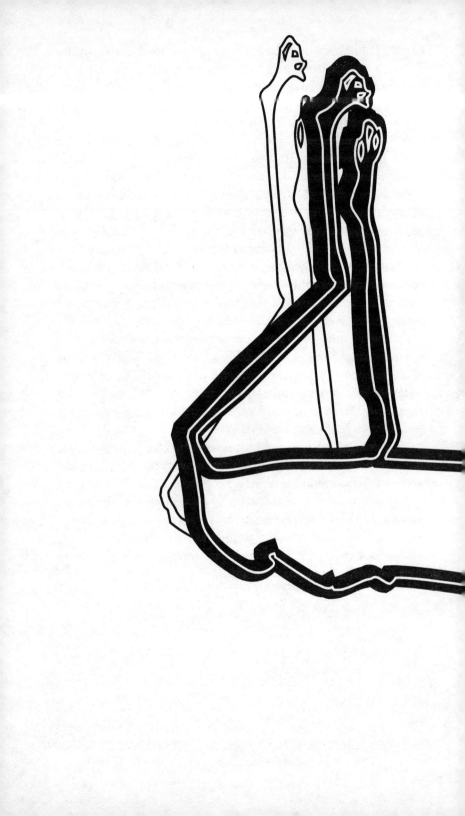

At the end of that summer we got off to do the next album, *Pills an Thrills an Bellyaches*, in LA. Paul Oakenfold an Steve Osborne had been drafted in to do their magic. We knew it was goin to be a good relationship with them. They understood exactly where we wanted to go with the sounds on this album.

By the time we'd arrived in LA, everyone in the band was fucked. We'd just done a three week tour of America that no one had wanted to do. No way should we have been sloggin round the States immediately before recordin an album. The workload was gettin ridiculous with the constant on the road thing an all anyone wanted to do when we got to LA was sit around. After all, we were by now multi-millionaires, weren't we? It felt like we were at the time. We'd just done the whole of America in pure luxury an it was costin us an arm an a leg, blowin out gigs because the venues were too small like proper spoilt babies.

We were out there for about twelve weeks on about £500 plus with nothin to shell out for. It was fuckin brilliant! With nothin else to spend the cash on, I went an laid out on a watch that had been teasin me in some hotel shop I walked past every day. It had my name on it, even if I did have to get a sub of two weeks' money to get at it. Top kettle.

We did our last gig in LA to round off the tour before gettin stuck into the nitty gritty of recordin. It wasn't supposed to be the last gig but it was all we could muster at the time. The exhaustion had taken over an the gigs were stoppin right there, no negotiations, no go. Some daft excuse was made up an we settled back by the pool to get some sun an finally chill out.

The first night out in LA was one for the history books. Well, one for this book anyway. I'd found a fuck-off warehouse party via a bunch of scousers who were livin over there frontin their lucrative business with various complementary trades: locksmith, decorator, set builder. The party turned out to be a proper

LA do with all the trimmins. Halfway through the night, some good-lookin bird came saunterin over an began to give it some chat. I thought I was dreamin, she looked just like somebody really famous but I couldn't quite put my finger on who. She told me her name was Julia Roberts.

I came over all apologetic an tried to smooth over the cracks of my ignorance in the conversation by offerin the sad excuse that I was always shit at recognizing real stars. By way of an apology, I told her that I probably wouldn't recognize Bet Lynch either if she happened to walk on by. She wanted to know who the fuck Bet Lynch was. Oh well.

I was completely shittin myself by now, gettin in a right old fluster. I decided to go with the I'll call your bluff routine, just in case I was bein sent up. She started to get all defensive, sayin she'd just had her hair done which was probably why she didn't look like her characters in the films. Then, to totally get me in a spin, she offered to take me out to the car park to show me her ID. What an idiot – I blew her out in my panic an struck up a conversation with her bodyguard instead who was busy smokin a pipe of some description. Talk about throwin a golden opportunity to the wind. What a prick. Next time.

A few days later, we'd settled right into our luxury Oakwood apartments, commandeering the outside jacuzzi an starin out all the wannabe bit part actors an directors talkin scripts. The place was full of 'em, all loungin about sportin porn-style muzzies an neat little trunks. It was a right mixed bag of Hollywood triers with the odd failed English actor thrown in for good measure.

We sorted ourselves out with hire cars. Mine was a shiny blue leather interiored convertible Chrysler Le Baron somethin or other. It was fuckin beautiful, what a machine, a real bird puller. The first night out in it I slammed it into a kerb, tryin to negotiate a turn into a garage, bucklin the front wheel back under the wheel arch. I couldn't believe I'd done the same stunt yet again. I was too scared to take it back to the apartment an admit that I'd fucked up on the car front again. I stayed out all night with the scousers, so I didn't have to face the music like a kid too worried to face his mam. I spent the whole of the next mornin tryin to iron out the mess by replacin it with an identical blue one so that no one would notice. I got one exactly the same, but white. It was a long shot but I thought they might not notice the drastic change in the colour scheme with it bein the same shape.

They noticed. Fuck. I've got to get a grip with this car thing, I promised myself, as I screeched off out of the underground car park, roof down, tunes a-blarin, on a mission to find the beaches.

I spent the next few weeks doin all the beaches an shops, burnin up an down the freeways findin excuses to go to Malibu or Venice Beach or Santa Monica or Universal Studios or anywhere that I could drive around in the sun with the tunes pumped up an my shades on. I liked the way you could change lanes from every side on the freeways an with five lanes to choose from, I did it a lot, just for the fun of it. I loved it all an didn't want it to end.

I popped by the studios from time to time to see what the developments were. The band were all workin at different times of the day as everyone scattered themselves about LA, goin shoppin with girlfriends or just soakin it all up in case we never got the chance to come back an do it all again.

On one of the nights out, there was a peace night goin on between the rival gangs. Me an Oakey decided to go an have an idle about to see if anythin interestin was goin on. It turned out to be more excitin than we'd ever anticipated, or wanted for that matter. It soon became apparent that in a city like LA, the notion of holdin a peace night an expectin all to comply was an impossible task. The communities are far too fragmented for the inhabitants to ever unite peacefully on common ground.

The night's activities had nothin to do with peace. There was an uneasy tension as people cruised the streets, cautiously testin the waters with all senses on full alert for possible danger. The sounds of the city at play were rudely interrupted by a series of loud cracks. Four people dropped to the tarmac like puppets with their strings slashed; at least one of them was dead. I've never seen a peace night end so unpeacefully, there was fuckin mayhem goin on all around. The crowd dispersed as fast as you fuckin like. It was a mad scramble as people tried to get indoors away from danger. There were people screamin hysterically all about me as I walked on by as if in a dreamscape. It was totally surreal. There was nothin I could do but take it all in my stride. My memory took snapshots of the bloody scene as my mind raced to digest it, offerin up rational actions I could take in order to survive myself. The old adrenalin finally kicked in an provided the answer: leg it to the car an get the hell out of there, back to the safety of the apartment complex. From then on it was concluded that peace night celebrations were a bad idea an shouldn't be entered into on any level.

There's a certain natural element of safety in chaos; get too ordered about things an you're a dead man. It's a topsy turvy world out there.

We took to finishin off our nights out in the relatively tame BBC bar on Venice Beach where in the mornins you could catch up on the football from back home. One such mornin, we'd dragged a shitload of celebrities down there with us to watch the footy. It was shenanigans goin down in the back. We singled out one famous British actor who had recently divorced from his millionairess wife. He was enjoyin his newly reinstated bachelorhood with the proceeds from the settlement an we thought we'd help him along. The lads were busy tryin to set him up, gettin him to snort daddy lines of charlie off the bar. All of a sudden he burst out cryin, just like that, out of the blue, askin why we all hated him so much. Hollywood paranoia had set in double bad. It's not as though we were even bein malicious, it was purely an simply a bit of a laugh aimed at the character he used to play back home rather than the person sittin before us. I felt a bit sorry for him, but there you go. I suppose he just had one of those faces that begs to have the piss taken. An I know all about that, but I don't go around cryin in bars when the footy's on, for fuck's sake.

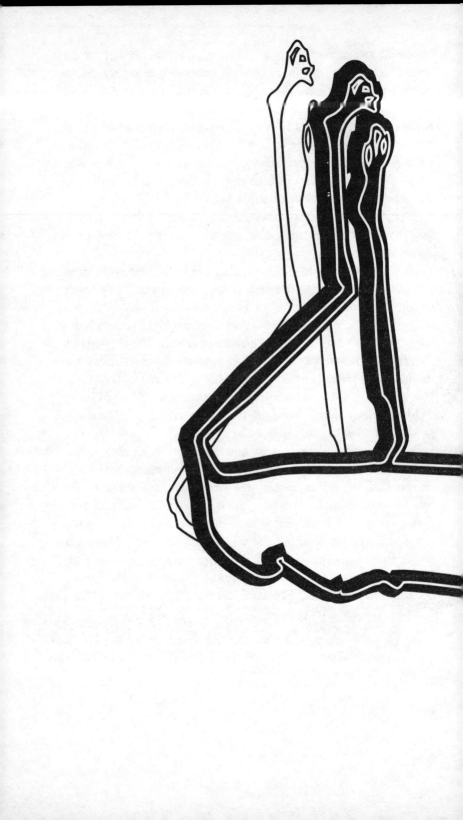

For the last couple of weeks, I'd arranged to have Debs join me. She was a few months pregnant by this time an so the partyin had to stop. I didn't mind 'cos I'd been at it for a good long stretch by then – about ten years I think – an it was time to chill out an gear back down for normal existence. I'd have to get used to it from now on anyway, I reasoned, with fatherhood loomin on the horizon.

Nathan, on the other hand, was busy being a top fuckin nuisance: never around when you needed him, out every night, nausin up his manager status by generally not doin his job when he should have. The whole swingin LA scene was too temptin for Nathan as he flitted from one little clique to the next, gettin up to all kinds of nonsense along the way. There were rumours that I couldn't possibly repeat but after one memorable night on the razzle, suffice to say, he did seem to have a hint of the John Wayne to his gait. That'll be the LA thing then.

Luckily I wasn't afflicted with any of it bein the staunch, well brought up an emotionally balanced individual that I am.

By the last few weeks of recordin, we knew that the album was a belter. I rode round the boulevards in my super-duper convertible, listenin to the tape over an over, all day long. That sounded fuckin ACE. It wasn't just the heady backdrop of the sprawlin city an the constant sunshine affectin my judgement either. I really believed that it was a fuckin monster hit of an album that we had on our hands. Everyone was buzzin to get back an lay the tunes on the waitin public.

All the band members felt pretty confident of their futures by now. Horse even went as far as gettin married to his long-time girlfriend while we were out there 'cos he was feelin so good about himself. It was a good do, apart from Nathan who, havin been requested to step in an organize the evenin's recreation, made a complete balls up of it 'cos he thought it wasn't in his contract to be doin such things. We ended up in some small-time club on the outskirts eatin pizzas, but everyone was happy enough.

The realization that we might never have to scrimp an scrape our way through life again felt fuckin great. We'd all come a long way from the scuzzy backwaters of suburban Salford an nobody ever wanted to return to that way of life again. We'd had our bite of the apple out there in sunny California an now we wanted to consume the whole fuckin fruit bowl, startin with the cherries.

Little did we know then that one year down the line, the very mechanism that had propelled us to the top would crush us mercilessly in the final hour.

We got back home to rave reviews. The album was receivin massive critical acclaim from all corners as one of our best to date; it was to be pure stadiums an arenas from now on, somethin I hadn't really contemplated with any seriousness until I heard that our first gig was to be at Whitley Bay ice rink.

We got in there an set up the PA, crankin it right up, blastin away to our hearts' content while no one was around. It was good fun, we were enjoyin the novelty of playin really loud music on such a massive scale without the horrible pressure of havin the 10,000-strong audience in front of us. Unfortunately, there was one security geezer who'd just finished his nightshift an was busy tryin to get some kip in before the start of the show. The noise was deafenin an no way was he gettin any shut eye with sound engineers revellin in the freedom to abuse the airways as much as us, givin it their all from the mixin desk.

As a solution to his problem, he came up with the lunatic idea of phonin in a bomb scare. Now we're really makin waves, we thought, if someone out there thinks we're so important that they want to blow us up. He must have been demented with exhaustion to think such a harebrained scheme would pay off. He got arrested for it, poor geezer, an the show went on as scheduled.

I've kind of forgotten how fuckin BIG we'd actually become. That night, as I walked on stage in front of the sea of upturned faces I nearly died of fright as I was physically hit by the wall of sound from the crowd. The noise penetrated every cell in my body; it was an amazin feelin. They surged forward shoutin an screamin, louder an louder as the rest of the band took their positions. Bodies were bein pulled over the barriers in the press pit before we'd even started. People just get so excited at the silliest things. It's that mass hysteria thing that takes over. I never dreamt that we would be the cause of such madness though. It's a strange thing to get a grip on, an to know how to react to it. I just set off dancin, lost in a rush of adrenalin for the first few tunes with everythin in my vision havin a funny sort of fuzziness to it. Once I'd got my heartbeat back to a manageable level, I decided to test the reaction of the crowd by walkin over to a section an raisin my hands to see if they'd get on it. Hundreds of people saluted me back. YESSSSS! I thought, I'll try that one again, an so I crossed to the other side an tried it over there. Hundreds more waved back at me. I began to relax into the character they so obviously responded to an we got along the whole show just fine. The music sounded massive. I was really proud to be such an integral part of the whole set-up. It was one of those BIG moments in life that you wish you could catch in a jar, to sniff at an remember some time else down the line when you're lost in some mid-life crisis, thinkin about what the fuck you've done with your time.

One of the best times we ever had was in Brazil at the Rock in Rio Festival. Originally, we were only supposed to be goin there for three days. Everyone else was spendin a week there. We were fuckin gutted, but fate was to be on our side. On arrival we heard that their national paper had it all over the front page that we were bringin two thousand E's with us an that we were goin to be slingin them off the front of the stage. We were fuckin shittin ourselves goin through their customs. The rumour wasn't true, of course, but I did have my usual supplies to get me through what I had to do, so I was double cackin my pants at the thought of gettin a pull an missin out on the party.

We got through customs without a hitch an I assumed it was all over, but then, after we'd walked into the terminal there was a reception party waitin for us an we got led off to a separate room. This is it, I thought, the fuckin shit is goin to hit the fan an it's about to come right on top here for you Bezzy boy. Luckily, everyone else from the plane followed us through the same way as we were all workin the Rock in Rio event an interviews had been set up to do right there an then at the airport before everyone had a chance to disperse, never to be rounded up again. I suppose for them it was the ideal time to get the lot of us in one place at the same time. A massive sigh of relief went round as we settled back, ready to lap up the VIP treatment all the way to the hotel.

On drivin into Rio, everyone alighted at one hotel together but our lot were instructed to stay with the transport as we were to be delivered somewhere else. The paranoia began to creep back in as we realized that we were bein purposefully kept apart from the main body of artists. It turned out that Guns 'n' Roses an ourselves, the two most disruptive bands with the worst reputations, were bein shipped out to the International Hotel, about six miles up the coast, out of harm's way. I can't think why they thought that was necessary.

Like I said, we were only supposed to be there for a three day jaunt, playin the next day an then gettin straight off, but our equipment didn't turn up on time an we had to hang about waiting. No one complained, we were all buzzin at the prospect of what we could achieve with the spare time we had been given.

It turned out to be a good thing as we got to play the very last night of the festival to a crowd of about 98,000 people, supportin George Michael, believe it or not.

Somehow, someone organized a trip for us to go an meet Ronnie Biggs, who had become a sort of national hero over there for his part in the Great Train Robbery, what with his total commitment for evadin doin the slightest part of his sentence. Nice one Ronnie. Poor old Jack Slipper is still bitter.

At the barbecue we mingled with Ronnie's mates, swiggin beers, crackin jokes an eatin chicken, like you would at any other garden get-together. The company was really enjoyable, with a carefree an relaxed atmosphere presidin over the goins on. It turned out to be a pretty good stroke of luck, meetin so many of the influential locals, as they took it upon themselves to take us under their wing on a guided tour of the town, visitin all the little gems that we would never have found on our own, shelved away in little enclaves of culture dotted around the coast. We came across some serious lambada dancers down in a bay, struttin their stuff, an settled down to watch, orderin up some fresh calamares that had come off the boats that mornin.

We were also shown where to score the cheapest coke in the world; at the equivalent of ten pence a gramme it was laughable. Of course, we got a bulk buy in that we couldn't even possibly have finished durin the time we'd planned to stay. There was a fuckin small mountain of the shit that didn't seem to go down even with every man on our team snortin for England.

The night times were spent trawlin the clubs an on one such night I was out in the company of one of our security team, whose nickname was John the Spunk, for obvious reasons. We ended up in a club goin by the apt name of Help. We stood in the doorway with our jaws grazin on the ground, hardly believin the scene that was goin on before our eyes. There were loose women everywhere, accostin men in every corner. We made our way cautiously to a table an sat down. A second later, one of the women was on to the Spunk in a big way. I was shittin myself, havin heard all the rumours about geezers gettin on the prostitution thing to make the same money as the women.

The Spunk was lookin dangerously like he was goin to play along with it, till I butted in shouting, 'Look at his fuckin hands man! Check out his Adam's apple!'

It was a close shave. My paranoia must have been enough to put the Spunk off 'cos we left the club a few minutes later, laughin our heads off all the way back to the hotel in our nervousness about the lucky escape. I could always have been wrong but there's nothin wrong with exercisin a fair bit of caution in these matters. One slip in that department an you'd be physically an psychologically damaged for life.

The final night we were there, we finally got to play our set in the Mecacan; it was fuckin amazin. Walkin out on stage in front of 98,000 people completely took my breath away an I didn't know which way to look there were so many of 'em. We put on a good performance an won the Brazilian crowd over, who'd never seen us before with our adrenalin-fuelled ecstasy-

driven set. Towards the beginnin, there were a couple of cans
thrown up on the stage an I managed to catch one perfectly, an
kept it up doin some footy tricks right across the front of the
stage, headin it, flippin it with my foot on to my knee, over my
shoulder an finally volleyin it back into the crowd with a top
boot. It was one of those perfect stunts that only happen as a
complete fluke of timin an I couldn't have asked for better luck.
From that moment on, the crowd were with us 100 per cent,
goin absolutely wild an gettin right into the vibe.

After the gig, me an the Spunk managed to drag everyone out
with us, intent on showin them just how mad it could get in the
thick of it. It was a Saturday night an it was absolutely heavin
everywhere. There were about thirty of just our lot tryin to stick
together so that no one got the paras with all the inundations
from the hordes of prostitutes. One of our press officers was out
with us an bein a blonde white girl all the prostitutes thought she
was some Dutch bitch trying to muscle in on their patch an pinch
their trade. She thought she was goin to get murdered an nearly
broke down cryin in the panic of tryin to get back on the bus
alive.

A good few of us left the partyin an went back to the relative
safety of the hotel but a lot of them stayed out up to no good,
causin a scene of pure bedlam in the hotel the followin mornin.
One of the lads came down to breakfast complainin that he
hadn't fully realized that the top bird he'd pulled was a brass. He
thought she'd actually fancied him rotten at the time an his manhood was smartin a bit at the truth of the matter. The situation
had been resolved with him payin her for the services with a
chocolate bar from the fridge in his room.

Horse had sorted his out with a good swig from his
methadone bottle an had quietly packed his bags an changed
rooms while she was asleep. There were women screamin the
place down all over the gaff; thank fuck we were leavin that
mornin before it turned really nasty.

On the flight home there was none of the VIP treatment that
we'd encountered on the way in. As far as the organizers were
concerned, we'd done our bit an could be left to slog it home
with the rest of 'em in economy class. It was fuckin horrible.

We'd been up for days an sweat was pourin from every pore with the comedown an the heat. My lips were sore as fuck from constantly lickin them on the five day charlie binge an they cracked every time I attempted to laugh or smile, so I stopped smilin to compensate.

By the time we got to the plane, we were the last ones to be boardin an there was a mad scramble for seats. I couldn't believe my luck, spottin an empty seat in a boss position, right at the front of the screen. I made a mad dash for it, hurdlin seats an bags, determined to grab it before anyone else. When I got there, I realized instantly why no one had wanted to sit in this seat. My neighbour was Piers Morgan, who was at that time the gossip columnist for the *Sun*. I turned round to see everyone was laughin their fuckin heads off, but I wasn't bothered. As far as I was concerned, it was a top view of the telly an not much else mattered. Besides that, it wasn't long before I had Piers pretendin that he was asleep so that in no way could he be connected to me. I think it was somethin to do with the fact that I kept puttin the blanket over my head, as I tried desperately to snort the remainder of the coke I had on me before we got home, an lightin spliffs after each session.

Similar goins on could be seen happenin in other secluded pockets of the plane but they all thought I was mad doin it next to a *Sun* journalist. It was sweet. Piers wouldn't even talk to me in case the other journalists thought he was up to the same nonsense. He shit himself every time I disappeared under the blanket an crumbled every time I lit another spliff. He probably didn't want to talk to me anyway, which was just fine an dandy by me. I was perfectly content to be goin about my leisure activities in complete isolation an after a few good sessions was feelin quite cheery about the whole set-up.

Luckily, it was a Brazilian Airlines plane so we got away with murder, again.

Up the Rio! A good do by any standards.

The Rio trip was about the last time I can remember that the band worked together as a harmonious whole. It was an ironic truth that, as things had really started to gel for the band in terms of musical recognition an a certain amount of financial stability, the internal goins on within the set-up had already started to crack under the strain. We were tourin the world, visitin every country you could think of, but all was not well in the Happy Mondays stable; the rot had set in, eatin away the very foundations of what we thought had been an indestructible force.

Certain members of the band, an I'm not goin to start gettin tacky an pointin the finger at individuals, but some of them were beginnin to make it clearly known that they weren't happy with the set-up an the way the money was bein divided. Now, I never bigged up my own role in the band at all, but the thing is, once the media get on to somethin, whether they are slaggin you off or kissin your arse, it tends to get blown out of all proportion an now that the band were ridin high, it seemed that X an I were gettin all the attention. A lot of people wasted their breath discussin my exact role in the band, which to me was irrelevant; they either appreciated the show I put on or they didn't, an what the fuck business of theirs was it what I got up to in the studio with the band? To be honest, I really didn't take a great deal of notice of what was bein said in the press or on the street, I just got on with it.

The rest of the band, though, didn't like the way I was bein given more coverage in the press than they were. I found myself in the unlikely position of adorning front covers here, there an every fuckin where I looked. It was a bit strange, especially as I'd never really anticipated that kind of attention.

X lapped the attention up an his stories became more elaborate, baitin the media with the kind of juicy snippets that had them lined up an pantin for more. Unfortunately, the other lads weren't gettin a look in on the press front, which fired them up even more. Certain people began to get far too serious about the whole thing, forgettin how to enjoy themselves an what we were all about. Money changes people, an with serious money comin in, that change was magnified.

We got to the point where we were gettin far too much attention from the papers, hittin the headlines every other day, or so it seemed, for this an that. Everyone must have been gettin totally sick of the whole affair because even we were gettin sick of hearin about ourselves.

The crunch point came one day when a reporter, I can't remember his name now, it happened so long ago, came up from one of the weekly music papers to do an interview with the intention of highlightin our ignorant Northern ways. He obviously thought we'd been given too much of an easy time in the press an that it was high time the situation should be redressed.

His line of questionin didn't ring true from the start. He kept bangin on about what our opinion of the gay community was, an it was apparent afterwards, when we'd had time to digest an munch over the questions again, that he was tryin to stitch the band up, to swing the tide of public support against us in some way. We'd always been painfully honest, vergin on naïve about the way interviews were conducted an the way they would be reported.

At the time, all I could see was some uptight reporter gettin into our heads about the way in which we viewed the whole gay community an what we thought of their appreciation of our music. I was really suspicious of where he was comin from an what his ulterior motive was for gettin on to the subject. The other lads were bein very polite with him, but I couldn't help but get wound up by his interview technique. I was in no mood for playin the game that day, an apart from that, I suspected he was a screamin, closet gay himself, the way he was probin an pushin for answers. Finally, I confronted him an he denied the accusation flat. I wasn't havin it an took the point further with X addin to the pressure by insinuatin that we knew how his mind worked an what kind of dark, perverted thoughts crept into his consciousness late at night. I admit it was bullyin tactics, but he had brought the subject up an hadn't let it drop.

The sad thing is, I knew he was scared by the intimidation he was gettin but, in my mind, if he'd admitted the fact an had been either man enough or gay enough to stand up for himself, the subject would have been shelved an I would have come away from the interview with more respect for him. It probably would have cracked the ice an he would have got a better, less gruellin interview under his belt too. Maybe he was pleased with the result anyway, an his little claim to fame was that he helped to cast a shadow over the popularity of the Mondays, who knows.

The piece was printed an the backlash was fuckin horrible. All fingers pointed at me an X, but especially at me. The rest of the band were askin for me to be sacked as a result, which fitted in perfectly with the fact that they all thought I wasn't a value for money proposition any more. I was despised for all the attention I was gettin, especially as some of the attention was as damagin to their overall image as this last piece of journalism proved to be. X, once again, came to my rescue, tryin with all his might to paper over the cracks for my sake. He might be a bastard at times but on occasions, he can have the biggest heart goin. He stood up for me against the rest of the band, larger than large. I couldn't help people bein interested in what I had to say, however stupid it might be.

That incident really marked the beginnin of the decline of the Mondays an the morale within the band hit an all time low. It was the fact that X had made a stand for me an no one had the power to overthrow the decision that led to a rancid, bitter undercurrent which tainted everythin we did together from then on.

It also seemed like we'd been on tour for years, zippin backwards an forwards across the globe without a proper break. It was cripplin us mentally, an physically we were fairin no better, with the constant, steady drip of narcotics poisonin our bloodstreams an messin with our metabolisms while on the road. We were all sick of each other's company an we desperately needed a rest, but that wasn't about to happen. Factory had been makin some big time moves, shiftin their base from the cosy set-up in Palatine Road, which had suited them just fine for years, to a shiny, spacious office complex in the city. They wanted to polish up their image an put on a charlie big spuds front, gettin swept along with the massive tide of success of The Haçienda. It was now hammered every night of the week as a direct result of the expansion of commercial interest in the whole E scene.

The two main breadwinners for Factory, ourselves an New Order, seemed to be doin well, but Tony Wilson was insistent that he sign up all these shit bands that had mushroomed from nowhere out of the rejuvenated club scene, throwin ridiculous amounts of money at them under the misguided conception that they would be guaranteed hits.

A large, grimy, industrial-lookin buildin on the fringe of the city was earmarked to become the new Factory headquarters, but it needed massive renovations to be converted into the avant-garde showpiece that they had in mind. Grotesque amounts of money were poured into the rehashin of the huge white elephant which sported such useless objects as a phenomenally priced, glass boardroom table that was decoratively suspended on metal wires from the ceilin. On one of the first forays around the refurbished buildin, we chose the boardroom to do a photo shoot an promptly broke the table by simply sittin on it. Very practical, if you're lookin for a large smooth surface for choppin the lines out, that is.

The banks an creditors began to put pressure on Factory to start payin back money after all the big talk of certain success. Factory, in turn, looked to the two most likely ventures to make some sure money to pull the company from the brink of disaster. We were called upon to make another album but we weren't in any fit state to even be contemplatin a return to the studio. I think that New Order were havin some problems too, of a completely different nature to ours, of course, an as a consequence they weren't in a rush to do anythin.

The finger was firmly pointin in our direction to produce the goods but by this time X had really got himself a dirty, filthy habit with the smack, which wasn't goin to help matters in the slightest. All the time I'd known him, he'd insisted that he was not to be cast in the same mould as your average smackhead. With the recent pressure on him to clean up, he'd dug his heels in even more, recitin the labels an extravagant cost of his clothes as testament to the fact that he was in a different league to the addict on the street. His favourite way of explainin his actions was to turn to me, saying: 'Bez, it doesn't matter to me, I'm not a normal smack'ead. I'm all right, look, I've got my Armani this an my fuckin Patrick Cox that, that cost me blah, blah, blah. I'm not a smackhead who needs to go out on the rob to pay for any of it.'

He'd been kiddin me for years that his behaviour was nothin like that of the thousands of others who lined up at chemist's up an down the country, in every city, every day to get their methadone. He was pullin smackhead stunts left, right an centre an it couldn't be ignored any longer that he had become exactly what he'd been denyin all that time. His habit of tellin everyone the price of his clobber increased in direct proportion to the amount of smack he was takin an the need he felt to reassure everyone of his supposed respectability.

His habits an his awkward ways had been grindin away at the rest of the band over a long period of time by now, an they could have done with a serious break from it all too. Everyone was gettin really sick of the constant nonsense surroundin the real issue of music. X could have done with a chance to try an clean himself up properly before embarkin on anythin more challengin than a photo shoot.

I knew that the album wasn't goin to go right by the simple fact that X really wanted to work with Paul Oakenfold an Steve Osborne again but they were too busy with other commitments. With the emphasis bein put strongly on getting out another album as quickly as possible, we had to start lookin round for another producer.

Nathan took it upon himself to take Horse out to meet Chris Frantz an Tina Weymouth in America. It was decided that their Talkin Heads background could help us to pull some weight with the American audience. A lot of muso bullshit, record company talk went down in the process; all the kind of big-time crap that gets you exactly nowhere but up someone's arse. It was also decided that the project should be undertaken on some luxury Caribbean island, in the sun, without a trace of smack in sight. The plan was seriously lackin in foresight in that no rehab time was allowed for X to get his shit together.

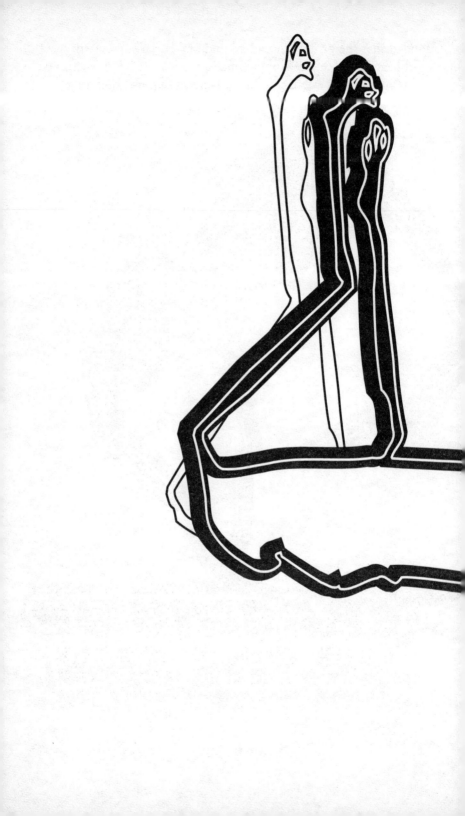

We were all actually made up to fuck that we were gettin off to the tropical setting of Barbados. It had given all of us a much needed lift of spirits, even though the signs were there in full view, for all to see, that this was not goin to go at all smoothly.

Everybody – wives, girlfriends, sound engineers, mothers, fathers, babies – I mean everybody, was comin, an we were all buzzin at the prospect of some relaxin tropical sunshine an sea.

Manchester Airport, early in the mornin: we were all clustered together around the small mountain of pushchairs an suitcases, decked out in our finest for the trip. The babies were behavin, everyone was smilin an the chatter was all palm trees an white beaches. Then X arrived, late as usual. He'd been bombin around all mornin, tryin to sort out his medicine an all the other bits of shit he needed to get off to another country. He strolled up, grinnin, everythin sorted an in order.

He promptly threw the weighty bag off his shoulder, on to the floor in front of the waitin brethren. Boosh! We all heard the explodin sound of the glass bottle that contained his medicated comfort syrup as it splintered loudly in the bottom of the holdall, spreadin stickiness all over his already hummin socks an trainers. The colour drained from his face as the horrible fuckin truth hit home. No methadone, no go. It was a sight to see. For a moment he stood paralysed, rooted to the spot in a petrified panic. Then the spell broke an he began stampin his feet in a top tantrum, hissin at Horseman, with his mouth curlin up in a lopsided grimace. He was goin fuckin ballistic, threatenin to cancel the flights if somethin wasn't sorted out, NOW.

A grim silence fell all around as our lot held their breath an turned their attention to the parked planes on the tarmac, hopin that he would manage to retrieve some sanity along with the crunchy green liquid he was frantically tryin to scoop into the empty container that Horseman had produced from somewhere.

The band played on; we were goin come rain or shine or loss of medication. Determination set in as X was assured that things would be all right once we got in the sun at the other end. In retrospect, maybe he should have held back for more supplies. It might have staved off the madness that was to come for a few more weeks so that we could have all got on with the task in hand. You can't foretell the scale of such disasters, though, until they are starin you in the face an it's too late to turn the clock back.

On landin in Barbados, we all crammed into an awaitin minibus an set out to Eddie Grant's studios on the windswept side of the island, takin in the undulatin panorama of green an yellow sugarcane fields, dotted here an there with pockets of lush natural forests.

Before too long, the bus swerved off the main road an headed up a series of rough tracks where we glimpsed Barbados green monkeys scatterin into the bushes an brilliantly coloured wild parakeets flittin about in the amazin subtropical greenery. A fresh ocean breeze wafted in through the open window, whettin the appetite an promisin good clean livin. It was a complete lie but it really looked convincin at this early stage of the proceedins an all around there was nothin but fuck off grins as we looked out on an assumed paradise.

The studio was a cluster of whitewashed villas of varyin sizes set in a plantation in the middle of nowhere, surrounded by flowerin bougainvillaea vines an elongated trees, all bent an deformed by the constant rush of the trade winds. Eddie Grant's large family house sat bang in the centre of the plot, a grand old plantation house with stone pillars an a flight of steps that led down to a terrace overlookin the vast, sun-parched prairie land. The outdoor pool occupied another terrace that in turn looked down on to a fuck-off garden complete with pavilion an pond. It was a pretty fuckin tasty set-up he had goin, to say the least.

The staff at the studio were at pains to tell the band of their most famous friends an guests that had previously occupied the spaces that we were unloadin into. Mick Jagger came into the conversation quite often, which wasn't such a bad thing to my mind.

Me an X were thrown in the apartments at the studio to keep

us away from the rest of the gang, due to our track record of gettin up to mischief an also due to the fact that everyone was a bit pissed off with us still. It also meant that X was never very far from the studio an couldn't go missin quite so easily. That was the theory anyway. It suited me just fine.

It was hot, hot, hot but with a constant wind, but the wind was hot, hot, hot as well. It was fuckin great. The whole set-up was fuckin great an we were ready to burn in the studio. Actually, we were all just ready to burn to tell the truth. The first thing that everyone thought was SUNTAN, but the climate was deceptive, what with the constant wind. We just couldn't get enough of it, havin flown out of a dreary winter climate back home. There was a certain novelty to baskin in the sun in the middle of January, a sense of encounterin a pure luxurious state. The mad dogs an Englishmen were out in force, turnin a nice shade of lobster-pink within hours.

We geared down a notch or two to fit in with the lazy pace of the island, an feelin like we had all the time in the world all serious matters were put aside while the band settled in an everyone took time to get to know each other a little.

Chris an Tina were surprisinly easy to get on with an I found myself chattin away to Chris an swiggin beers, engrossed in nice an easy conversations over the dinner table about David Byrne an about the famous musicians that had stayed over at these studios in the past.

The first night there, we were all pretty calm due to the fact that we'd taken a small amount of percy to smoke. On the second day, advantage was taken of the momentary lull in proceedins to go an explore the immediate surroundins, with a view to securin a source of supplies for the forthcomin nine weeks.

Some of the band an crew were stationed over at a luxury complex called Sam Lord's Castle. Curiosity got the better of us so we all squashed into one car, me, X, Trish, Debs an the babies, an sped over to check out their accommodation. The road over there passed through a number of wooden shack villages an it wasn't long before we were approached by certain entrepreneurs from these establishments, offerin their wares down on the beach.

Along the stretches of craggy coastline nestle pure white beaches where the surf crashes in from the great expanse of the Atlantic. Here the locals are happy to supply an barbecue fresh fish from the sea, collect an cut fresh coconut from the trees an cook an serve up rocks from the finest white powder, to order. It was too easy on this side of the island, away from the tourist confines of decorum. We were teeterin right on the edge of the dark side of reality an all it needed was just the one nudge for the shit to hit the fan. That nudge came the very first day that we'd decided to venture out, followed by an avalanche of shit that never stopped flyin the whole time we were there.

The local word for rum is acid; says it all really. A half dozen bottles an a bountiful supply of weed completed the picture nicely. Whoever thought that this would be a clean an easy alternative, away from the temptation to sin, was trippin. Rehabs an recordin don't mix. It's like the long-distance runner tryin to stop the momentum of his poundin limbs dead on the finishin line. It's just not an option. We'd just legged it round the stadiums of the world, fuelled by a mixture of adrenalin an drugs an there was no chance of amendin the diet at this late stage in the race.

The recordin session might as well have ended right there an then. Everyone, bar about two of the band, had their sneaky little lick of the rock an came back for more, makin recordin an almost impossible task. It was naughty stuff an bein stupidly cheap, too difficult to resist. You can take the boy out of Salford, but you can't take Salford out of the boy. Chris an Tina Weymouth stood by, clockin in the mountin madness with a parental concern. Occasionally they tried, tactfully, to give some sound advice on the pitfalls of takin crack while workin, but it fell on deaf ears. They knew what they were talkin about, havin worked in this dirty industry long enough to see what the effects are likely to be, but the lads had their fingers stuck firmly to the self-destruct button an nothin an no one could persuade anyone otherwise. We knew in our hearts that it could cause murders, but for now, it all seemed to be goin along pretty much all right an everyone still had a tentative hold on what the overall objective of the mission was: to make music.

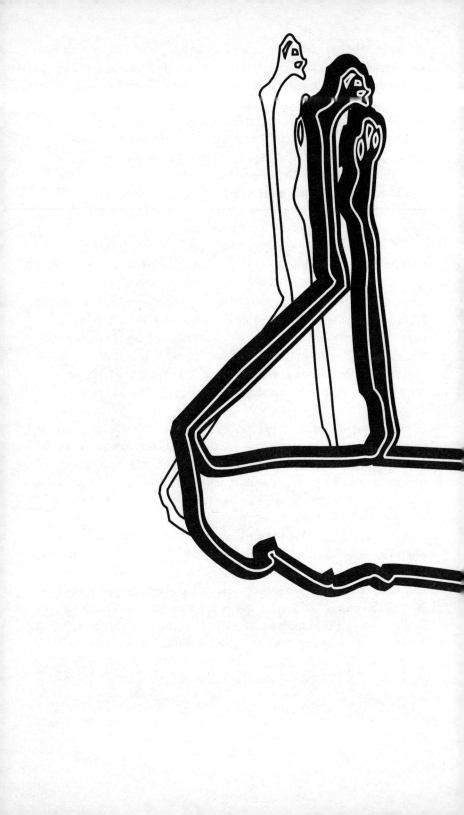

I managed to get myself sorted out with a Vitari Jeep on about the fourth day an spent a few hours doin handbrake turns around fields an in the garden by the studio, happy as a pig in shit. Every now an then I popped back into the studio to see what was happenin, if anythin, but then I couldn't hold off any longer an set about rippin about the island on a voyage of discovery in my new plaything.

Comin back from a local shanty bar that afternoon after a serious rum session with X, I'd been shown a top shortcut to the studio by a friendly Bajan through a bit of jungle an up through a sugarcane field. We were absolutely steamin drunk an seein our intoxicated state, the lads decided they'd like some of the same. I volunteered to go back an get the supplies in, so that I could get another drive in before work commenced. I thought I'd have no problem negotiatin it on my own. It wasn't so much the route that was the problem, but the speed I was takin it in my heightened spirit; ridin roughshod like a mad March hare with a terrier on its tail. I'd noticed the bumpy patch on the way down an made a mental note of where it was for the return journey. I was proper enjoyin myself, burnin about in the open-top car in the sun.

I reached the gaff with no problems, scored four bottles of wine an two bottles of rum an stashed them under the seat, in the box that I'd got them in. I set off back at a rate of knots, really enjoyin slingin the Jeep about, pushin it to its limit. I remembered the bumpy bit an was just thinkin about it as I ripped down the last mile of dirt track when I hit it full on, doin about fifty miles an hour an still acceleratin. I fuckin took off, doin somersaults in the air an landed upside down facin the way that I'd just been comin from. At first I just hung there in my seat, thinking, Fuckin hell, I can't believe I got away with that one. Then I noticed that my arm was swingin above my head at a funny angle, but I didn't have any pain, just a mad rush of adrenalin coursin through my body.

I knew that I had to get out of the car, fast, in case it blew up or it could be a serious case of hasta la vista an goodnight Barbados. My brain sent a hasty message to my limbs to move it, quick style, or fry. My right arm was apparently ignorin the situation at large so my left arm worked overtime to try an free the safety catch on my belt. I couldn't reach it from the position I'd landed in; crushed an twisted an upside down. By this time I was in a flyin panic, lookin about an trying to reach over to turn the ignition off, but I couldn't get to that either. The only option left was to try an escape, Houdini style. I spotted a little gap about fifteen inches wide that no one could believe, when they saw the wreckage afterwards, that I could possibly have got out of. I didn't have time to weigh up the pros an cons of gettin myself an a broken arm out of such a tiny gap. I simply picked up my arm an moved it forward an inch at a time while wrigglin the rest of my body like fuck, until I'd prised myself out.

No doubt about it, that last blast on the coke saved my life, keeping me conscious an aware when I should have been out cold. After wrigglin free of the twisted wreckage, I looked around shoutin a feeble 'Help!' but there were no crowds gatherin in this corner of the field. I realized I'd have to walk the rest of the way up to the studio. The blood was pumpin fast an every nerve screamed for me to stop an lie down, to surrender to the pain. I'd have only had to try again later though, by which time the numbin effects of the alcohol an drugs would be wearin off an shock would have set in properly. There was nothin for it but to grit my teeth, put my head down, an plod on.

A lifetime passed before the familiar surroundins of the studio swam into view. It was a swelterin 35°C an sweat was drippin from every pore, makin me feel completely dehydrated as well as exhausted. The fact that I'd been knockin back the rum an smokin rocks had made my mouth even drier. I felt like the walkin dead, stumblin up the garden, cranin my neck to see if there were any signs of life around the pool. I tried shoutin again, but as the rest of the band were holed up in the studio, no one was goin to hear me. Luckily, Trish, X's girlfriend, spotted me as I was on the point of collapse an came rushin over as she sensed that all was not well. I think it was somethin to do with the deathly shade of grey I'd turned when only a few hours earlier I'd been a healthy shade of sun-kissed brown. The same few hours earlier, I'd offered to give her an baby Jael a lift home on the very route I'd trashed myself. She must have been thankin her lucky stars for possessin the kind of intuition that comes free only with the full motherhood package.

Thank fuck for that, I thought. It had been the loneliest trudge of my life an I was desperate for some assistance as the very last vestiges of energy drained from my body.

My arm was doin S-bends, fallin this way an that. Not a pretty sight to see in any circumstances. More help arrived in the shape of Tina an a few studio hands an they dragged me the rest of the way to the house where I slumped on a sofa an prayed for the early arrival of an ambulance. Just my endurin bad luck that I had picked a national holiday to snap a major limb; all the ambulances were out on call an it would be three long hours or more before one could be dispatched to my aid.

Tina, as it goes, is pretty hot on reachin higher levels of meditation an she took it as her personal duty to clamp herself rigid, cross-legged an yoga style, with an icy compress, to my right side, hardly flinchin for the whole three hours as she held my arm together in a fix position to try an ease the pain. I was really grateful that someone could take on such a task, with no thought for their own discomfort, to try an lessen my pain an distress. Nice one T.

Debs, I gathered, was havin an afternoon nap an bein three months pregnant with our second child, it was a unanimous decision that she shouldn't be disturbed until necessary. As if by sixth sense, a few minutes after my arrival back on the scene she awoke an immediately asked of my whereabouts. Apparently, it was suggested that she should sit down before the news was given to her, upon which she instantly flew into a massive panic an assumed the worst. When she found out I'd only broken my arm, she shot across to the main house with the intentions of killin me off anyway, for bein so fuckin stupid.

My mind was still bendin sideways from the crash but all I could think about was a good long toke on a loaded spliff. Surely it would make things seem better, I reasoned with myself. I insisted that someone roll me one an after one drag I was pukin as the shock intensified ten fold. It wasn't a good idea at all, but all I could think about was smokin it to the end, if only to divert my attention away from bodily matters.

The ambulance finally arrived an a makeshift splint was applied to steady the snakin limb. I mentioned earlier that the studio was located up a web of rough dirt tracks an now I could feel every ridge an dip as the ambulance slowly made its way down to the main road. Every minute felt like an hour an it had been about four since the actual accident. I was seriously flakin by now an Debs was lookin on all concerned as she'd taken over where Tina had left off, gingerly holdin my arm an wipin my brow every nudge an jerk along the way.

The studio had called ahead for a friend of the family to meet me at the hospital. She was a British nurse workin in the accident an emergency unit an it had been her day off until now.

The casualty department in Barbados was a pretty wild place to be; there were all sorts of injuries an nasty goins on at every turn. The weirdest case was that of a girl who'd been brought in with a serious bite from a monkey. The monkey had achieved a certain amount of celebrity status on the island an was bein billed as 'Jack the Ripper' for his frequent attacks on women an girls. I could hardly believe what I was hearin, but there I was, sat right next to one of its latest victims. Apparently, it had attacked a right few of 'em an there was a massive hunt on for this rogue monkey. There was news that the thing had been trapped an shot while comin in for another victim, before we eventually left the island.

The British nurse arrived an rushed me through the waitin room an into the X-ray department where she personally did the necessaries, cuttin my wait by hours. I could have kissed her. The news wasn't good. The X-ray showed that the bone had snapped clean in two an the consultant could do nothing for me. I was given an appointment to see the specialist the next day an sent off to get a makeshift plaster put on. The nurse supervised the plaster cast an arranged my transport back to the studio with a small bag of painkillers.

The pain I was in that night was fuckin unbelievable. I couldn't wait to get back to the hospital the next day to see the specialist. After more X-rays, it was decided that he would have to operate. He told me that he wouldn't be able to operate for another week an that he strongly advised that I should go back home to England to have it done straight away.

I'd only been away four days in total an no way was I goin home an miss out on everythin. I was resolute in the decision that I was stayin till the bitter end. What a major, lifetime mistake that was. I wish to fuck that I'd taken more heed of his advice, but, like a fool, I decided to wait on the island an spent the next week walkin about with my arm swingin loose, in pure agony.

The local doc came round with his bag of tricks an handed out the pethadine. I ended up goin through about thirty a day as X soon got on the quality of the pills an nicked nearly half of my prescription. I ended up just mongin around, pinned to fuck, not even able to roll my own spliffs. I never even looked at another pipe of crack all week. I spent all day, every day, just fidgetin about, tryin to get in a comfortable position so that the wobblin arm could feel somethin like straight.

Finally, the day came for the op. I was buzzin an couldn't wait to get on with it; the pain was ragin by now. The only trouble was, I wouldn't lie down because the torment was too great to lie flat. The nurses compromised an gave me the shots to get me off while I was still sittin in an upright position.

When I awoke on the ward, I felt as if the whole team of nurses an surgeons had jumped all over me to get me down an keep me flat. Later, I found out that it could have been the anaesthetic they used that was makin me feel as if I'd been battered on every muscle a hundred times over.

My arm felt brilliant though, solid as a rock for the first time in a week. All that remained was to sit back an relax for four weeks in the sun while the bone knitted itself. That would be too easy though, an I had to get caught up in smokin the fuckin stupid stone again.

On the third day of my recovery, I went down to the tourist side of the island, where the sea was calm as a mill pond, lappin up on to soft, white, palm-fringed beaches an the wind quietened to a gentle breeze. This was the Caribbean of the brochures, with people doin water sports an enjoyin themselves to the max. Like I said, the sea looked as flat as a mirror so I thought, Fuck that, I'm goin to join in, broken arm or no broken arm.

I called the speedboat attendant over an told him of my plans to sit in the back of the rubber ring an be pulled, GENTLY around the bay. I emphasized the fact that my arm was in plaster an that he was to take it at a nice, slow, steady pace. I prepared myself, wrappin a plastic bag over my arm while the rest of the crowd looked on, tellin me I must be fuckin crazy. I was adamant that all would be well.

The first two laps went like a dream an I was beginnin to feel confident about havin the kind of fun that everyone else was havin. The speedboat driver wasn't happy with the proceedins though, an on the second lap he decided to speed things up a little. The next minute, I found myself rippin along, tryin to hold on for dear life with the one good arm, screamin at the geezer to slow the fuckin thing down. It was gettin harder an harder to keep hold an then he launched me into the corner at what felt like a hundred miles an hour, bouncin me across the sea. I couldn't hold on any longer. B-boom, I went tumblin like a top skimmer across the water. Straight away, I felt the fuckin arm go. I managed to get up on the side of the boat an made it back to shore. I knew that somethin wasn't right. Not right at all.

That afternoon, I went back off to the surgery an made up a top lie about how it had happened. Yet another X-ray showed that the pin had come away slightly, not too much, but enough to aggravate the injury. I could feel the arm was swingin loose again but they weren't havin it. I was really fucked off with myself by now. So fucked off, in fact, that I started tannin huge amounts of stone again with X. It had got to that really dangerous point though, where everyone was sneekin off to do their little cache in by themselves. I was totally reliant on others for my little pleasure in life an couldn't even light a pipe by myself; an absolute invalid. It was a sad situation on all counts.

The number of hire cars bein written off was slowly increasin, an I seemed to be the jinx that caused half of them. X was the next in line for a crash with me sittin by his side. He'd been tamin all kinds of crap: downers, painkillers, stone, booze – the lot. He was in no fit state to be drivin an it was terrifyin me, especially as I already had one broken limb. I was beggin him to stop as he weaved about all over the road, but he didn't want to be driven by some one-armed, pissed-up loon either.

Thinkin that we'd seen someone familiar drivin past in the opposite direction, we both turned to look an wave. Obviously, it's not such a clever thing to do if you're drivin at the time. The next minute, we were off the road, goin straight up the side of a hill, rippin the exhaust off on the bumps an rocks an finally smackin into a tree. Another car bites the dust, but at least we were in one piece. The person we'd waved at never stopped.

By this time, me an X knew nearly everybody who was anybody on the island. The first week we'd been there, we'd gone for a meal at the openin of a top restaurant where we'd met the prime minister, the chief of police an all the other top nobs of the island. So our knowledge of the inhabitants of Barbados ranged from the very top right down through the social stratosphere to the crack dealers at the six cross-roads at the bottom. This made for some interestin gossip, all the way across the island, about all the mayhem goin down in an around the studio. Most worryin, to Mrs Grant anyway, was the talk of us gettin busted by the police.

By first daylight, me an X took to buildin our own personal den by the side of the pool, out of the mornin rush of babies an cleaners. One night we'd been at it till the wee small hours when X took it upon himself to go off an get in fresh supplies. I decided to stay back home, takin the sensible option, for once. A few hours had passed by when Horse appeared by the pool lookin for some action himself. I told him that there was nothin doin as X had taken off a few hours earlier an that he was yet to return. We thought it best to drive over to where we knew he was holed up: some notorious crack den at the six cross-roads.

On the way up there, we spotted X's car upside down in the middle of the road an got out to make a closer inspection of the wreckage. Yet another car bites the dust. Shit happens.

X was nowhere to be seen, but the bonnet was open an the battery had been taken out. Surveyin the scene further, we realized that he'd hit a big lump in the road, ran up a steep embankment an the car had toppled over. He'd struggled all the rest of the way over to his new mates' house to swap the battery for rock. We got up there to find X battered to fuck from the accident, his nose all over the place, an cuts all over his head, but happily smokin away with token grapefruit by his side, ready to take home. The dealers at the six cross-roads always sent us away with the odd present of a grapefruit, no matter what time of day or night we'd descend on them. They must have thought that we needed the vitamin C boost, in our emaciated state; even the hardened crackheads were concerned for our health by now.

By this time, we'd spent every penny we had on the shit an X thought it a good idea to get on the phone home, holdin the part-finished tapes in one hand an the receiver in the other, threatenin to destroy the lot if more dough wasn't wired over for us imme-diately. It was plainly obvious to everyone by now that the plot had seriously gone sideways. Stories had been flyin back about all the happenins an everyone at Factory was panickin.

To say that things were gettin completely out of hand has to be the understatement of the century. X was now totally an utterly right off his fuckin box an way beyond any reasonin.

By now, I'd thankfully come to the conclusion that enough was enough an begun to redress the situation by tryin to do the normal, everyday things alongside the rock binges, like goin out for meals an takin days trips about the place. The kind of things that ordinary, sane people do when they're in such a beautiful place as the Caribbean. X continued to hammer his body an mind an not one man in the entourage could stand bein in his company for any minute longer than they had to. It had developed into an impossible situation that couldn't be resolved in the short space of time we had left in this supposed paradise.

He'd taken to stealin furniture from the studio to feed his crack habit but, in his twisted mental state, he thought it was sweet; a kind of robbin the rich to feed the poor opportunity, convincin himself that, morally, he was somehow in the right. The Grants were not impressed, to say the least.

The money had all but run out along with any speck of com-radeship that may have been present at the onset of the venture, makin for one of the worst atmospheres that you could ever have the misfortune to be existin in.

I looked around me an saw the biggest explosion imaginable formin on the horizon an calculated that we had approximately one week of luxury left to make the most of. I made up my mind to squeeze as much enjoyment out of this last week as possible before the annihilation of the band an consequently the whole Factory set-up took place. It was time to get at least seven days of proper holidayin out of it all, so that I could look back an say that at least somethin good came out of the time we'd spent there.

I moved down to the beach-side villa on the tourist end of the island to join Debs, who'd already been at this choice location for the last few weeks. She'd cut out from all the crap at the studio a few weeks earlier when it had got too crazy to be dealin with, with a baby in tow. She'd organized Arlo's first birthday party down there an there was to be a top do with a barbecue, right on the beach. Everyone attended an it was a welcome respite from all the mayhem of the previous weeks. Horse took charge of the cookin, erectin an old oil drum for a makeshift barbecue an we had the best feast of the entire time we were there.

I'd completely sacked goin into the studio as I wasn't at all interested. In fact, I just didn't give a flyin shit for any of it any more as I'd totally lost heart in the whole thing. I looked around at the rest of the band, who were supposed to be friends, an realized just how snide the entire enterprise had become. To me, it was no longer what it had all initially been about; takin the piss out of the system an havin a top time with a bunch of mates, smashin it together an makin real dough to boot. The time for such idealism had sadly passed by an was now resigned to history.

Eventually, I got off back home a week earlier than planned with a few of the others who'd had their fill an wanted to simply go home. I couldn't take any more of the nonsense an I also wanted to get my arm fixed properly in a nice clean hospital with competent surgeons, modern equipment an pristine sheets on a bed in a private room.

One serious lesson that was learned from the experiences in Barbados was that crack cocaine is one motherfuckin nightmare if you intend to try an make music on it – it creates the complete antithesis of the mood you need to make music. In fact, anyone ever thinkin they can make music on the nasty shit needs to stand well back an take a good long look at the work ethics they are employin, because you might as well scrap the whole fuckin project then an there because it will, without a doubt, end in tears an debt.

The next six months were spent racin against time, tryin to get myself in a fit state of mind an body to go on tour. X was in some fuckin expensive detox clinic, goin through the motions of at least pretendin to detox so that he could attempt to finish his vocals off with Chris an Tina in England. None of the rest of the band were invited as we were all seen as a destructive influence. You have to laugh; the band weren't even allowed to go down an be part of the final arrangements on the album they were expected to play live on the forthcomin tour.

Fuck that for a game of soldiers then, I thought, an settled back in my new house to get on with everyday family life in a nice, orderly, clean way.

The enormous relief of bein back home, doin nothin more dangerous than delvin into the tabloids of an afternoon, was fuckin fantastic an I wallowed daily in the serenity of sittin in my little cottage, practisin couch potato manoeuvres. One such afternoon, I was loungin around, doin nothin in particular, when Debs came in an slumped down beside me, accidentally puttin her entire weight on the mendin limb. This was the final break to end all breaks. The pain seared through every nerve endin in my arm. I couldn't even scream out, it was so intense. All I could do was run round the room in silent agony, beads of sweat poppin out of my head as I tried to convey the extent of the damage she had done.

It was back to the ozzie again. It turned out that actually she'd, in some perverse turn of luck, done me a massive favour. My arm was badly infected from the unclean screws used in the Barbados hospital an it was eatin away at my whole arm.

Another operation was quickly arranged an it turned out that I was to be in the broken limb ward at the very same time that Debs gave birth to our second son, Jack, over in maternity. It was a double whammy for the family, with Jack arrivin at some unearthly time in the middle of the night, givin me just enough time to spend a few hours with them both before stumblin back over to my ward to get ready to go down to the theatre. I was tired an in pain, but happy.

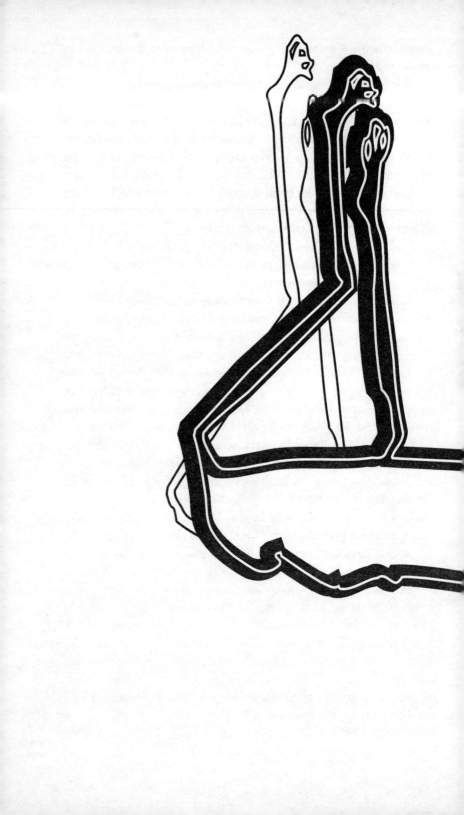

When we finally got our shit together to take the band on tour, it had degenerated into a fuckin horrible, disastrous ordeal as no one wanted to be there at all. The spirit of the band that had kept us up an runnin through the years of strugglin to make it had completely disappeared, leavin nothin but an empty performance on stage an the punters knew it. The rest of the band had signed letters sayin that they wanted to sack me an X, but obviously that would have been totally unfeasible on the brink of tourin.

It didn't make for a comfortable atmosphere an I was in even more physical discomfort due to my arm bein strapped up still, with a metal rod runnin from the shoulder to the elbow. The painkillers I was on were so strong that I was mongin out all over the place, with not a single fuckin groove inside me. I literally couldn't feel the music, an to add to the overall confusion, we had some snide E on board that I foolishly took to counteract the effects of the painkillers, but they just made me feel really weird. It was the worst possible scenario you could imagine for attemptin live gigs. I knew for sure then that it was all over. Rock 'n' roll, this was not. It hadn't actually blown up yet, but we all knew that it was comin, soon.

To make matters worse, if it could get worse, X's coffin was havin the final nails banged into it by Factory Records, who were teeterin on the brink of goin bust, big-time. It was goin to be the end of the Manchester legend. The legacy that they handed down through the years to the people of the city through their pioneerin of new music was about to evaporate, leavin nothin but a vaporous trail of back catalogues an stories. It was a sad time for everyone involved: Factory Records, Tony, Alan Erasmus, all the bands they had supported, the whole lot of us. It was a cryin shame that the whole scene had collapsed in such a sorry débâcle after so much input from every angle.

Amazinly though, through all the messiness, a light was twin-klin at the end of the tunnel as immediately other record com-panies began to show interest in the future of the band. One of the more lucrative offers on the line was from EMI. It looked a pretty good deal, an as the band had been back in the rehearsal rooms, workin against all the odds at buryin the hatchet so that we could at least try an salvage a bit of professionalism from the ashes of the past mistakes, we thought we'd give it one last shot at gettin it right.

It seemed that everyone was willin to forgive an forget so that we could get on an build up a bit of a future – but had they? Maybe it is my suspicious nature that leads me to wonder if it was all an elaborate plot by Nathan, who knew in his heart that it would never work out an therefore set up one last money-spinner so that he could grab his percentage an run. The accountants were desperate to get this deal sorted also, to polish up their reputations within the business an neatly clean up the messy debts that had accrued due to sloppy administration of the funds.

This leads me to believe the ulterior motives theory even more. But then, what do I know, being merely a member of the band an not a business head? Like I said, it's just a theory . . .

A series of meetins were set up with EMI an to this day I'm completely pissed off with how their representative went about handlin his business an I'd have no qualms about tellin him that to his face, preferably with the aid of a fist to drive the fact right home. Credit to X though, who throughout all the mess an his addictions could see right through the fuckin con. He disliked the geezer as much as I did, as the day before the final meetin, he'd received phone calls from EMI, passin on loads of stupid, baitin messages about rumours within the band about personal matters. Basically, it was a shit-stirrin ploy to see how strong the internal structure of the band was, but he was stirrin up old dirt that we'd all agreed to put to rest so that we could carry on, the prick.

The final meetin was set up that was to be our ultimate twist or bust move. X had, by now, taken a total fuckin dislikin to the geezer as I had, if not more. We turned up to meet the suits an X took one look at him before announcin, 'Fuck that, I'm goin for a Kentucky.'

It was his coded call to say that he wasn't talkin to the prick now an wouldn't be at any point in the future either. He walked straight out an never came back, leavin them all standin there, waitin to get their cocks sucked, like they were used to gettin from all the other people in the industry. They were waitin around for about three hours before it actually sunk in that the deal was off. The gods from EMI had been stood up spectacularly an they weren't happy.

That was final straw for the rest of the band; they were infuriated. They'd been plottin to break away from me an X, to go off on their own, thinkin that they didn't need us any more. Me an X pleaded for them to change their minds as we'd fought tooth an nail to keep the band as a whole unit all this time. We were adamant that we could get a new deal sorted that would benefit us all; a real rock 'n' roll swindle that would piss on any offers we'd had in the past. We didn't want the band to split up because we knew that we had a future an that we were nowhere near finished with the business. They were havin none of it, preferin to buzz on the false premise that they'd fucked us off an that they were goin to leave us behind in the gutter.

The best thing about the whole affair was that it was the very fuel that X needed to finally straighten up properly. It was the straightest I'd ever seen him in over ten years. I was happy as well because it had meant that we'd all gone down together in this miserable event, which was quite funny from my point of view, considerin that it was only supposed to be me eatin dirt initially.

X had started goin to the gym an eatin bodybuildin supplements to put weight an muscle on. He kept the gym thing up for a couple of weeks an then sacked it, but kept on the bodybuildin stuff in replacement for downin pints, for a further six months. He piled weight on like you wouldn't believe an grew a muzzy to add to the transformation. Everyone told him to stop with the supplements, but he wouldn't fuckin listen. He wanted to be fat. It was the strangest thing I've ever seen. He wanted to visibly prove his new, healthy, clean-livin regime of rebellin against drugs, determined to show everybody that he'd given it all up by putting on loads of weight. He put loads too fuckin much on though in the process, which was really funny at the time.

His other stimulant was a picture of PD on the dartboard, which he would stand throwin darts at while plottin his revenge. Each dart that hit the target was a metaphor for each new move that would take us one step further, towards a new future. A shape of the plan to get us back up an runnin was slowly formed durin the dartboard sessions. We were down, but we weren't beaten.

The plan was to come back an give everyone the biggest fuck-off salute that they'd ever fuckin seen in their lives. We refused point blank to be written out of the picture so easily. We wanted to show them that we meant business, an so we did.

RIP – see you in a big bit.